Praise for

THE MOST DANGEROUS
MAN IN AMERICA

"Fascinating...rigorously researched...[THE MOST DANGER-OUS MAN IN AMERICA] offers the pleasures of the tick-tock genre. Much like Leary himself, the book is plenty of zany fun."
—*New York Times*

"A rip-roaring tale of hallucinogenic drugs, revolutionary politics, and an intercontinental standoff...Minutaglio and Davis have taken a largely forgotten chapter from the recent past and turned it into a vigorous page-turner." —*San Francisco Chronicle*

"One of the decade's most audacious and exciting stories, told with page-turning panache." —*Boston Globe*

"A pitch-perfect, exhilarating work about one of the strangest chapters in the American experience, one so exciting that even the postscript rivets...A stroke of narrative genius."
—*Booklist* (Starred Review)

"A rollicking tale that brings to life the antic atmosphere of America in the 'Me Decade.'" —*Wall Street Journal*

"A brisk, riveting book that, thanks to the use of present tense, novelistic color, and frequent cross-cutting between characters and locations, moves a ton of information with crackling immediacy... THE MOST DANGEROUS MAN IN AMERICA has 'movie' written all over it." —*Dallas Morning News*

"THE MOST DANGEROUS MAN IN AMERICA is a wild ride across time, space, and multiple cosmic planes during an era when America came close to losing—or finding?—its mind. Leary and Nixon: Surely no other country on earth could have produced such a perfectly, surreally antithetical pair. Crack open this book and prepare to have your mind blown by the reality of this very strange tale."

—Ben Fountain, bestselling PEN/Hemingway and O. Henry Prize–winning author of *Billy Lynn's Long Halftime Walk*

"The glory of [THE MOST DANGEROUS MAN IN AMERICA] is its fast-paced, rollicking narrative that brings the freakishness of the revolutionary 1970s to life. Bill Minutaglio and Steven L. Davis have pulled off a meticulous observation of their subjects with turns of phrase that pop with pleasure. I galloped through the book; could not put it down."

—Jan Jarboe Russell, *New York Times* bestselling author of *The Train to Crystal City*

"A riveting international chase between a tenacious but paranoid cat and a wily but delusional mouse...Minutaglio and Davis are superb storytellers, and throughout the narrative, they nimbly move between their two converging subjects. Their account is expertly detailed and blessedly fat-free." —*Kirkus* (Starred Review)

"Our intrepid authors, pounding the present tense like the brake pedal on a runaway eighteen-wheeler, narrate a story more wild, inventive, and sex-drenched than a Dennis Hopper movie."

—Glenn Frankel, Pulitzer Prize–winning journalist and author of *High Noon: The Hollywood Blacklist and the Making of an American Classic*

"A vivid, eye-opening alternate view of an especially bizarre period of American history...Far too strange to be fiction, the book brilliantly details an American tragedy of two men, each of whom considered the other to be the most dangerous man in America."

—James Fadiman, PhD, microdose researcher and author of *The Psychedelic Explorers' Guide: Safe, Therapeutic, and Sacred Journeys*

"There is enough high-quality hash, weed, acid, booze, and tobacco in THE MOST DANGEROUS MAN IN AMERICA to make Hunter S. Thompson blanch. [This] book should be taught in journalism, history, and political science departments nationwide...a triumph of the reporter's art." —*Texas Observer*

"A deeply researched, entertaining, and informative look at the symbolically joined paths Nixon and one of his nemeses, LSD guru Timothy Leary, followed in the early 1970s, the era that would ultimately be defined by Watergate." —*St. Louis Post-Dispatch*

"Fast-paced and suspenseful, [THE MOST DANGEROUS MAN IN AMERICA] captures a mad—and menacing—moment in American history. Clearly, Minutaglio and Davis have done their homework...THE MOST DANGEROUS MAN IN AMERICA is awash in authenticated details, by turns outlandish and outrageous, that illuminate 1970s American culture and politics." —*Minneapolis Star Tribune*

"Fascinating...The personalities that make appearances read like a Who's Who of counterculture figures and political insiders." —*Santa Fe New Mexican*

"In the hands of Bill Minutaglio and Steven L. Davis, the true-but-really-weird saga is a warp-speed revolution-and-heist film. It's a real page-burner." —*Austin Chronicle*

"Not unlike our current reality, [THE MOST DANGEROUS MAN IN AMERICA] proves that truth can indeed be stranger than fiction." —*San Antonio Current*

"Seems as if it takes place on a completely different planet...[THE MOST DANGEROUS MAN IN AMERICA] would make an insane HBO miniseries." —*Austin American-Statesman*

THE MOST DANGEROUS MAN IN AMERICA

THE MOST DANGEROUS MAN IN AMERICA

Timothy Leary, Richard Nixon, and
the Hunt for the Fugitive King of LSD

BILL MINUTAGLIO
and
STEVEN L. DAVIS

TWELVE

NEW YORK · BOSTON

Twelve
Hachette Book Group
1290 Avenue of the Americas, New York, NY 10104
twelvebooks.com
twitter.com/twelvebooks

Originally published in hardcover and ebook by Twelve in January 2018.
First Trade Edition: August 2019

Twelve is an imprint of Grand Central Publishing. The Twelve name
and logo are trademarks of Hachette Book Group, Inc.

The publisher is not responsible for websites (or their content)
that are not owned by the publisher.

The Hachette Speakers Bureau provides a wide range
of authors for speaking events. To find out more, go to
www.hachettespeakersbureau.com or call (866) 376-6591.

Library of Congress Cataloging-in-Publication Data

Names: Minutaglio, Bill, author. | Davis, Steven L., author.
Title: The most dangerous man in America : Timothy Leary,
Richard Nixon & the hunt for the fugitive king of LSD /
Bill Minutaglio and Steven L. Davis.
Other titles: Timothy Leary, Richard Nixon and the hunt for
the fugitive king of LSD
Description: New York : Twelve, [2018]
Identifiers: LCCN 2017032575| ISBN 9781455563586 (hardcover) |
ISBN 9781478923664 (trade pbk.) | ISBN 9781455563609 (ebook)
Subjects: LCSH: Leary, Timothy, 1920–1996—Travel—Foreign countries. |
Fugitives from justice—United States—Biography. | Escapes—California—
San Luis Obispo County. | Psychologists—United States—Biography. |
Radicalism—United States—History—20th century. | Counterculture—
History—20th century. | LSD (Drug)—History—20th century. |
United States—Politics and government—1969–1974.
Classification: LCC HV8658.L43 M56 2018 | DDC 150.92 [B] —dc23
LC record available at https://lccn.loc.gov/2017032575

ISBNs: 978-1-4555-6359-3 (trade pbk.), 978-1-4555-6360-9 (ebook)

Printed in the United States of America

LSC-C

10 9 8 7 6 5 4 3 2 1

For Michael Horowitz and Robert Barker,
for saving the archives.

For Rosemary, Joanna, and everyone
who shared their stories.

Richard Nixon famously called Timothy Leary
"the most dangerous man in America."

—NEW YORK TIMES

When Nixon called me that, I was thrilled. The president of the United States, whom many Americans and the rest of the world thought was a crazed, psychotic danger, for him to be calling me that . . . that's my Nobel Prize, that's my bumper sticker, that's my trophy on the wall.

—TIMOTHY LEARY

If Richard Nixon is not sincere, he is the most dangerous man in America.

—DR. MARTIN LUTHER KING JR.

AUTHORS' NOTE

Timothy Leary met with one of us many years ago on a humid, rainy day in Houston. It was a time when he was trying desperately to uncover what had been done to him during his life as a fugitive running from the president of the United States.

As he sipped some beers and curled up in a creaky wooden chair in one of the oldest bars in the city, he said he was having little success getting to the deeply hidden truths that might detail how he was once hunted by Richard Nixon's FBI and CIA as "the most dangerous man in America."

In several subsequent conversations, Leary began to look forward, predicting, accurately, that the world would be connected via computers and that space exploration and travel might become more commonplace. But still, he remained achingly wistful about the massive secrets he'd never fathom while he was alive—the specifics of how, in one burst of time, he had been at the utter mercy of bomb-throwing revolutionaries, gun-toting militants, an international arms smuggler, secret agents on four continents, and even the occupant of the Oval Office.

This book is not a biography of Timothy Leary. Its goal is to finally reveal a dramatic, hidden piece of modern American history—a madly careening, twenty-eight-month global hunt for one man.

Thousands of freshly available and unexamined primary resources were used: court documents, personal letters, criminal files, secret government cables, internal paperwork from foreign governments, and audiotapes recorded clandestinely at the White House. Hundreds of boxes of archival material from New York, California, Washington, Texas, the District of Columbia, Algeria, Afghanistan, and

Switzerland were consulted, many for the first time. Key foot soldiers in the hunt for Leary gave their first interviews.

News accounts translated from sources in Europe unearthed fresh details. Previously sealed FBI documents—publicly available for the first time—were used to construct the chronology and conversations. The once-elusive facts behind Leary's life on the lam were also finally corralled with help from Leary's longtime personal archivist—and the New York Public Library curator who oversaw the unveiling of Leary's personal papers. This book is built on primary sources and firsthand accounts. Strict attention is paid to exact dialogue and quotes from Leary, Nixon, and others. Interior thoughts and monologue derived from memoirs and primary sources are presented in italics. A complete list of endnotes is available on our websites.

In the end, a startling truth emerged: Timothy Leary and Richard Nixon had much more in common than they ever knew. Each led an outsize, prolific life. Each saw truth as a cosmically malleable enterprise.

Each man thought the other was leading America to hell.

—*Bill Minutaglio and Steven L. Davis*

PRELUDE

Some Bad Guy

July 23, 1971

*I*t is high summer in Washington, DC, another blistering day, and President Richard Nixon is stepping from the Oval Office into the adjoining Cabinet Room. He can see the Rose Garden outside, but he orders the drapes drawn shut. He is feeling surrounded by enemies:

Anti-war radicals are bombing the Capitol and other government buildings. Black Panther militants are calling for Nixon's execution. There are explosions and fires in cities around the nation. Even worse, as far as Nixon is concerned, are the attacks from the Democrats and the media that threaten to undermine his reelection campaign.

He has decided to strike back, to wage war and do it hard.

Today he is putting the final touches on the creation of a top secret White House counterespionage team, an elite group of loyalists who have sworn to destroy Nixon's political enemies. The president is thrilled with one of its chief operatives—an ex-FBI agent named G. Gordon Liddy.

Inside the Cabinet Room, Nixon's aides and trusted cabinet officers file in behind him. The president takes his seat in a leather chair taller than the others. Only Nixon knows that two microphones are hidden underneath the wooden table, with wires that run to a voice-activated recorder hidden inside a locker in the basement.

Today the president is disturbed by the latest polls. Although he has declared a war on drugs, the American people say he is at his weakest when it comes to fighting the counterculture.

"We got to keep talking about it, we got to keep hitting it," he tells the others. Nixon is growing testy, musing aloud about those enemies, like the Democrats and Teddy Kennedy, being friends with "the hopheads"—with pot smokers. Why can't people understand him or appreciate what he's doing for America?

"I have done a lot ... but it doesn't seem to get through," Nixon says glumly.

Treasury Secretary John Connally speaks up in his thick-as-molasses Texas drawl, suggesting that Nixon hasn't picked one clear "drug enemy" that he can target.

"You are not identified vis-à-vis an identifiable character or an identifiable incident, something that stays in the minds of people," explains Connally.

"Some bad guy!" adds a suddenly intrigued Nixon.

Connally suggests that Nixon needs to find a single figurehead to crucify as the poster child for the drug problem in the United States. Someone who is "head of the drug business in this country," Connally adds.

"That's right!" responds Nixon, his mood brightening. "That would be something quite dramatic."

Several of Nixon's aides begin chattering at once, talking over one another. Everyone agrees that Nixon needs to find an identifiable villain, like the notorious Mafia warlords Carlo Gambino or Lucky Luciano, whom he can turn into the face of the enemy.

Someone Nixon can capture and hold aloft as a symbol.

"We've got to find a way to identify him," Nixon says as more shouting erupts. "Good guy against bad guy!"

Connally interjects again: "Well, there is this guy, the guy who went to Algeria," he drawls.

"Leary, Leary, Leary ... Timothy Leary, Timothy Leary!" Nixon and his aides begin shouting.

The room convulses in excited laughter.

Nixon bellows triumphantly to the others:

"Well, we've got room in the prisons for him!"

PART I

YOU SAY YOU WANT A REVOLUTION

Fourteen Months Earlier

John . . . people used to say to me . . .
"Did the Buddha use drugs? Did the Buddha go on television?"
I'd say, "Ahh—he would've. He would've."

—Timothy Leary, in conversation with John Lennon

WE THROW AWAY THE KEY

Morning, May 13, 1970

Inmate 26358 is behind a wire cage, swaying with the movement of a California prison bus curling along the Pacific Coast Highway. It's Wednesday, Dr. Timothy Leary's eighty-fourth day of captivity, and he is being reassigned to a new prison home. He's carrying all his possessions in a small cardboard box—two packs of Bugler roll-your-own cigarette tobacco, two ballpoint pens, and rubber shower shoes that are a good-bye present from a murderer he met in another state facility.

He is turning fifty in a few months and he's hard of hearing but with a full head of wavy, silver-threaded hair. Lean and tan, he has the rakish good looks of an aging tennis pro at a country club, albeit one with a genius IQ, who can quote Socrates and the Bhagavad Gita while lecturing on the seven levels of consciousness or the physiological nature of a woman's orgasm. The other prisoners on the bus—killers, thieves, and rapists on their way to Folsom or San Quentin—know his reputation. He is the godfather of the psychedelic 1960s, the High Priest of LSD who advised young people to "Turn on, tune in, drop out."

The black-and-white prison bus rattles past Ventura, and Leary tries to glimpse the whitecaps of the Pacific Ocean from behind the grimy windows. He sees a group of wetsuit-clad surfers paddling out to catch some waves. At a stoplight in Santa Barbara, he glances over and sees a man in a convertible with a beautiful woman riding shotgun, her long hair blowing in the breeze. Leary sighs and looks away.

A few hours earlier, at 3 a.m., he had been immersed in a sultry dream: *I'm in an exquisite house in Santa Monica, the ocean lapping outside. There is a naked woman lowering herself onto a fur rug in front of a fireplace. Some bluesy Janis Joplin music is oozing from a stereo. The reclining woman whispers to me in a velvety, druggy voice: "All I want is to feel good . . . just keep me high."* It was getting good, much better, until the guards suddenly barked at him in midslumber and told him to gather his shit for the trip to his new prison.

At Pismo Beach the bus chugs through the mountains and when the road opens again, Leary can see the city of San Luis Obispo ahead, surrounded by soft green hills. Soon they are passing the sprawling Cal Poly university campus, just reopening after California governor Ronald Reagan shut it down for four days following nationwide student protests.

Suddenly, another prisoner on the bus is shouting and pointing. Leary and the others turn to look. The con is gesturing toward Poly Mountain, with its fifty-foot-tall concrete *P* overlooking the university. Next to the giant *P*, some renegade students have added two new letters. Now the hillside spells out *POT.* The prisoners laugh and cheer.

Two miles past the campus, the California Men's Colony–West comes into view. Clusters of simple white wooden barracks are spread out against the foothills, dotted with blooming trees. As they draw closer, Leary sees a group of old inmates playing shuffleboard while others waddle across cracked tennis courts. In the distance, out on the stark prison golf course, another prisoner is taking a practice swing before launching a drive.

CMC-West is a minimum-security facility, designed for older men who pose little threat of violence. The perimeter is patrolled at night by gun trucks with sharpshooters inside, but the only physical barrier to the outside world is a twelve-foot-tall chain-link fence, topped by three looping strands of barbed wire. Leary has been trying to get himself transferred here ever since he got sentenced. When he took the standard prison personality test that would help authorities determine where to assign him, Leary knew exactly how to reply in order to seem as docile as possible. He had designed many of the test questions himself in his earlier incarnation as a nationally respected psychologist.

As the bus lurches to the drop-off zone, one of the prisoners suddenly shouts at Leary:

"Hey, man, this is the end of the line. The Department of Correction sent you here to die."

Leary lets the words wash over him.

He is already studying the prison layout.

❈   ❈   ❈

In Washington, Richard Nixon's White House is anxious for any new FBI leads about the wave of extraordinary bombings splintering the nation. Even as Leary's bus ferried him up the California coast, a massive dynamite attack rocked the police station in Des Moines, Iowa, shattering windows and setting nearby cars on fire. In Salt Lake City, Utah, a homemade bomb blew apart the entrance to the local National Guard building.

Meanwhile, agents are still pursuing suspects from a bloody tragedy in New York City. Revolutionaries calling themselves "the Weathermen" had been working on a nail bomb, plotting to detonate it during a military dance at Fort Dix in New Jersey. Instead, the bomb exploded in their hands, reducing a four-story townhouse in Greenwich Village to rubble. Three of the radicals were killed. Two women emerged from the smoking ruin, bloody and dazed. Taken in by unsuspecting neighbors, they showered and were given clothes—and then they vanished.

Just last week, at Kent State University, National Guard troops fired sixty-seven shots at students protesting President Nixon's escalation of the Vietnam War. Four underclassmen were gunned to death, including two young women. Two of the slain students had simply been walking to class. Nine others were wounded by gunfire. Nixon, who'd denounced student demonstrators as "bums," defended the National Guard and blamed the victims: "When dissent turns to violence, it invites tragedy," he lectured. California governor Ronald Reagan had already demanded a crackdown on campus protesters: "If it takes a bloodbath, let's get it over with," Reagan warned. "No more appeasement."

Since Kent State, millions of college students across the country have gone on strike, taking to the streets. At the University of Wisconsin, Molotov cocktails ignited buildings and bonfires blazed as students hurled bricks, stones, and bottles at six hundred riot police and guardsmen. At the University of South Carolina, a thousand students smashed into the administration building, ransacking offices and destroying files. At the University of New Mexico, eleven students were bayoneted by National Guardsmen after taking over the Student Union Building. At the University of California, Berkeley, protesters torched an ROTC truck and tore down an American flag, setting it on fire and chanting: "*Burn, Nixon, burn.*"

In the White House, and sometimes in public, Nixon is increasingly brooding, even scaring his aides when his ire toward his enemies explodes into rage. "We live in an age of anarchy . . . We see mindless attacks on all the great institutions which have been created by free civilizations in the last five hundred years," he thunders in a speech to the nation. *Who is turning these kids, the most affluent and entitled generation in history, against America?*

In Nixon's Oval Office and Ronald Reagan's governor's mansion, it is becoming easier and easier to connect the unrest to one man, to link Dr. Timothy Leary with the violence, to see him as a Robespierre on acid, a kingpin hell-bent on unraveling the normal order. He is a subversive, a hippie rebel leader summoning his army, a sociocultural terrorist whose real master plan is to blow up the nation's moral compass in the name of free love and drugs.

Leary is becoming, in the words of Richard Nixon, "the most dangerous man in America."

A decade ago, as a prominent Harvard psychologist, Leary had achieved a comfortable life. He was the son of an Irish Catholic dentist from a quiet town in Massachusetts. He had attended the College of the Holy Cross and then became a cadet at the U.S. Military Academy at West Point. He had been court-martialed for a variety of minor infractions, honorably discharged, and then had begun his march through the academic ranks. At Harvard, he easily nestled into an Ivy League cocoon of faculty parties, scholarly articles in scientific journals, and blowing off steam with a round of martinis. But he knew something was missing: "I was a middle-aged man involved in the middle-aged process of dying."

On the cusp of his fortieth birthday, he ingested psychoactive mushrooms considered sacred by the Aztecs. "I came back a changed man," he said. "I learned more in the six or seven hours of this experience than in all my years as a psychologist."

He cofounded the Harvard Psilocybin Project and began researching the curative powers of hallucinogenic drugs, experimenting on himself, his friends, and even his children. Soon, he found his way to a little-known chemical, lysergic acid diethylamide, a drug so powerful that a microscopic dose could rocket him into the same transcendent realm sought by shamans and mystics.

LSD's creator, Albert Hofmann, viewed the drug as "medicine for the soul." Leary concurred—and went even further. If nuclear weapons represented man's grip on the universe's destructive power, LSD was the opposite: "The exact antidote to atomic energy. People take LSD and FLASH! They get the message and start putting things back in harmony with the great design. Stop war. Wear flowers. Conservation. Turning on people to LSD is the precise and only way to keep war from blowing up the whole system."

Leary's experiments brought disagreeable publicity, and Harvard finally dismissed him for his psychedelic zeal. But he no longer cared about advancing his Ivy League career. Instead, he wanted to share his realizations with the world.

He envisioned leading a mass conversion, a planetary spiritual awakening guided by LSD. And he turned out to be a natural showman, very good in front of crowds. He flashed a knowing smile as he promoted LSD's mind-expanding capabilities, suggesting it could cure many of society's ills. To prison authorities he claimed it would reduce recidivism. To politicians he whispered that the Kennedys had already turned on. To religious leaders he vowed they would see God. To the readers of *Playboy* he said, "There is no question that LSD is the most powerful aphrodisiac ever discovered by man...In a carefully prepared, loving LSD session, a woman will inevitably have several hundred orgasms."

He shelved the tweed jackets and began wearing American Indian headbands, Tibetan meditation beads, and dashikis. Soon his beaming face was everywhere, from magazine covers to television talk shows. His easily memorized mantra—*Turn on, tune in, drop out*—appeared on bumper stickers and was splashed across T-shirts, quoted by millions of kids around the world.

Jimi Hendrix, the Doors, and other famous new friends sought him out, hoping to glean some knowledge. John Lennon absorbed Leary's advice on tripping and composed some lyrics for the Beatles: "*Turn off your mind, relax and float downstream / It is not dying, it is not dying.*" And when Lennon and Yoko Ono decided to stage a famous "Bed-In"—curling up for days in a hotel room and hoping that world peace would break out—they invited Timothy Leary to join them. The grinning ex-professor was there, shirtless and at the foot of John Lennon's bed. He joined in, clapping and happily singing "Give Peace a Chance." In midtune Lennon shouted a joyous salute: "*Timmy Leary!*"

In Washington, Nixon and his aides were watching. They were stunned at how Leary garnered so much attention, how he dominated the airwaves and headlines, how huge crowds came to see him. He was not just an LSD Lothario rolling in drugs and orgies, not just another Pied Piper sybarite luring hippie girls. He was talking about leading a mind revolution: *Congress shall make no law abridging the individual's right to seek an expanded consciousness.*

When Nixon tried to stanch the flow of marijuana across the Mexican border with Operation Intercept, Leary promptly announced his countermove: Operation Turn-On. "They've lost the war in Vietnam, and now they are using the same techniques in the war on pot," Leary proclaimed, urging kids to grow their own marijuana and turn it into a national industry.

The government convicted him for failing to pay the federal marijuana tax, sentencing him to thirty years in prison. But Leary remained free on bond while he appealed, fighting all the way to the Supreme Court. In *Leary v. United States*, he won unanimously, defeating the Nixon Administration's lawyers and striking down key marijuana laws.

He celebrated his victory by declaring he would challenge Ronald Reagan in the California gubernatorial election. "Don't you think I've had more experience than Ronnie?" Leary joked to reporters. He promised to legalize pot, selling it through officially sanctioned stores with the tax revenues going into state coffers. He said he would never live in the governor's mansion—instead he would pitch a teepee on the front lawn and conduct the state's business from there. His campaign slogan, *Come Together, Join the Party*, inspired John Lennon to write a song for him that the Beatles recorded as "Come Together."

But even as he was joyously leading his cultural revolution, Leary could see that things were spinning beyond his control. He had always been careful to portray LSD as a religious experience, emphasizing the need for trained guides to lead people to enlightenment. But too many kids were swallowing LSD like Halloween candy, for kicks. And not everyone was seeing LSD as a manifestation of the inner God. For the unready, the unfit, it had summoned inner demons. Dark stories were spreading about wickedly bad trips, people flying out of windows, and the CIA using LSD for mind control.

And then the nation recoiled in horror in 1969 when a Medusa-haired drifter named Charles Manson—who had dropped acid and divined messianic prophecies in the lyrics of the Beatles—unleashed a bloodbath in California. Manson sent his handpicked cult members to murder five people in a mansion north of Beverly Hills, and then out the next night to stab two more people to death with...*forks and knives*. Millions of Americans assumed that LSD, Timothy Leary's sacrament, was driving people insane.

"I'm terribly frightened by LSD," Governor Ronald Reagan announced. "I think there's been a great deal of misinformation by those who seem to see no harm in it."

And now, Nixon, Reagan, and other unnerved leaders are convinced that Timothy Leary has been waging chemical warfare. That he has been brainwashing a generation of young Americans.

To them, there is no real difference between Timothy Leary and Charles Manson.

※　※　※

Even before the White House zeroed in on him, prosecutors and police had been hunting Leary for years. Among the first was G. Gordon Liddy, who invaded Leary's spiritual retreat in upstate New York. Liddy found nothing but a kilo of peat moss on the first bust. But he kept coming back, finally driving Leary and his family out of the state. At a border crossing at Laredo, Texas, cops unearthed a tiny stash of pot in a snuff box hurriedly tucked inside his teenage daughter's panties.

There was one more big bust: The day after Christmas in 1968, Leary parked his family station wagon on a dead-end street in Laguna Beach, California. A police cruiser pulled up. The cop insisted he could smell marijuana and began searching the car. With a grunt of pleasure, he finally extracted two charred joints from the ashtray and held them up, victorious. Leary, who had hurtled the cosmos on hundreds of acid trips, saw the officer's paltry prize and scoffed: "Big deal!"

But the two roaches were a felony in California. They were enough to disqualify Leary from running against Reagan for governor—and to finally send him to prison. The Reagan-appointed judge who imposed the maximum sentence, up to ten years, called Leary an "insidious and detrimental influence on society...A pleasure-seeking, irresponsible Madison Avenue advocate of the free use of LSD and marijuana."

When Leary was first put behind bars, the jailer slammed the cell door shut and sneered: "For you we throw away the key."

※　※　※

On the very day that Leary enters the bowels of his new prison, Richard Nixon's aides are arriving at the Oval Office to brief him on the latest spasms of violence. All week, there has been one explosion after another. When one hundred thousand anti-war activists converged on Washington, a bomb roared inside the headquarters of the National Guard Association. There have been attacks at the Selective Service offices in Hollywood, Oakland, and Detroit. Detonations at military buildings in Longview, Washington; Kent, Ohio; Reading, Pennsylvania; Mankato, Minnesota. Government offices were blown up in Portland, Oregon. There had been an eruption at the Atomic Energy Commission office in Rocky Flats, Colorado. Explosions and fires at Ohio University, Illinois Wesleyan University, the University of Alabama, Valparaiso University, the University of Virginia, Case Western Reserve University, Colorado State University, University of Nevada, DePauw University, the University of Missouri at Columbia, Loyola University in Chicago, and John Carroll University in Ohio.

The FBI is sending reports to Nixon's aides suggesting that homegrown revolutionaries are holding enough dynamite to bomb a building in the United States every day for thirty straight years— and that they would surely love to blow President Nixon to hell.

THE GREAT FEAR

Afternoon, May 13, 1970

Inside CMC-West, a burly guard hands Tim his new gear: a small padlock and key for his metal locker. A blue denim jacket. Three pairs of denim pants. Three denim shirts with his prison number stenciled on them.

A trustee leads him past a shaded patio where a bridge tournament is in progress. Inmates look up and shout his name. He walks past garden beds where elderly prisoners are on their hands and knees as they turn over the soil. The trustee points at the tomato plants and brags that the prison grows much of its own food.

Tim walks inside building 324, identical to the other wooden barracks. There are no bars on the windows and the front door remains unlocked. *We don't call them cells here*, the trustee says. *This is your dormitory*. Inside, there's that sour tang of stale cigarette smoke mixed with the odor of ancient men. Several lifers are gathered like gray seals clumped on the rocks, hunchbacks with parchment-paper faces and homemade tattoos. They begin to move toward him, faces flickering with recognition.

He is led to bed number 7, and he surveys the tiny space Richard Nixon and Ronald Reagan want him to occupy for the next ten years: a narrow cot, a dented locker, and a gray metal desk. He dumps his clothing down, along with his tobacco, pens, and shower shoes. The other inmates bounce around him, each dressed in the same standard-issue denim pants and bone-colored sneakers. They slap palms, pandering, flattering, promising to help him. Suddenly a loudspeaker crackles to life and the prison intercom blares a message:

"Will all gardeners please report to the yard crew office for your garden seeds."

❋   ❋   ❋

Slumping on his cot, Leary has time to try to hover above his own new reality. He rolls a cigarette and fires it up. In many ways, he expected to end up here.

"Of the great men of the past whom I hold up as models," he tells people, "almost every one of them has been either imprisoned or threatened with imprisonment for their spiritual beliefs: Gandhi, Jesus, Socrates, Lao-tse...I have absolutely no fear of imprisonment... I know that the only real prisons are *internal*."

Years ago, he and some of the other pioneers of hallucinogenic research had developed a theory that your essential coding was changed when you ingested the psychedelic sacraments. That portals were blown open. That, perhaps, after you experienced the enlightenment...you had somehow physically evolved. In a way, the LSD stayed with you. It was as if you were simply operating on another, higher level, all the time.

Among his peers and devotees, Leary is legendary for his Herculean ability to ingest frequent doses of extraordinarily potent LSD without ever being gripped by the monster of panic—*the Great Fear* that overwhelms so many users. His friends chalk it up to his sweeping intellect, his ability to outwit fear; or maybe it's just his Irish pluck letting him mock the demons. He can take hit after hit of pure LSD and appear to be perfectly normal, whether he's trading jokes with a glib TV talk show host or charming a millionaire hostess at a lavish dinner party in San Francisco. Leary grows more lucid on LSD, laughing easily as he becomes the smartest, wisest, most *superior* person in any setting.

Some of those who've known him the longest are fascinated but also disturbed by the way he gravitated so easily to the celebrities, the bright lights, the big money. Some had a theory: His ego, the very thing he was telling everyone else to be free of, was steadily devouring him.

❋   ❋   ❋

From his prison window, he glimpses nine weathered hills in the distance. The Nine Sisters, as they are called, are lined up like a giant's steppingstones to the sea. Ten miles to the west, winds rise from the Pacific and push toward the hills, sailing over moon-kissed Morro Bay and aiming for the prison. The breezes can carry aromatic blends of sagebrush, coyote bush, and monkey flower—heady reminders of free and wild California.

As he lies on his new prison bunk for the first time, the winds can reach him through the open windows and it must feel like something achingly familiar that's fading from memory. Maybe it's only with that sense of things and people being forgotten that the Great Fear really rises up. The celebratory 1968 Moody Blues pop hit about him, "Legend of a Mind," now sounds almost cruel: *"Timothy Leary's dead . . ."*

PURPLE LIZARDS

May 17, 1970

Today is Sunday, visiting day, and Tim's wife, Rosemary, is at the sign-in desk after making the trip from their home in Berkeley. She has just been in New York, where she staged a high-profile fundraising benefit with Jimi Hendrix to help pay her husband's legal bills.

As Tim enters the visiting area, he is ordered to stand at attention, both arms raised high. A guard studies his wrists to make sure he is not wearing a watch—it could be used to smuggle things in and out of prison. His arms, legs, and crotch are patted down.

On the other side of the visitors' center, the guards have been warned that Rosemary might try to sneak in LSD for her husband, perhaps by hiding a tiny speck inside a fingernail or by dabbing some onto her shirt collar for him to lap up with his tongue. They nervously search her, scared of accidentally touching the acid and having it seep into their pores—and losing their minds.

Tim pushes through the swinging doors, the guards trailing him. He sees Rosemary, serenely elegant in a flowing hippie skirt and Indian blouse. She is thirty-four, fifteen years younger than him, tall and slender with dancing dark eyes and long chestnut hair.

They rush to embrace and kiss. This is the first time they've been able to touch each other in eight weeks. The guards watch closely—the couple has already been warned against trying anything "lascivious."

She might be slipping him some acid under her tongue.

✵   ✵   ✵

Rosemary Woodruff Leary has taken her own long journey. Born in St. Louis, Missouri, she grew up in a conservative household with

Baptist parents. She gravitated to New York and became a model, finding that slipstream inside the beatnik and cutting-edge jazz world that was moving away from opiates and alcohol and downers—and toward hallucinogens, magic mushrooms, and eventually LSD. She knew the Beat writers like Jack Kerouac, had married a Dutch jazz accordion player, and began hearing about Timothy Leary and his experiments in Millbrook, ninety miles north of New York City.

After leaving Harvard in 1963, Leary had been invited to live on a 2,400-acre estate by heirs to the Mellon fortune. Anchored by a sixty-four-room nineteenth-century mansion, the Millbrook domain held forests, lakes, orchards, gardens, and creeks. Leary had moved in with his two young children, several colleagues who had also left Harvard, and a growing retinue of poets, artists, and musicians who had heard about the higher-consciousness experiments—and about Leary forming what he called the League for Spiritual Discovery.

With little buildings seemingly airlifted from a Bavarian forest, stone bridges, fields of sunflowers, and rows of ripe corn, Millbrook became the world's most important site dedicated to the pursuit of psychedelic awakening and the parallels found in Eastern transcendental religions. Jack Kerouac, Aldous Huxley, Allen Ginsberg, Charles Mingus, and Ken Kesey and his Merry Pranksters all came to see Leary at the estate—and the once-quiet experiments with LSD began to attract notice: A local prosecutor named G. Gordon Liddy led a task force checking into rumors of LSD, pot, and hash—and skinny-dipping hippie women, hulking jazz men playing flutes for audiences of squirrels, body-painting orgies, and men with flowers in their hair riding white stallions.

Rosemary met Leary at an art exhibition in New York, and he invited her to visit the estate. It struck her as a psychedelic playland, a magical place, but she also thought he was lonely inside of it, even with the hubbub of seekers and trippers arriving at the door. She eventually moved in and Tim began telling others that he and Rosemary had been married "several thousand years, in many forms."

Over the past five years, the two soul mates have dropped acid dozens of times together. They have consulted tarot cards, horoscopes, and the ancient Chinese divination text, the *I Ching*. They have chanted together, breathed together, done a locked-together Tantric form of yoga to expand their consciousness. They've made love in teepees, in mansions, and outdoors in a waterfall under a full moon. In 1967 they were married three different times: by a Native American shaman at Joshua Tree National Monument while everyone else was vomiting from having ingested too much mescaline; during a simple Hindu ceremony at their pleasant home in Berkeley; and at their estate in New York the day after one of Liddy's midnight busts.

Since moving in with Tim, Rosemary has been arrested three times and jailed twice. It was her peat moss that Liddy confiscated on his first raid. She refused to testify against her husband and once served thirty days in solitary confinement. She was in the station wagon with Tim when the cops found those two minuscule roaches in the ashtray, and now she's facing her own six-month jail sentence.

✸   ✸   ✸

Tim and Rosemary look around at the drab visiting room with its weathered wooden tables, crappy wicker chairs, and walls dotted with slogans from Alcoholics Anonymous. They head outdoors to a little garden, with wooden benches set out on the grass.

He leans in close to her, inhaling her scent as he lights their cigarettes. They know that someone, somewhere, is watching them very carefully.

He asks about the fundraiser in New York. They were hoping to collect at least $100,000 for his defense. The other organizers included John Lennon and Yoko Ono, though John couldn't appear because the Nixon White House had barred him from entering the country.

Rosemary is quiet for a moment. Then she tries to explain what happened. Tim listens, beginning to frown as she speaks:

Somebody drizzled heavy-wattage LSD into the punch bowls...and it was as though the avenging avatars of Vishnu suddenly crashed the party. Jim Morrison of the Doors tried to read some of his poetry, but nobody listened. People's fingers turned into hissing snakes.

Some of the guests began cowering under tables, shielding their eyes from the yakking purple lizards. The famous hippie activist Abbie Hoffman wobbled on the stage and shoved aside Beat poet Allen Ginsberg, who had been chanting a peaceful "Ommmmm" to calm the crowd. Acid eating his brain, Hoffman began screeching about Kent State, how everyone would have to fight like hell to end the Vietnam War. As he writhed around, offering up nonsensical hallucinations, several of the wealthy would-be donors began crawling for the exits, fighting frantically against the first stages of full-blown LSD panic attacks. When Jimi Hendrix emerged onstage, right after midnight and striding into the purple haze, most of the audience was barely aware that they were in the presence of a sonic messenger dispatched by the psychedelic gods—and the next day some couldn't remember hearing Hendrix play.

Tim is silent for a second, and then he asks:

"How much money did you collect?"

Rosemary tells him reluctantly that they only raised about $5,000.

Tim offers a half smile.

"It could have been worse."

Rosemary slowly answers:

No, it is worse. It cost us $8,000 to put the benefit on.

They sit quietly for a moment, each of them dragging on a fresh Camel cigarette. She adds that she is talking to other people in the rattling caravan of seekers, leeches, hangers-on, moochers, rock stars, poets, radicals, liberal lawyers, trippy sycophants, and true believers who have affixed themselves to their orbit.

Maybe some of them can help you.

Tim looks around and whispers in her ear.

She stiffens and nods. When he had first been sentenced, Rosemary had pressed her face to the prison window glass separating them, stared into his eyes, and sighed:

"I'll free you love."

ARES, GOD OF WAR

May 24, 1970

The guards have been studying the infamous Timothy Leary since he was processed into the prison eleven days ago, and they've concluded he is probably harmless.

After the 7 a.m. wakeup whistle, he reports promptly to the captain's office and works as a desk clerk. When his shift ends, he takes music lessons, trying his hand at the organ and the flute. Sometimes the guards see the middle-aged man out on the grass, standing on his head, focusing his attention on the roses in the flower beds.

It's yoga, he tells them.

During the head counts, they come upon him sitting cross-legged on his cot, chanting and mumbling in some sort of hoodoo-voodoo, weird-ass language. He's been in for less than two weeks and already there are some cons seeking him out for advice about their legal cases, their medical conditions, and their drug problems.

A few of the guards worried about his followers, the ones who might try to free their guru. From the moment he arrived in prison, there had been some strange long-haired freaks hanging around down by the highway, probably trying to gather the courage to troop up to the gates and see their master. But as Leary's days inside the prison march on, the freaks have scattered—as if they've given up on ever seeing him again.

Every day, he uses more and more yellow prison paper, writing long letters to Rosemary and decorating them with psychedelic sketches, numerological references, and peace signs. All of them are filled with a kind of secret alphabet, cosmology or Hindu symbols that only they know, that the guards or whoever is reading the letters will never understand.

Leary keeps to himself and tries to read books from the prison library—and to follow the news from the free world. On a Sunday in May, he can see that the blood-curdling details from the Manson prosecution are being joined by other spectacular news: The shadowy revolutionary organization that went underground after that deadly townhouse explosion in Greenwich Village has just issued a "Declaration of a State of War" on Richard Nixon:

> This is the first communication from the Weatherman Underground. All over the world, people fighting Amerikan imperialism look to Amerika's youth to use our strategic position behind enemy lines to join forces in the destruction of the empire... We've known that our job is to lead white kids into armed revolution... Revolutionary violence is the only way...
>
> Guns and grass are united in the youth underground. Freaks are revolutionaries and revolutionaries are freaks... Within the next 14 days we will attack a symbol or institution of Amerikan injustice.

This Sunday, there are also news reports that in Ames, Iowa, the FBI has been called in to help figure out who detonated a massive dynamite bomb inside city hall that injured nine people and blew up portions of the adjacent police headquarters.

✹   ✹   ✹

As he weighs what the hell is going on across America, Leary is informed that another visitor has arrived. It's his new lead lawyer, Michael Kennedy, an intense thirty-three-year-old man with scowling blue eyes and huge round glasses that give him the unblinking appearance of a large owl. Kennedy wears his sandy-colored hair long, over his suit collar, and he's recently grown a bushy, horseshoe-shaped mustache.

Tim has given Kennedy a nickname, a code name: Ares, after the Greek god of untamed, violent war. The attorney is known for his brusque, agitated manner in the courtroom.

"I am not a gentleman," he told one jury. "I am an advocate, a fighter, and we are in a jungle, and we are outgunned, and we have to fight hard."

After one of his cases ended in a mistrial, the prosecutor sidled up to him and said, "Well, Mr. Kennedy, it looks like we will be trying these clients of yours all over again. We'll do better next time."

Kennedy shot back: "Is that what you think, shithead? Why don't you and I step outside right now and let's settle this."

He keeps an office in an 1895 Victorian home in San Francisco's Fillmore District. It is decorated in revolutionary colors, black and red—the doors, the walls, even the typewriters. He started his career representing conscientious objectors and farmworkers but has broadened into heavier, increasingly militant cases. He's becoming one of the counterculture's most famous lawyers. He has ties to the Black Panthers and is widely assumed to be advising various fugitive radicals who have gone underground. He conducts much of his business from pay phones so federal agents can't trace his calls.

He has other, aboveground clients, including two San Francisco porn impresarios, the Mitchell brothers, who are battling obscenity charges over their X-rated theater. They are paying Kennedy's bills, helping him buy a purple Porsche and a fine Pacific Heights abode where Jane Fonda and other celebrities sometimes gather. Kennedy's wife is a designer who works with the elegant clothing shop in San Francisco where Marilyn Monroe bought her wedding dress when she married Joe DiMaggio. The store, Joseph Magnin, is famous for its "Wolves Den"—a men-only lounge where preferred customers smoke cigars and are served gently shaken martinis by the staff's prettiest women.

Inside the prison, Tim greets his lawyer and leads him to a table out in the visitors' garden. Tim is in his wrinkled denims; Kennedy wears a neatly pressed suit and tie.

Kennedy has bad news:

Our attempt to get Supreme Court Justice William O. Douglas to grant an appeal has failed.

And in New York, Tim is facing eleven outstanding charges. In Texas, he's facing a decade for the pot found inside his daughter's underwear. The Texas judge denounced him as a "menace to the country."

Tim studies his attorney and does what he has been doing most of his life as a trained psychologist. He scans his face, seeing if it will help him read Kennedy's mind. Kennedy has been steering every facet of Leary's legal drama: Kennedy urged him to plead guilty, promising Tim would be freed on appeal. Kennedy predicted that the Supreme Court justice would help him out. *But none of it has happened. Instead, Kennedy's legal advice has turned to shit—and now he's suggesting that I could be in prison until I die.*

Tim bends forward and tells Kennedy exactly what he wants to happen.

Some hippie friends, some drug smugglers, can help get me out of prison. They're good at moving millions of hits of Orange Sunshine acid and tons of Thai sticks and Afghani hash.

Kennedy snarls in response: "The hippies aren't going to get you out. It's going to be the politicals that have the power and the will to get you out."

A few minutes later, Kennedy signs out on the prison visitors' log and walks to his Porsche, knowing that Timothy Leary, the king of LSD, wants to get out of jail by any means possible—and that his wife, Rosemary, will raise the money to make it happen.

MADMAN

June 1–5, 1970

Tim sits at his little metal prison desk, pecking away on his portable Olivetti. He's one of the few inmates with a typewriter, and now he's working on a last-ditch personal plea to Justice Douglas, hoping that the court's most liberal member will intervene on his behalf. Tim is composing a prose poem, "The Eagle Brief," to attach to his final appeal:

Rosemary and I are American Eagles.
Totem animals of this land.
Wild. Free. High. Proud. Laughing...
Fierce, stubborn wild birds.
We are in prison because we are American
Eagles.
We are not free because we have become
symbols of freedom.
They have gone and passed laws against
eagles.
They have hunted us to the ground.
Rashly, wickedly, and in violation of our
national law...
Because we laughed and cried
FREEEEEEEEEEEEEEEDOM!

Tim looks at the page and keeps typing:

We sit trembling in our cages.
Soon we will die if we are not freed.
Do you want us dead?

❁　❁　❁

On Friday, June 5, President Richard Nixon finishes his usual working lunch inside the Oval Office—a canned pineapple ring topped with a scoop of cottage cheese.

Now his senior aides are shuffling in, eyeing him nervously. Among them is Henry Kissinger, his national security advisor. It is Kissinger who colluded with Nixon to invent the "Madman" strategy. The idea is simple: Make the Russians and the North Vietnamese believe that Nixon is so psychologically erratic, so impulsively violent, that he might launch a nuclear strike in a fit of rage. Nixon and Kissinger believe it could force the Communists to submit to American demands at the negotiating table. They have even staged a full-scale nuclear alert, buzzing the Soviet Union's borders with nuclear-armed B-52 bombers while Kissinger warned the Russians: "The president is out of control."

Now, as Kissinger enters the Oval Office, he really is worrying about the president's state of mind. Since the invasion of Cambodia and the explosion of campus protest, Nixon has been veering into uncharted waters, even drinking his way through sleepless nights. He's picked up the phone at 3 a.m. and issued slurred orders:

"Bomb the shit out of them," he'll say, ordering strikes against North Korea or Syria. Kissinger and the other staff will discreetly put things off until morning, when Nixon will inevitably have little memory of what happened the night before.

"If the president had his way," Kissinger complains to his aides, "there would be a nuclear war each week!"

Beyond his drunken declarations of war, the president's behavior just seems...increasingly loopy.

One afternoon a Secret Service agent stood vigil as the president fed treats to his Irish setter, King Timahoe. As the agent stared in disbelief, the leader of the free world briefly examined one of the dog biscuits, then popped it into his own mouth.

The whispers were caroming in the White House hallways, especially about how the president behaved last month when one hundred thousand protesters converged on Washington after the Kent State shootings. The president stayed awake all night, playing classical music at top volume, sipping cocktails, and peeking through a window at the demonstrators' candlelight vigils. Then he began making phone calls—more than fifty in all—jarring dozens of surprised friends and advisors out of their sleep. Finally, after 4 a.m., he summoned his Cuban American manservant, Manolo Sanchez, and ordered Secret Service agents to drive them to the Lincoln Memorial.

Climbing up the steps with Manolo beside him, Nixon entered the lair of the hippies. The student demonstrators crawled out of their sleeping bags, astonished to see the president of the United States, the bogeyman himself, interrupting their dreams. "I know most of you think I'm an SOB, but I want you to know that I understand just how you feel," Nixon announced.

As the students rubbed sleep out of their eyes, the president rambled on about his desire for peace and his admiration for Winston Churchill, whom Nixon had originally believed "was a madman." Secret Service agents tried to pull him away, but he kept talking. He discussed college football and traveling abroad, and he recommended the students surf the beach near his home in San Clemente, California.

The kids were spooked. "He didn't look at anyone in the eyes; he was mumbling," one said later. Another told a reporter, "He looked scared and nervous like he was in a fog. His eyes were glassy."

The Secret Service tried to coax him back to the White House, but Nixon insisted on taking Manolo to Capitol Hill. It was nearly dawn when the president ordered the House of Representatives unlocked. He took a seat and asked his manservant to make a speech from the speaker's dais, from the same podium used for State of the Union addresses.

Manolo hesitated.

"Manolo, say something!" the president commanded. Finally, the reluctant man, speaking in fractured English, stepped forward and spoke briefly about how proud he was to have become an American citizen. The audience—Secret Service agents, a nighttime cleaning woman, and two of the president's aides who had been alerted to what was happening—stared at the scene. As Manolo concluded his brief remarks, Nixon's hands slowly slapped together, the lonely clapping echoing through the nearly empty chamber.

Nixon's chief of staff, H. R. Haldeman, had arrived just in time to see the president applauding his personal valet in the House chamber. At home, Haldeman wrote in his diary:

"The weirdest day so far. I am concerned about his condition... there's a long way to go and he's in no condition to weather it."

✺   ✺   ✺

In the Oval Office, Haldeman, Kissinger, and Nixon's other senior aides watch carefully as FBI director J. Edgar Hoover and CIA director Richard Helms arrive and take their seats. Nixon has summoned them—and all of his intelligence chiefs—for an emergency strategy session to deal with the enemies at home.

The president launches into an angry tirade. He says that young people are "determined to destroy our society" and are engaging in "revolutionary terrorism." He is certain that the provocateurs are being financed by a worldwide Communist conspiracy, all with the goal of bringing America to her knees.

"Good intelligence," he says, is "the best way to stop terrorism."

Next, Nixon demands a tight, coordinated plan to defeat and destroy the enemies. He has ideas about how to proceed: widespread electronic surveillance, a secret campaign to intercept and monitor private mailings, burglarizing homes and offices, planting bugs, rewarding informants, planting undercover spies everywhere.

His intelligence advisors are stunned. The plan the president is proposing is clearly illegal. Nixon goes even further. He says the CIA has to become involved in domestic espionage against American citizens, in clear violation of national law.

Nixon's words settle in. No one says it out loud, but several are scared by his recklessness. If they get caught carrying out any part of the plan, it will ruin their careers and probably bring down the administration. Nixon preempts any resistance from his aides: "When the president does it, that means it is not illegal."

The president's aides exchange quick glances. Maybe the whispers are true. Maybe Nixon's no longer simply pretending to be a madman. Maybe he is *becoming* one. And maybe he's taking them all down the same road.

WARGASM

Inside the California Men's Colony, the mealtime whistle is shrieking and Leary looks up to see a scramble of old men hiking up their drooping, faded pants. The lifers are scurrying past him like blind crabs, all of them ready to nab food trays and bump in line.

After dinner, the men gravitate to the TV room, slump into their usual chairs, and cheer at the *Bonanza* wranglers or giggle at *The Carol Burnett Show*. Even though the sound is turned up full volume, several geezers begin to snore and flail their arms as they tumble into sleep. Tim has already been hearing stories about the cons who refuse parole, preferring to live out their lives in the west wing.

It's just a carefully designed velvet coffin.

He sits on his prison cot, fingering a strand of meditation beads and chanting "Om" over and over again. His crazy-ass personal appeal to Justice Douglas, in the form of a hallucinatory prayer, has been rejected. He studies a paperback copy of the *I Ching*, trying to predict the future in the splay of hexagrams. He obsesses over his horoscope, consulting the stars. When he turns on his transistor radio, he hears the Beatles' newest hit, the melancholy-tinged title song from their brand-new album, *Let It Be*. The record's release coincides with Paul McCartney's announcement that the band is breaking up. If *Sgt. Pepper's Lonely Hearts Club Band* felt like the beginning of an era, this new album feels like the end of one. The lyrics are meant to be a balm, but Tim finds them oppressive.

The last thing he wants to do in prison is *Let It Be*.

❈   ❈   ❈

After a month inside, he is talking casually with a few inmates, quietly learning everything he can about how the California Men's

Colony is run and guarded. The place feels loose around the edges, even with the barbed wire and patrolling sharpshooters in trucks. He learns that just a couple of months ago, a convict escaped by doing the most unlikely thing imaginable—he nonchalantly hopped onto a visitor's bicycle and briskly began pedaling away in broad daylight.

An especially weathered-looking inmate, a grinning man named Bellinger, sidles up. He is obsequious and mumbling about his own spiritual quests. Tim quickly recognizes him as a classic heroin junkie, a user in his midfifties. Bellinger suggests a game of horseshoes and he whispers.

I know who the snitches are. I can name the prisoners who will turn you in to the guards.

Bellinger adds something else.

I know every inch of the prison and what happens—or is supposed to happen—during each minute inside.

Bellinger looks directly at him.

I know how to get you out of here.

❋   ❋   ❋

More bombs are erupting across the country, from New York to Chicago to Oakland. The Weathermen, the tight-knit clique of former campus leaders who have gone underground as guerrilla revolutionaries, are careening toward notoriety. They've taken their name from Bob Dylan's "Subterranean Homesick Blues"—"you don't need a weatherman to know which way the wind blows"—and are led by Bernardine Dohrn and Bill Ayers. Dohrn is a twenty-eight-year-old with a law degree from the University of Chicago. Raised in an upper-middle-class Milwaukee suburb, she was a dance student and high school cheerleader before turning to revolutionary terrorism. Her coleader, Ayers, is the twenty-five-year-old son of the president of Commonwealth Edison in Chicago. When people call him a rich radical, Ayers bristles: "Kill all the rich people. Break up their cars and apartments. Bring the revolution home, kill your parents, that's where it's really at."

When news leaked out about the Weatherman "Wargasm" council meeting last year, many Americans assumed Dohrn was in solidarity with Charles Manson's "family." She had shouted, "First they killed those pigs, then they ate dinner in the same room with them, then even shoved a fork into a victim's stomach." Dohrn was mocking, but the audience cheered and the other Weathermen began greeting each other by spreading three fingers—the sign of the fork.

Besides the bombings, the Weathermen are issuing more ominous communiqués, most of them authored by Dohrn:

> Our job is to lead white kids into armed rebellion...The pigs of this country are our enemies...Political power grows out of a gun, a Molotov, a riot, a commune, and from the soul of the people...kids are making love, smoking dope and loading guns.

The Weathermen orchestrated the bombing of the National Guard Association headquarters in Washington, DC. They've bombed three banks in Manhattan. On June 9, they pull off their most audacious attack, aimed at the five-story headquarters of the New York City Police Department, in the heart of Manhattan. At 6:42 p.m., after most employees had gone home for the evening, a caller phoned with a warning:

"There is a bomb set to go off at Police Headquarters."

Fifteen minutes later, as cops searched the building, a huge explosion went off on the second floor, injuring seven people, shattering windows, and blowing glass, bricks, and mortar into the street.

YOU GOTTA PITCH

June 12, 1970

On day 114 of Tim's captivity, arsonists set fires at the campus ROTC office at UCLA. In another part of Los Angeles, a twenty-five-year-old pitcher for the Pittsburgh Pirates named Dock Ellis is wrestling with a terrible hangover. Nearly instinctively, he reaches over to the nightstand and gobbles some LSD. A young woman he's with is flipping through the morning newspaper.

"Dock," she says, "you better get up. You gotta pitch."

He is stunned. He thought *tomorrow* was his day to pitch.

"Oh, wow," he says. "What happened to yesterday?"

A few hours later, he's on the mound in San Diego, facing the Padres. As he launches a fastball toward the catcher, he can see a fiery comet tail trailing behind the pitch. He smiles. *This* is the fastball he's been looking for. As the game continues, the ball changes size. Sometimes it becomes huge, like a fat balloon. Other times it feels very small, like a pockmarked golf ball. By the fifth inning he is certain that the umpire must be Richard Nixon. The batters swim in and out of focus. He hits one of them and walks several more. The opposing players are nervous, diving into the dirt at times to avoid getting hit. He can't tell if he's pitching to Babe Ruth or Mickey Mouse. Yet, somehow, by the end of the game his team has won 2–0 and Dock Ellis has pitched a no-hitter. He is a hero, mobbed by his teammates.

Later, when he tells them about the LSD, he boasts:

Dr. Timothy Leary personally gave me the drug.

LOVE REVOLUTIONARIES

Mid- to late June 1970

Tim's celebrity status has won him admirers inside, even as the guards grumble about the deluge of fan mail. Some prisoners salute him, and when Rosemary visits he tells her that he feels like a general in a POW camp.

She can see that Tim is getting tanner; he's going out on the handball court, shirtless and laughing. He's easy to recognize from a distance—he's the only prisoner without any tattoos. He's getting better at the flute and he practices while sitting cross-legged in the grass.

Bellinger, the old junkie, remains coy whenever Tim presses him for details about their plan. He makes vague references to finding the right time—of the day, of the week, of the season. Bellinger says his carefully researched method is so secret that he can't disclose the specifics until everything is in order.

It's foolproof, Tim hears him say.

For now, there's just one thing that Tim needs to know, Bellinger adds:

"You're going to have to be in the best physical shape of your life."

✶   ✶   ✶

In late June, Rosemary arrives for another Sunday visit, sweeping in buoyantly. He can see her eyes lighting up as she nears him.

Tim presses into her as she pumps quarters into the grimy prison vending machine, waiting for the packages of Marlboros and Snickers bars to tumble into his hands. Tim can sense that she's gaining strength, independence.

She has news: *I've been spending time with the attorney Michael Kennedy and his wife.*

They are asking her out to dinner or inviting her to their posh home and engaging her in long, serious talks about the future of America. And Michael Kennedy and Rosemary have been conferring about what kind of operation, what kind of money, would get Tim out of prison, into hiding, out of the country.

Tim and Rosemary agree: *There's only one outfit capable of raising huge sums of money in the blink of an eye—the Brotherhood of Eternal Love.*

A loose-knit posse of LSD-worshipping young hippies from Southern California, the group has tabbed Tim its spiritual godfather. The off-the-grid soul mates are a barely tethered collective of bikers, surfers, college kids, and mountain people who had welcomed Tim and Rosemary when they decided to flee from G. Gordon Liddy and permanently relocate to California. Tim could see that they are far from the entitled Ivy League dropouts, professional Bohemians, hipsters, and arty types from the downtown scenes in San Francisco or New York. The Brotherhood members are working-class Johnnies and Jills who swallowed acid—and called it freedom. They want to drop out—with no polemics, diatribes, or politics. They have a spiritual code, a philosophy inspired by Tim, of turning the entire world on to LSD. They manufacture millions of hits of a highly visionary form of acid called Orange Sunshine, often giving it away for free. They tell people they are *love revolutionaries.*

Tim and Rosemary spent several months living in a teepee at the Brotherhood's mountaintop commune. The people there liked Tim's stamina, his sexual energy, and his ability to guide them on trips as they floated in the ranch's pond. And as Tim and Rosemary moved deeper into the California counterculture, the Brotherhood members morphed into pot and hash entrepreneurs.

"We deal because that's our thing," one of them told Tim. "Dope is the hope of the human race."

The Brotherhood perfected laughably sly ways of making huge amounts of money from smuggling—by hollowing out surfboards in Hawaii and stuffing them with hash, or by shipping hash-filled Volkswagens overseas from Afghanistan. Leary praised them in the underground press as modern-day Robin Hoods.

Tim and Rosemary once thought they might stay on the

Brotherhood ranch forever—until a teenage girl, high on LSD, drowned while skinny-dipping in the swimming hole. The cops came and Leary was arrested for contributing to the delinquency of a minor.

The pressure on the commune became unbearable, especially after Nixon established his "Western White House" a few minutes away in San Clemente. Finally, the Brotherhood abandoned their mountain hideout and funky old houses in Laguna Beach. Like stoned Vikings going to Valhalla, several of them fled to Nicaragua, Canada, and Hawaii, especially to Maui and its most remote, inaccessible regions, where they are harvesting pot and carrying out their smuggling operations protected by the spirits, by the fire goddess Pele.

Rosemary whispers to Tim that she was driven to the prison today by one of the key members of the Brotherhood, an old friend of theirs who has miraculously escaped detection, hiding his tracks better than anyone else. He is waiting outside, keeping a safe distance from any suspicious guards.

Tim looks out toward the parking lot and sees a tall, sinewy man standing under a tree.

Michael Randall, a former business student, was there at the beginning of the Brotherhood in Laguna Beach. He had managed Mystic Arts World, a bookshop, meditation center, and homage to Leary. When Randall would emerge from the clouds of incense, he struck visitors to the store as having a quiet, strong demeanor. Women, including Rosemary, found him reliable and attractive. So did rock stars: After Randall met the Moody Blues backstage at a Los Angeles show, he invited them to the Brotherhood's ranch. Some of the visitors dropped acid and watched the young kids romping in the fields and past the teepees. The next Moody Blues album was called *To Our Children's Children's Children*.

At the Newport Pop Festival in Costa Mesa, California, Randall and the Brotherhood were allowed to sell organic food and juices. The Brotherhood dosed thousands of bottles of vegetable and fruit drinks with Orange Sunshine. One of the bottles was handed to a cop; the policeman disappeared and later a crackling announcement blared over the crowd, telling all cops to avoid consuming anything they were offered.

The Brotherhood still has trucks filled with millions of hits of Orange Sunshine. Randall has told Rosemary that he remains a true believer in Tim, that he still has a deep spiritual commitment to turning the world on.

From inside the prison, Tim studies the handsome, bearded Randall, a man half his age.

Surely the Brotherhood will help free their spiritual leader.

ARE YOU SLEEPING WITH HIM?

July 1970

Tim is staring at Rosemary as she settles herself on the wooden benches in the prison garden. The skies are Easter-egg blue and a soft wind is coming from the west. In the background, there is the grunting and shuffling of the old convicts sweating through another game of handball. Rosemary seems animated, edgy, as she chats about politics, about the coming revolution. He's wondering how much influence Kennedy is having on his once-serene wife. Tim knows what she must see when she looks at him—his skin feels saggy, his eyes are puffy.

"What news of the escape?" he blurts out.

Rosemary whispers that Kennedy has made a secret connection with a group that has agreed to help pull off the breakout. She doesn't know anything about them, other than that they're political dissidents, longhairs who live in the mountains.

"They'll get us out of the country," she says.

Tim rears back: "Where?"

Rosemary replies: "I don't know yet. Maybe Cuba. Or Algeria. Or Chile. It all seems like a faraway dream to me."

They lean closer to each other, the fear beginning to wrap around them as Rosemary tells him what she knows.

The operation will be expensive. We'll have to go underground and then sneak out of the country. We'll need scouts, drivers, getaway cars, safe houses, birth certificates, driver's licenses, motel money, and airline tickets.

Tim pauses for a moment and ponders the loose, runaway details of the plot: *How much is it going to cost?*

Rosemary tells him: *The asking price is $25,000.*

Tim turns away and peers at the old-timers walking with their families around the visitors' area, drooping men with their hands behind their backs.

I'm still not sure about Kennedy—Ares was a brutal god, blood lusting and wickedly, mindlessly committed to his version of victory.

The loudspeakers are blaring with the announcement that visiting hours are over. Rosemary stands to leave and Tim looks over her shoulder and through the prison fence.

Michael Randall, the stealthy stalwart from the Brotherhood, is again standing just far enough away from the prison guards to avoid attracting any attention.

Tim and Rosemary have an open marriage, but now a thought coils in his mind: *Who the hell is she fucking on the outside; who is she balling while I'm trapped inside?*

Tim lifts his hand in greeting and Randall nods in return. Tim hugs Rosemary and watches her walk away.

❀   ❀   ❀

By now the guards are accustomed to seeing their most famous prisoner in a yoga position, staring into space. But what they're not prepared for is Iron Man Leary, the prisoner who is working out, doing a hundred push-ups a day. He's playing handball with a passion now, working up a sweat and furiously dispatching younger opponents. He's doing what Bellinger advised—getting into the best shape of his life.

When Rosemary visits the next Sunday, Tim can see that she's wearing expensive new clothes. She's breathless with excitement, whispering about being a secret agent working with dashing radical lawyers taking her to Martha's Vineyard, on private yachts, to good restaurants.

Lowering her head, she confides that she's been noticing strange cars parked along the street outside their home in a pleasant part of Berkeley. Even more suspicious, telephone repairmen are often working on nearby lines. Strangers have been knocking on their door, offering to sell her dope or guns—and she knows that they're narcs hoping to set her up.

She adds that Mike Randall has made contact with the

Brotherhood of Eternal Love fugitives, especially the ones who disappeared into the jungles of Maui. It sounds like they will donate the $25,000 that "the politicals" want for their part of the escape plan.

Tim looks out through the fence. He can see Randall again, once more waiting for Rosemary under the same tree.

He turns to her: *Are you sleeping with him?*

Rosemary is startled, but she can't lie. Blinking back tears, she admits that she is.

Tim nods, fighting the anger and wondering if he wants her with him anymore—whether he wants her at his side if he can manage to break out.

"Well, you don't have to come on this," he snaps. "You can tell your probation officer you're going to divorce me."

❀   ❀   ❀

On July 26, an explosion blows apart a sculpture of a Nike Ajax missile housed inside the Presidio, the iconic army base in San Francisco. The Weathermen issue a new communiqué: "Today we attack with rocks, riots and bombs the greatest killer pig ever known to man— Amerikan imperialism." They sneer at Nixon's blustery attorney general, John Mitchell, who has been targeting them: "To General Mitchell we say: Don't look for us, Dog; we'll find you first."

A few hours later, at 3:30 a.m., a pipe bomb explodes in the front lobby of the Bank of America in the heart of Wall Street. Chunks of marble and glass from the doors rocket into the street.

Twenty minutes after the bomb goes off, the *New York Daily News* receives a phone call:

"This is a Weatherman. Listen close. I'll only say it once. We have just bombed the Bank of America... Tell John Mitchell that no matter what he does, we cannot be stopped."

HOW DO YOU FEEL ABOUT
OFFING PIGS?

August 1970

On August 5, Black Panther leader Huey P. Newton is freed from prison after a court overturns his manslaughter conviction for killing a cop. Hundreds of Newton's supporters are cheering outside the courthouse in Oakland as he appears. The news is crackling with reports about his release, as well as updates on some fellow Black Panthers, dubbed the Soledad Brothers, who are on trial north of San Francisco in Marin County.

Newton jumps onto the roof of a car and raises his clenched fist, the Black Panther salute:

"You can see I am free! Now I want you to do the same thing for the Soledad Brothers!"

Two days later, a seventeen-year-old named Jonathan Jackson sneaks a cache of weapons into the Marin County courthouse. He frees two of the Black Panthers on trial and together they take hostages—three women jurors, the prosecutor, and the judge. A sawed-off shotgun is taped to the judge's neck—and in the mayhem, the weapon goes off, killing him instantly. The teenager and escaping Black Panthers are shot down in a hail of bullets.

❁　　❁　　❁

Inside his dormitory, sitting cross-legged and barefoot on his cot, Tim absorbs the news of the failed Black Panther escape attempt. He fingers his meditation beads, trying to concentrate.

My wife is sleeping with the hippie who might get the money to fund a prison break; my lawyer is in bed with some radical revolutionaries; my prison confidant, Bellinger, is a fucking junkie who has been promising for two months to help spring me.

Tim pushes off his cot and searches the prison for Bellinger:

I need to know the details, now.

Bellinger nods gravely. He motions to Tim to follow him. They aim for a building set back from the road that circles the prison. Cautiously, Bellinger lays out the plan:

Tim has to wait until a Sunday morning, when the guards often take an extended coffee break. Preferably a cloudy day, a foggy day, probably in the fall or winter. While the guards are making their Nescafé and slurping from their grimy coffee cups, Tim has to come to this very particular, very remote section of the twelve-foot-high fence. He'll have just a few seconds to race up the fence and claw through the three strands of twisting barbed wire—and then hurl himself to the ground, sprint for cover, hurtle down the hill, and get to a wooded part of the highway before anyone notices. The old junkie nods happily as he speaks, pleased with the simple genius of his plan.

Tim is staggered, brimming with fury. Finally, he turns his back and trudges away.

He has no choice—he will have to cast his lot with Kennedy, with Ares, the god of war—and whoever the fuck "the politicals" really are.

❊   ❊   ❊

Mike Randall, the rangy financial wunderkind of the Brotherhood of Eternal Love, travels to Maui and begins a bumpy journey into the jungle paradise. The east side of the island has the most dangerous roads in the nation. Nudge the steering wheel on your jeep one inch in the wrong direction and you plummet into a waterfall-lined ravine, crashing through the mountain apples, the breadfruit, the palm-like pandanus plants, and the waves of almost iridescent hibiscus. People who don't know the way, who get lost and plunge all the way down into one of the sacred pools on Maui—the ones who are not protected by Laka, the goddess of the forest—are sometimes not found for days or weeks, if at all.

In Maui, Randall knows what the FBI and the drug agents don't. He knows how to find the still-active Brotherhood of Eternal Love members who escaped to deep, ancient Hawaii—trying to keep it together in paradise. One by one, he reaches five Brotherhood members. Some are surfing, some are just wandering unbothered along the pristine coves and beaches, maybe picking up translucent green globe-sized glass Japanese fishing floats that have washed ashore and adding them to the other treasures that you could find in the hardest-to-reach places—cloudy hundred-year-old Chinese opium bottles, turquoise-colored sea glass, the Shiva's-eye seashells that can tamp down negative energies and dark forces.

Each of the Brotherhood members agrees to donate $5,000, and Randall flies back to California.

☀   ☀   ☀

Kennedy is arriving for another visit. Tim can see his attorney glaring at the guards as they search him. Kennedy seems more intense than ever.

He lowers his voice as he confers with Tim: *Everything is carefully coordinated. They're working on getting you set up with ID cards, a passport, a safe house, and airline tickets—there's a good chance you'll need to go to some foreign country where you'll be shielded from the FBI, CIA, and anyone else that Nixon sends after you.*

Tim is impressed. This is real, certainly better than Bellinger's half-assed heroin-addict fantasy of climbing the fence.

These are very sophisticated people. That's all I can say for now. But they want something from you in return: They want you to endorse the revolution, to support their fight to liberate America from Nixon and stop the war.

Now Tim is beginning to understand.

I've played right into Ares's hands. He's plotting to marry drugs and revolution—trying to shove the love-and-LSD brigade to join the bomb makers on the front lines.

Kennedy leans in again:

There's something else. You're going to have to figure out a way to break out on your own. If you do, a car will be waiting for you.

Tim isn't sure what he had expected. A helicopter, a secret tunnel, maybe a tank plowing through the chain-link fence?

Kennedy is staring back.

Can you get yourself over the fence?

Tim nods nervously and chuckles.

No problem.

Kennedy fixes his blue eyes on Tim: "Would you approve of guns being used in the escape? You know, some of the people involved in this…are on the run and are not about to be caught."

As Tim absorbs the question, he hears Kennedy ask something else:

How do you feel about offing pigs?

❋   ❋   ❋

On the last weekend of August, Rosemary shows up for her Sunday visit. Tim checks the tree outside. This time, there's no sign of Mike Randall.

Rosemary says: *I haven't seen him in two weeks.*

As they walk through the visitors' yard, she seems nervous. She says she has been stewing over the escape plan. She's traumatized by the botched Black Panther escapade and the bloody nightmare in Marin County. She wants to be absolutely sure that Tim's breakout will be successful. Although she's an accomplished amateur astrologer, she can't trust herself for such an important matter. She has contracted for access to Astroflash, an IBM computer programmed by a French astrologer. Tim's exact moment of birth has been entered into the computer and coordinated with the position of the planets for the coming month. An eighteen-page printout has been generated, providing a detailed forecast for his life in September.

Now Rosemary is sharing the results with him: "*You will be full of energy and determination and this will enable you to overcome any obstacles which may appear.*"

He nods noncommittally, waiting for her to continue. She looks deep into his eyes: "*It is as if a bright new future were about to open up, that you were to be 'readapted' to a fresh life unlike the present frame of your existence.*"

He begins to grin as she continues:

"Thus you may easily make a 'sudden leap' which is bound to take you farther along your climb to success."

He nearly laughs out loud. He wants to hug her, but Rosemary's not finished.

"Lady Luck smiles on you," she reads, glancing up. *"You will be rewarded in the end. Take advantage of this new breath of vigor to seek higher, loftier aims."*

They embrace each other, nearly weeping with joy.

Rosemary drops her voice and draws near to him, her face nearly touching his: "I'm going with you."

He strokes her hair tenderly. Maybe she'd be better off staying here, maybe with Mike Randall or some other lover.

"You don't have to flee with me," he says.

She is nearly laughing as she puts her hand inside his. "I have to go with you," she says merrily. "They'd bust me the day after your escape."

JUJU EYEBALLS

In the darkness along Highway 1, just outside the California Men's Colony–West, one of America's most wanted fugitives sits casually in the passenger seat of a two-door compact car as it slows and pulls over to the side of the road. Bill Ayers, a cofounder of the Weathermen, steps out and looks around.

Ayers, whose girlfriend was killed in the New York City townhouse explosion earlier in the year, has a lightning-and-rainbow symbol tattooed on his neck—the same symbol that the Weatherman Underground uses on its communiqués. He studies the area: This looks like a good place for the pickup. Even at night, old man Leary should be able to find his way from the prison to this spot; there's a turnout here, and a prominent landmark—three tall trees that appear to be growing out of a single trunk. Ayers looks back at the prison lights, about a half mile away. If Leary can just get himself past the fence, it'll be easy enough to meet him right here.

Ayers is the chief strategist for this new Weatherman operation. He has named the plan "Juju Eyeballs" in homage to some lyrics from the Beatles' song for Leary, "Come Together." Ayers prides himself on being a tactician, and he helped coordinate the bombing of the New York City police headquarters. He has studied the Vietcong's methods, and he and his fellow fugitives have become exceptionally skilled at planning operations down to the last detail. They pick targets very discreetly, probing for weaknesses, anticipating the enemy's reactions. They rehearse over and over again until all the gears mesh and everyone knows their role.

They are here outside the prison tonight on a scouting mission, a practice run. They are checking to see how much traffic there is, to see whether any prison guards patrol the highway and where exactly patrol trucks with sharpshooters are stationed. Now they've settled on Leary's pickup location, the place where he can slip through the darkness and climb into a waiting car without being seen.

Ayers finds it nearly ludicrous that his hard-edged band of fugitive dissidents would risk their necks to bust a middle-aged hedonist out of a minimum-security prison. Freeing a single freaky, grinning old white man isn't going to jump-start the revolution.

Why not break out some Black Panthers, or, hell, Charlie Manson if you really want to stick a fork in the pig's eye?

Despite the successful bombings and their ability to elude the FBI, the Weathermen are suffering. The feds have been closing off corners, breaking up their supply network, getting uncomfortably close. Ayers and the Weathermen desperately need cash for food, shelter, cars, fake documents—and more dynamite to keep the war on Amerika in full attack mode. Maybe Leary can help.

❈ ❈ ❈

On Wednesday, September 2, Rosemary is preparing to board a flight to Chicago with a new friend, a straight-looking young blond woman who calls herself Pam. A few days earlier, Michael Kennedy had alerted Rosemary to be waiting for a certain call, and now the women have spent the last two days together, building a new identity for Rosemary. She and Pam went into San Francisco and picked up a roundish-looking wig, orange-pink lipstick, eyeliner, and fake lashes. They found a plain-looking dress, the kind a secretary at a car dealership would wear. Pam steered Rosemary to the pantyhose section. Finally, she handed Rosemary a push-up bra. Rosemary hadn't worn a bra in years; reluctantly, she went into the fitting room to put everything on. When she saw her reflection, she was horrified—she looked like one of her Baptist relatives from Missouri, people from the Middle America she fled years ago.

Rosemary checks in for the Chicago flight under the name Sylvia E. McGaffin—a name once given to a girl born May 22, 1943, who died as an infant. Rosemary is carrying a birth certificate for McGaffin and other ID cards, some of them forged. The last step in creating a new identity was to obtain a passport. Chicago has the most overworked passport office in the country, Pam tells her. They simply don't have the time to carefully scrutinize each individual application; the chances of getting caught are lower in Chicago than anywhere else.

Rosemary's young comrade is totally at ease. She's only eighteen and moves fluidly through the airport security checkpoints. Rosemary's legs feel like jelly. She's still on bail for the California marijuana bust that landed Tim in prison. If she's captured with fake documents, or arrested for passport fraud, she's facing felonies and decades behind bars.

As they fly together, Pam quietly tells her that the revolution is at hand, and that she's one of its advance troops:

Nixon will be overthrown, perhaps within the next year; the young people, the blacks, the Chicanos, and the women will all come together to form a revolutionary government. The draft will be abolished, the war will end, and pot and LSD will be legalized. Everyone will be treated equally, even the greedy capitalist pigs—though they'll soon learn to share their hoarded riches.

In Chicago, Pam checks them into a hotel near the airport. The next morning, she leads Rosemary to the new federal building, a dark, imposing steel-and-glass skyscraper. As they make their way to the second floor, Pam plots out the situation for Rosemary:

The lines will be long, but when you get to the window you can request an emergency passport, which costs an extra two dollars. Your passport will be ready in half a day, instead of the normal three to four weeks.

Rosemary fills out the forms, trying to keep her hands from shaking. She lists national holidays as the birth dates of Sylvia McGaffin's parents. For her occupation, she writes *student*. When she finishes the paperwork, she joins one of the lines, reaches the counter, and hands the forms to the clerk. She raises her hand and swears allegiance to the United States. She pays the fourteen-dollar fee and is told that she can come back in the afternoon to pick up her new passport. In a daze, Rosemary nods and turns away.

As her heels echo on the shiny floors, she braces for a squadron of cops to storm the area, shouting her real name and pointing guns at her head. She follows Pam blindly and they push their way through the glass front doors, past the security guards, and out onto the honking streets of Chicago. It's sweltering outside. Rosemary is dripping, sweating inside her dress. She sees a little health food station and grabs a cup of carrot juice, downing it with trembling hands.

At 4 p.m., Rosemary nervously returns to the passport office. She scans the room, still bracing for something bad to happen. When she reaches the counter, the clerk asks her name. *Oh, shit. My name. What's my name?* Her face goes blank. She lets her purse slip out of her hands and it falls to the floor. She bends to pick it up and tries, desperately, to remember who she is supposed to be.

She slowly stands straight again and offers the clerk a weak smile. "Sylvia McGaffin," she finally says.

When she arrives back home in Berkeley, Rosemary sees another telephone repair truck parked on the street. The paranoia comes zooming back. Inside the house, she shuts the curtains. After dusk, she tiptoes to the redwood deck and hides her fake identity papers and passport under a patch of bamboo.

THEY CAN CARRY GUNS

September 6, 1970

Tim is admiring Rosemary as she signs in for her weekly prison visit. She's wearing a new dress, one suggested by Kennedy's wife. Tim looks her up and down. She seems chic, like she could still make her living by modeling.

They walk outside and into the visitors' garden and Tim quickly presses her. He needs to know what Kennedy has planned:

"What happened?"

Holding his gaze, she says, "His people have come down from the mountains...dozens of them waiting around." And they're growing impatient. "It's costing them time and energy and money to sit around week after week."

Tim says he's decided when he's going to try to get over the prison fence: "Next week."

The September breezes are pushing across the prison yard and the roses are still putting out new blooms. The guards are circling, watching their most famous prisoner and his beautiful wife.

Rosemary whispers that there is one final thing: Kennedy wants to make absolutely certain that Tim will be cool in case "the politicals" pull out some guns and get into a battle with the pigs.

Tim examines Rosemary's face. She's flushed, excited. He says he is going to compose a political manifesto—an ode to the revolution—and leave it behind when he tries to escape.

He looks carefully at Rosemary and adds:

"Tell them they can carry guns."

ACID IS GROOVY

September 11, 1970

It's Friday, Tim's 204th day of captivity. Bomb threats are clearing skyscrapers in Chicago, a military contractors' headquarters outside of Los Angeles, and government offices in Maryland. Police in Kansas have found a cache of eighty-one sticks of dynamite, intended to destroy the National Guard building at the University of Kansas. In Tyler, Texas, six people are arrested in a plot to blow up a school administration building. A group of mayors, worried about more attacks, is asking to meet with Attorney General John Mitchell.

In North Carolina, a Green Beret doctor named Jeffrey MacDonald is still insisting to Army investigators that four hippies had broken into his home and slaughtered his pregnant wife, his five-year-old daughter, and his two-year-old daughter—clubbing them and stabbing them dozens of times with knives and ice picks. The soldier claims that one of the attackers had been holding a candle while chanting: "Acid is groovy, kill the pigs."

Halfway across the world, guerrillas from the Palestine Liberation Organization are holding dozens of Americans hostage after hijacking three planes on a single day—all bound for New York from Europe. Their attempt on a fourth plane failed when the passengers fought back. The PLO is demanding the release of political prisoners. To show how serious they are, they will blow up the empty $25 million planes. Under direct orders from President Richard Nixon, security is being tightened at American airports—and dozens more federal agents are being dispatched to serve as armed air marshals.

❋   ❋   ❋

At 10:20 in the morning, Tim is ordered to report to the Legal Office in building 310. He knows what's coming. His lawyers have told him that he has to travel to New York to face those eleven out-standing charges from G. Gordon Liddy's midnight raids. All the traps are snapping down—he's facing ten years in California prison, ten years in a Texas prison, and maybe another decade in New York. He'll be eighty years old before he gets out.

When Tim gets to the Legal Office, there is a beefy, seasoned sergeant from New York who has made the winding drive through the coastal hills to the hidden prison. He is here to escort Tim to New York to face Liddy's charges.

"Timothy, we have to take you back to New York. We came early to find out if you're willing to fly back. If you won't fly then we leave today by car," the husky cop tells him.

Driving means packing up right now. Flying means leaving on Tuesday. "Why don't you take the weekend off and we'll fly in? That's fine with me," Tim suggests brightly.

The cop is happy, they all agree, and Tim disappears back into his wing of the prison. Maybe the cop is going to go out and *really* blow his per diem money tonight. *Why miss out on a free weekend in California?* Leary spent years as a clinical psychologist sizing up strangers. Maybe this officer is a good-time Charlie ready to lope into a downtown bar and knock back a few. All in the name of pris-oner retrieval duty.

❁   ❁   ❁

In the afternoon, Tim is told to report to the visiting room. Some-one from Kennedy's legal office has been allowed to make a special non-Sunday visit because of the pending legal action in New York. Kennedy's law partner, Joseph Rhine, is waiting for Tim, his face highlighted by very thick glasses that make his eyes look ridicu-lously huge.

The two men walk out to the visitors' garden and sit at a picnic table. They talk briefly about the upcoming New York trials before Rhine tells him the real reason for this emergency visit:

Everything has been set up for tomorrow night.

Tim nods, eyes locked on the other man's face. Rhine takes out a notebook, looking at Tim expectantly. He is ready to transcribe the communiqué Kennedy has demanded—a statement from Dr. Timothy Leary endorsing the revolutionary overthrow of the pig-state of Amerika.

Tim takes a deep breath. He quietly dictates a lengthy message he has composed in his prison bunk and precisely memorized. As Tim recites, he sees the lawyer's eyes bulge out even more, growing oddly enormous behind his Coke-bottle glasses as he scribbles furiously.

When Tim is through, Kennedy's law partner inches even closer and spells out exactly what will happen if Tim can get over the fence without being gunned down.

I'M NINO

September 12, 1970

Tim is at the window in building 325, studying the clouds. The moon will be nearly full tonight and he's going to need all the cloud cover he can get. He hears the old inmate in the next bunk complaining that the overcast weather will ruin visiting day. Tim retreats to his cot, shuffles his tarot cards, and then heads to the prison yard to do some yoga.

As he settles into his pose, he examines the wooden telephone pole alongside building 324, the dormitory next to his own. Attached to the pole is a snaking black cable that runs over the fence and connects to another telephone pole on the outside. Standing on his head, Tim focuses on the pole and the wire, concentrating, meditating, and visualizing himself crossing over.

Suddenly a guard barks, telling him to get back to the main yard with everyone else. Tim folds himself back down to the ground. For good karma, he brushes against the telephone pole before walking away.

✦   ✦   ✦

By midafternoon, the sun is breaking through the clouds and the inmates fall into their usual routines. Digging dirt in the garden, making prison art, looking for quiet places to jack off. Tim goes to the mess hall for an early meal. Walking to his dorm, he can see some friendly-looking clouds gathering in the west, out over the ocean. He sits at his typewriter and adjusts the shift key to ALL CAPS. He begins pecking out a statement that he intends to leave behind for the prison guards. After he finishes, he hides the paper in his locker. He retreats to the TV room and sits with some dull-faced cons watching Stanford's football team beating up on the Arkansas Razorbacks. After the game ends, he heads back to his cot, waiting for the four o'clock count. Once the four thirty "all clear" whistle blows, several men leave for the cafeteria. Tim remains behind. The dormitory is empty.

He opens the locker in his cubicle and sits on the edge of his cot, working quickly. He pulls the white shoelaces out of his sneakers and replaces them with brown ones. He covers his lap with a newspaper and twists open some dark blue paint he's pilfered from the prison supply room. Using a white towel, he smears the paint over his sneakers and his handball gloves. When he's finished, he shoves the stained towel under his mattress. Then he puts the shoes and gloves in his locker, slamming the door closed.

✺ ✺ ✺

As evening approaches in San Luis Obispo, the clouds in the west make for a dramatically dappled sunset. By the time Tim and the other prisoners move to their bunks for the first evening count, darkness has settled over the prison. Tim checks the window and gazes at the heavens. A waxing gibbous moon is already high in the sky.

At 8:15 p.m., prison guard Albert Butterfield makes his rounds, verifying that all prisoners are accounted for. Butterfield is responsible for monitoring the 174 men in this section of the prison, all housed in four adjoining dormitories. He passes through Leary's wing and sees Leary is on his cot, bed number 7, present and accounted for. The next bed check won't happen until 11:40 p.m.

With Butterfield out of sight, the inmates move out for their normal Saturday-night activities. Some watch TV, others play cards. Some sneak off in pairs to a secret place under the barracks, looking to grunt their way through furtive sex.

Tim opens his locker. He is nearly alone in the building. He slips on his darkened shoes and stuffs his handball gloves into a pants pocket. He pulls on his prison-issue denim jacket. He removes the pile of love letters from Rosemary and tucks them carefully into another pocket, along with his strand of wooden meditation beads.

There's just one thing left. He looks at the sheet of paper he typed earlier in the day. Squinting, he draws a peace symbol at the bottom of the note—only he makes the symbol appear upside down. From his days at West Point, Tim knows that flying a flag upside down indicates "a nation in distress."

He sets the note on the top shelf, assuming it will soon be discovered.

❧ ❧ ❧

With the clock ticking toward 9 p.m., Tim is walking down the long main corridor inside the west wing. Up ahead, he can see the guard, Butterfield, making his regular rounds. Tim turns toward a side door to the prison yard. He is just about to reach for the handle when he glances over and sees three inmates peering at him. He freezes for a moment and then keeps moving down the corridor, trying to appear casual. He turns the corner. There's another door up ahead that he can use, although it will put him on the wrong side of the prison yard. But there is no other choice. He slips out into the night.

The moon has disappeared behind the clouds, but it hardly matters, because the entire area is brightly illuminated with floodlights, like a football field, so escaping prisoners can be gunned down. Anyone looking out a prison window could easily see the middle-aged man skipping madly across the lawn to the lone tree that grows alongside building 324. He reaches for the branches and begins clambering up, aiming for the angled roof. He can see inside the barracks and there's a notorious snitch on the other side of the window, just two feet away. The old prison informant is yelling something at some other cons.

Is it about me?

Leary gulps, breathing heavily, waiting for the searchlights, the sirens, and the guards with raised guns. But there is nothing, just that sudden rush of wild California blowing in from the ocean and the hills, just his own furiously drumming heartbeat. He continues climbing and reaches a limb that grows over the roof. He hugs the sturdy branch and works his way along it until he can drop down to the roof, four feet below. He pauses for a moment, hoping the thud didn't give him away. He slips his sneakers off, the better to pad along in silence. He prances toward the telephone pole on the other side of the building.

He is in relative darkness here, above the floodlights. He can see the pole, the heavy black cable, the perimeter road, and the twelve-foot barbed-wire-topped fence beyond. He's going to have to wriggle his way along one hundred feet of wire without falling or getting shot. He's still breathing heavily from his climb up the tree.

Calm. Steady. Centered.

He slides his sneakers back on and pulls on the handball gloves. He lies on his back with his head facing the fence and the road beyond. He reaches up, wraps his fingers and legs around the cable, and launches himself into the night.

What was I thinking?

He is swaying twenty-five feet in the air, desperately hanging on. His mind is racing, each breath coming harder as he struggles to keep his grip on the wire, to keep from falling two stories and breaking his back. He couldn't have done this at age twenty, never mind that he's nearly fifty now.

Easy, easy, calm.

He grunts, getting used to the feeling that his muscles are tearing apart. Then he begins to pull himself forward, inch by inch. The night is cool, but he's sweating like Richard Nixon debating JFK. After several frantic minutes, he makes it about a third of the way across. His strength is failing and his lungs are about to burst.

Why didn't I quit smoking?

He clings for life, wrapping his arms around the cable, gasping, trying not to hurtle down.

Suddenly there's the sound of an engine. A patrol truck is making its way along the perimeter road, coming toward him, headlights piercing the night. Tim freezes, feeling naked on the cable, silhouetted against the sky, a perfect target. He can see right into the windshield, waiting for the guard's jaw to drop when he spots the old man who thinks he is a trapeze artist. At the last second, the guard abruptly looks down, stubbing out a smoke in the truck's ashtray. As red rear brake lights flash, the truck turns a corner and disappears into the night.

Tim breathes again and feels a gear shift inside his body, a mad, rushing energy. He begins forcing himself along the cable, inch by inch, and finally the fence is coming into focus. As he stretches one hand for the telephone pole on the other side of the barbed wire, his glasses suddenly fly off and sail into the night. He can feel the wooden pole with his fingers. He reaches his right hand toward the metal spikes on the pole. He grabs one—a move he's visualized a thousand times in his bunk—and then lets his feet swing away from the cable, twisting his body around and grabbing the air with his left hand. He hugs the pole hard, his legs slam into it, and then he squeezes the dry, splintered wood and slides twenty-five feet to the ground.

He tries to remember exactly what Kennedy's law partner told him yesterday when he was given the escape blueprint:

If you can get to Highway 1 outside the prison, you are going to be picked up a half mile north of the main entrance. Look for a small pullout, a parking spot near a cluster of trees. There are three trees that grow out of one root. A small car will come by with its right blinker flashing. If you are not there it will return every fifteen or twenty minutes until midnight. If you don't make it out by midnight, then the assumption is that you are not coming out of prison.

If you make it out, the code name you should use for yourself is Nino.

Catching his breath, bracing for shouts and barks and bullets, Tim skitters in circles in the dark until he finally spots his glasses near the fence. Jamming them on, he crouches and begins running serpentine style until he suddenly caroms down a rocky hill.

Still no sirens. Nothing. No one.

Chugging into the night, he can see the big official entrance sign, brightly lit by floodlights: CALIFORNIA MEN'S COLONY WEST FACILITY. To the west, toward the ocean, the clouds are painting the darkening sky the color of Mercurochrome. He sees the highway going north and the grassy ravine that runs alongside it. He begins to sprint, arms pumping. He's looking for the clump of three trees alongside a pullout. A car roars into view, headlights sweeping, and he flings himself down, pressing hard against the ground until it passes. He gets up and keeps moving. Another car comes zooming along the highway and he falls to the ground again.

Fighting his way along the ditch, he sees three trees, joined together as if they spring from one root. He pops up from the bushes for a second, swivels his head like a periscope, and spots a little path that leads off the highway, just as the lawyer told him. He lowers himself back into the brush and kneels down.

Nothing to do now but wait and hope that whoever is handling this end of the operation has their shit together.

He's trying to think what time it could be, how many minutes he has left before the prison guards do the 11:40 bed check. Car after car zooms by. He waits five minutes, ten minutes, fifteen minutes, hunkering in the darkness.

Maybe no one is coming. Maybe it's all an elaborate ruse. Maybe I'm a damned pawn. Maybe the cops caught everybody. Shot everybody.

After twenty minutes, one more car is coming down the highway, its headlights splaying a kind of eerie glow over the trees. It suddenly peels to the side with its right blinker flashing. It's a small, dark two-door American compact. It pulls to a stop just past the three trees.

Tim lopes to the automobile and the door swings open.

"I'm Nino," Tim says, trying to make out the faces hidden inside the dark car.

DYNAMITE AND HAIR DYE

10 p.m.–11 p.m., September 12, 1970

Tim climbs in the backseat and the car races away. The passenger up front is lanky and dark-haired, maybe twenty years old. The driver is short, with a freckled face and some baby fat. He looks like a young Irish kid.

The driver turns back to look at Tim. "Brother, we're glad to see you. We made two passes by the pickup spot. We were worried."

Tim is astonished. All he can think to say is: "How old are you?"

The kid glances back for a second and answers: "Eighteen."

The other man points to the backseat. "There's a new set of clothes. Change."

Tim eases out of his prison denims, now torn and dirty. He's scratched and bleeding in several places.

"Save these for my archives," he jokes, nodding to the prison sneakers, denim jacket, and pants.

No one laughs. The passenger says they've got better plans for Tim's prison uniform—to throw the cops off the trail.

Tim nods as he's told that Rosemary is waiting in a safe house in Seattle, and it'll take a couple of days to get there. He's handed a wallet with a fresh ID card, just in case a police car pulls them over. They are driving exactly the speed limit, aiming for the little seaside community of Morro Bay, about ten minutes away. When they reach the darkened village, they turn at an intersection and see a long-haired man standing in a phone booth. He is a lookout and waves as they drive by.

They turn onto a beach road and slow to a stop. The passenger gets out and Tim follows him, walking quickly over the sand. After several minutes they climb some dunes and reach a parking area. There is a 1964 Dodge pickup truck with a beat-up camper attached to the bed. On the rear bumper is a sticker: AMERICA, LOVE IT OR LEAVE IT.

Waiting outside the camper is a straight-looking older couple: a gray-haired blue-collar man who appears close to Tim's age and a pleasant-faced woman maybe ten years younger. There is also a child, a boy who might be eight years old. The family looks very Middle America.

Tim steps into the back of the camper. There's a built-in table and chairs along with a tiny kitchenette with a sink and a small refrigerator. The young man from the getaway car tells Tim they need to dye his hair. He reaches for a bucket already filled with brown hair coloring.

"The Weathermen are the ones sponsoring your escape," he says as he changes Tim's silvery hair to a darker hue. He pauses for a second. "We hope that's all right with you?" he finally says.

Tim lets it sink in. His only knowledge of the Weathermen is confined to some news stories, including one sympathetic magazine article he read. Sure, he'd written a political statement and dictated it to Kennedy's lawyer, but surely these people know that he never signed on for . . . *the revolution.*

Finally, he asks:

"The twenty-five thousand dollars went to buy dynamite?"

The man working on his hair laughs.

"Dynamite, hair dye, and fast cars."

BE FREE, PRISON GUARDS

11 p.m.–Midnight, September 12, 1970

At the Highway 101 intersection, the old man driving the camper parks the car and heads to the rear bumper. In one smooth motion, he pries off the California license plate, revealing a Utah plate underneath. He barks at Tim: *You can sit up front.*

The driver is Clayton Van Lydegraf, a sturdy, weathered-looking old-school Marxist who's been making his living as a handyman. He joined the Communist Party as a teenager in the early 1930s. Later, he became a pilot during World War II, earning the Distinguished Flying Cross. After the war he worked as a machinist at Boeing until he was fired for his Communist affiliations. He's been a fixture for decades among labor activists in the Pacific Northwest. Even as he's entered his midfifties, Van Lydegraf has never wavered in his belief that a revolution is coming to the United States.

After one Marxist faction expelled him, he gravitated to the Students for a Democratic Society, serving as a father figure to the most radical members—the founders of the Weatherman Underground.

Tim crowds in beside Van Lydegraf, the woman, and the little kid, and the camper rumbles up the highway. The woman is from the Midwest, separated from her husband and now living in San Francisco. The little boy is her son, deliberately chosen to serve as a front. He looks at Tim and grins.

As the miles click by, Van Lydegraf scans the road: *We've got to watch for roadblocks until we get to San Jose. Once we're there we'll be safe because the highways are too busy to stop traffic.*

He turns and looks hard at Tim.

"I was against this whole thing from the start," he says. "If it was up to me, you'd still be rotting in jail."

They're now seventy-five miles north of the prison, driving

through the Salinas Valley. It's still another two hours to San Jose. Lydegraf checks his watch. It's nearly midnight.

They should be finding out by now that you're gone.

Prison guard Albert Butterfield is making the second head count, walking the darkened dormitories and shining his flashlight on the beds. The 11:40 count is always the easiest. Most of the old-fart prisoners are already asleep. But bed number 7 is empty. Butterfield shines his flashlight around the room, then shakes the ancient inmate in the next cot: *Where's Leary?*

"He never came back," the prisoner mumbles, turning over to fall back asleep.

Butterfield sprints to the lounge, thinking that maybe Leary has nodded off watching TV. Butterfield barges into the bathrooms and the recreation room. He bolts up and down the hallways. Still no sign of him. Butterfield reaches for his walkie-talkie and radios the sergeant in the control room: "Leary is gone."

The escape alarm begins booming. Guards are running to scour the rest of the complex and the surrounding grounds. Butterfield races back to building 325 and uses his master key to open Leary's locker. Sitting on the top shelf is Leary's typed message.

Butterfield grabs it and reads:

In the name of the Father and of the Son and of the Holy Ghost, Ave Maria. Prison guards, listen. To cage living creatures is a sin against God, a crime against nature. Listen prison guards. You stand convicted in the court of history as criminals and as sinners.

In the uniform of Athens, you jailed Socrates.

In the uniform of Rome, you arrested Jesus Christ.

In the uniform of Germany, you caged 6,000,000 Jews.

In the livery of Nixon and Reagan, you have turned the land into a police state.

Listen guards, to the ancient truth. He who enslaves is himself enslaved. The future belongs to the blacks and browns and the young and the wild and the free. Oh prison guards, I pray that you will repent and reform. Open the gates of your hearts and be free. Break out.

Follow me to freedom and love and laughter.

Be free, prison guards, be free.

SUPPORT YOUR LOCAL UNDERGROUND

September 13, 1970

The camper is moving quickly north on Highway 101. Tim has climbed into the rear and is lying down, drinking some chilled wine from the refrigerator. He braces himself as they drive past the Soledad prison, but there are no roadblocks, and the camper keeps moving. By 2 a.m. they reach San Jose. They breeze through Palo Alto and roll by the San Francisco International Airport. Van Lydegraf steers the camper off Highway 101 and turns west toward the Mission District. It's nearly three in the morning when he drops Tim off at a modest second-story apartment near Fifteenth Street and Albion.

Waiting inside are the two Weathermen who picked him up outside the prison. The living room has psychedelic posters; the Rolling Stones are playing on the stereo. There's the smell of food cooking in the kitchen and a fresh mound of dope on a table.

Tim slumps into a chair, feeling the pain from his climb over the fence. He is sore and scraped; his knees and elbows are stiffening up. He wolfs down some bacon and eggs, smokes some pot, and then slips into the old-fashioned claw-foot tub for a hot bubble bath. Then he flops onto a bed and passes out.

❁   ❁   ❁

The J&D Ritchfield gas station is two miles south of San Luis Obispo, next to an all-night Denny's on the highway heading toward Los Angeles. The station is open twenty-four hours and the attendant, Ken Martinet, works the overnight shift, pumping gas, checking oil, and changing the occasional flat tire. Near the end of his shift, at 5 a.m., Martinet begins cleaning the restrooms.

Inside the men's room, he opens the trash can and discovers a pile of clothing stashed on top: a denim jacket, denim pants, a belt, and a full pack of Marlboro cigarettes.

He notices that numbers are stenciled onto the jacket and pants, just like on prison clothes. As he picks up the jacket and studies it, he can see a little orange button pinned to the front.

In black letters, it reads: SUPPORT YOUR LOCAL UNDERGROUND.

✺   ✺   ✺

At 9 a.m., Tim wakes up to city light streaming through the window. The two young Weathermen are making breakfast and checking news reports. His whole body is aching. He hobbles into the kitchen. One of the revolutionaries tells him: *The first radio bulletin about your escape just aired an hour ago. The cops probably think you're headed south, toward Mexico.*

After he eats, Tim is given a fake brown mustache to paste on. He's handed an old suitcase containing a change of clothes and a toothbrush. He fumbles with the floppy hair on his lip and steps into the morning sunlight. Two blocks away, Van Lydegraf is standing outside the camper, polishing it with a rag.

The veteran Communist grabs Tim's suitcase and tosses it in the back. The two men climb into the cab and the engine roars to life. They look like two wrinkled old fishermen out for a retirement adventure. They begin driving across the Golden Gate Bridge, continuing north on Highway 101. Van Lydegraf drives cautiously, constantly checking the mirrors.

After twenty minutes, a car pulls up alongside them. Van Lydegraf, astonished, begins fuming and cursing. Tim takes a quick look. The driver in the other car is waving. Van Lydegraf is still cursing, gunning the camper as they shoot forward. The other car falls behind and exits the freeway. Tim is craning his neck, looking back. The other driver is still waving at them.

"That was Mark Rudd," seethes Van Lydegraf. "He wasn't supposed to cross tracks."

Tim nods, relieved that it wasn't the FBI or the cops. Rudd

is the infamous student radical who led the takeover of Columbia University in 1968 and kick-started campus revolts around the nation. He cofounded the Weathermen and had gone underground with Ayers and Dohrn after the deadly townhouse explosion in New York. Rudd was supposed to help set up the safe house in San Francisco, make sure the camper was running, and then guide the camper out of Marin County—just to make sure the cops didn't have a surprise blockade. Rudd's last-second maneuver, chasing after the getaway camper, is his way of saying good-bye.

Van Lydegraf is livid: "That was very dangerous and bad tactics to have our trails intersect."

The two middle-aged men ride on in silence. They cut over toward Sacramento and then pick up Interstate 5 heading north. Lydegraf is talking freely now, complaining that the youth culture is hopeless, that too many young people are wasting their time on frivolous things. *Liberation comes only from the bosom of the revolution.*

Tim interjects: *True freedom comes from within.* The old Communist harrumphs. After two hours of bickering, they finally settle into a truce as they pass Shasta Lake and begin climbing into the mountains. Van Lydegraf is examining every road sign as the highway winds alongside the Sacramento River. Forests of towering pines hug the edges of the pavement. About an hour into the mountains, Van Lydegraf sees the exit for the small town of Castella and slows the camper. He putters along the narrow frontage road, separated from the interstate by the thick forest. He frowns as he drives, unfamiliar with the area. The road curves and they enter a tree-shaded park with picnic tables and parking spaces. Up ahead two long-haired young women are sitting on a log, facing the road. Van Lydegraf's face breaks into a small smile. These are Weathermen lookouts.

The two men climb out and walk over. The women appear to be teenagers and they are beaming, smiling at Tim: *Would you like a joint?*

Tim is laughing as he reaches for the fat cigarette and sucks back a big hit. Smoke swirling up into the trees, he sits next to the girls on the log. Van Lydegraf glowers and returns to his camper. He emerges with a bottle of whiskey, raising it in a salute before he takes a huge slug.

Tim is feeling the buzz coming on, the warmth of the sunlight peeking through the trees, when a rattling pickup truck suddenly comes bumping into the hidden picnic area. Three people step out of the truck. There is an attractive woman in her midtwenties, wearing a cashmere sweater with very tight, perfectly faded jeans. Two men, one tall and lanky, the other shorter, stockier. They seem cocky, almost arrogant. Tim can't take his eyes off the woman. He instantly feels . . . her unforgettable sex appeal . . . something sensual about her. It's as if he's channeling the buttery, languorous days at the estate in New York, dropping acid and lolling naked in the streams, making love with whoever was willing.

They don't introduce themselves. The woman says, *We wanted to make sure you got here safely. We've got a campsite set up in the mountains for the evening, but we're going to leave right now to make sure it's secure.*

One of the men adds: *You can go into Castella and call Rosemary from a pay phone.*

The man hands him a piece of paper with a number written on it. *It's for a phone booth outside a coffee shop in Seattle. Rosemary is waiting for your call.*

The trio retreat to their truck and disappear back up the old mountain logging road. Van Lydegraf is in the camper, still drinking from his whiskey bottle and frying up steaks on the little propane stove.

Van Lydegraf hands Tim a plate with a burnt steak and swigs more booze straight from the bottle. He peers out the door of the camper and begins ranting at the hippie girls:

Injustice, too much injustice!

Tim interrupts him:

Who were those three people?

Van Lydegraf is swaying, slurring his words:

You've just met the high command of the Weathermen.

Three of the most wanted people in the United States: Bill Ayers, who mapped out Operation Juju Eyeballs. Jeff Jones, who handled the $25,000 delivered by the Brotherhood of Eternal Love. Bernardine Dohrn, who had shouted out what many Americans took to be an endorsement of Charlie Manson's murdering "family."

Tim's mind is churning. He looks around the picnic site, wondering what else, who else, is out there. The two teenage girls have done acid and now they are falling all over themselves, tripping like mad.

Van Lydegraf is red-faced, shit-faced, and roaring:

I'll take you to the damned phone booth so you can call your wife.

Tim nervously climbs into the camper as Van Lydegraf guns the motor and barrels toward Castella, a two-street logging town a couple of miles away. Van Lydegraf manages to keep the camper on the road and weaves into the village, aiming for the only phone booth. Tim hops out and dials the number on the little piece of paper. After a ring a woman's voice answers.

"Hello," Tim says carefully. "Who are you?"

"Well...I was just walking by the pay phone and I heard it ring and I don't know why I answered it," says the voice.

Tim quickly hangs up. The Great Fear races up his spine. He can see the drunk old Communist glaring impatiently from behind the wheel of the camper. Tim breathes deeply and dials again. This time, Rosemary answers.

Her voice is full of warmth. He feels himself relaxing, breathing. He tells her that he loves her, that he will see her soon, probably on Tuesday afternoon. He hangs up the phone and rides with boozy Van Lydegraf back to the picnic area. The old organizer is in the gregarious drunk phase by now, and Tim keeps expecting him to break into some socialist songs, maybe "The Internationale."

The two hippie girls are floating off into their own world, seeing something beyond the trees, beyond the heady, earthy smell of the antediluvian forest.

Tim dips his head and rubs his temples as one of them tries to play a flute.

☀   ☀   ☀

The sun has fallen behind the mountains and an evening chill is coming on when the Weatherman leaders finally return to fetch

Tim. He climbs into the pickup alongside them, all four riding abreast as the truck rattles across the highway and begins climbing into the mountains up a rugged dirt road. They are heading into wild, remote logging country. Darkness deepens and the temperature is plummeting the higher they climb. A nearly full moon illuminates the forest. They arrive at a small cleared site. Tim is handed a sleeping bag and he spreads it out on the grass. Everyone huddles around a campfire.

Bernardine's eyes are glowing from the firelight.

"Three dear Weather souls were blown to pieces," she says, talking about the comrades killed in the Greenwich Village townhouse explosion. "That forever destroyed our belief that armed struggle is the only real revolutionary struggle. It's a spiritual revolution."

For a second, Tim locks eyes with her.

On the dark, windy mountaintop, the campfire begins to die down. Tim tucks into the sleeping bag and tries to crash. The moonlight is softly diffused as it penetrates the dense, dark forest.

YOU'RE TOO HOT

September 14, 1970

After breakfast the next morning, the four walk through the cool air and up the narrow, potholed dirt road. In twenty minutes they reach an overlook that gazes out over seemingly endless miles of wild terrain.

Tim sits on a boulder and looks at Bernardine. "If you can use us here, we'll stay underground in America."

One of the men tells him: "You're too hot. You should leave the country."

Tim understands. Rosemary already has a false identity and passport. And the Brotherhood of Eternal Love has so many cool refuges, so many connections in Mexico, Central America, and South America—places where there is ancient, sacred worship of hallucinogens. Tim snaps to attention as one of the Weathermen says:

"Maybe...Algeria."

He listens as they gush excitedly about how Algeria is a gurgling outpost for the revolutionary experiment. Exiled Black Panther leader Eldridge Cleaver has been given sanctuary there—and so have dozens of his followers from the United States. Cleaver is the author of the seminal sixties revolutionary tome *Soul on Ice*, and he has been on the run after being accused of trying to murder two Oakland cops. He was welcomed with open arms by the Algerians. There is word in the underground that the Algerian government is even going to give Cleaver and the Panthers their own official embassy in Algiers.

Tim feels a throbbing in his aching knees, still sore from scrambling along the prison cable and sliding down the hill. It has never occurred to him to flee to North Africa, except perhaps to Morocco with all its hashish.

Dohrn and the others keep talking about Algeria. *Other countries*

might grant you asylum, but only Algeria can give you the nurturing envi-
ronment, the freedom, to continue your work. You can establish a research
center. Do some writing. Spread your spiritual revolution.

And there's something else: *The FBI really has been closing in. The*
Weathermen might not be able to stay in the United States much longer. You
should go to Algeria. Check the place out. If it's a good scene we'll join you.

Tim can see out to the distant horizon from the remote mountaintop where he is marooned with three of America's most wanted
revolutionaries. If he were to accidentally fall over the edge of this
cliff, chances are his body would never be discovered. He slowly
agrees that it makes sense for him to go to Algeria.

Do you have my new identity papers? A passport and anything else I'll
need to get out of the country?

Suddenly, the Weathermen are gingerly explaining that they
don't actually have any documents right now.

It's a very complicated procedure, building a new identity.

They couldn't accomplish it on their own. It'll require some
dangerous, tricky work from Tim. He'll have to wear a disguise and
visit government and state offices. They assure him that it won't take
more than a week.

Tim marvels at the forest below, gauging the long distance
down. His mind is somersaulting.

The Weathermen couldn't arrange false papers?

He looks glumly at his rescuers. They are so young, so certain
of themselves, so committed to *the revolution.*

Now Bernardine Dohrn is smiling sweetly at him, asking if he
will also do something else. A gesture of goodwill:

Will you write a brief statement thanking the Weathermen for your escape?

She has even brought paper and a pen for him to use. She watches
closely as he scribbles out some words.

❋   ❋   ❋

By midafternoon, Tim and Bernardine return to the forested picnic
area along Interstate 5 to wait for Van Lydegraf and the camper. She
stretches out on the picnic table. Tim is edgy, certain the entire state is
crawling with cops, all looking for him. He blurts out that he'd

rather wait out of sight. He begins walking toward the woods and Bernardine hurries to join him. They stroll together, her body moving easily and fluidly alongside his. It's very hard to not want to take her hand, to lead her to a quiet spot under a towering sugar pine with its cinnamon-red bark and begin making love. Instead, they talk quietly as they make their way through the forest, keeping an eye on the rest area—watching for Van Lydegraf to return in the beat-up camper.

When he arrives, the Trotskyite looks like he is back on his game, rebounding from his whiskey rebellion. He grumbles hello and motions for Tim to join him in the front. Bernardine gives Tim a good-bye hug, promising that they will see each other tomorrow in Seattle. Tim slides into the camper, back to playing his part as the square old fogey wandering the Pacific Northwest in search of rainbow trout with another rocking-chair angler.

They pull onto the interstate, the two men resuming their debates about drugs, pleasure, and the revolution. Van Lydegraf is hard of hearing, so he often shouts to get his point across. When Tim looks out the window, he can see Mount Shasta, the slumbering volcano rising more than 14,000 feet into the sky. As the miles drag by, Van Lydegraf talks more about his role inside the Weatherman Underground. *The college-educated leaders may be brilliant in many ways*, he says, *but they don't always know how things really work*. He proudly shows off his calloused hands.

They cross the state line into Oregon and drop out of the mountains into the Rogue Valley, passing through Ashland and Medford as the sun touches the horizon. They cruise through a series of low hills, past Grants Pass, and Van Lydegraf pulls off the road at a rest stop. Tim looks around warily.

It's basically a glorified parking lot with a toilet. No forest to hide in, no place to escape if the cops corner them.

Van Lydegraf collapses on a bunk in the camper and immediately drops into a roaring snore. Tim lies in another bunk, staring at the camper ceiling.

Fighting off the Great Fear every time headlights turn off the interstate, he tries to slip into a dream.

ARMED AND DANGEROUS

September 15, 1970

Timothy Leary's escape from prison is dominating national headlines and TV broadcasts. Reporters are saying no one knows exactly how Leary disappeared from a state prison guarded by gun trucks. And penitentiary officials are scrambling to explain that Leary had been a model prisoner and seemed to pose no threat of escape—and now his wife is also missing and presumed on the run with her fugitive husband. Governor Reagan refuses to comment. Law enforcement agencies say they have one solid lead to follow:

Leary's denim prison pants and jacket were found in a restroom on a road leading to Los Angeles.

"We believe Leary is still in California," a prison spokesman announces. A massive dragnet has been set up across the state—roadblocks on highways and heavy security along all roads leading into Mexico.

"He could be anywhere," one police investigator concedes. "With the number of hippie communes around these hills, tracing him could be difficult."

❊　　❊　　❊

As Tim and Van Lydegraf begin the final stretch to Seattle, a communiqué is being delivered to the press:

September 15, 1970

This is the fourth communication from the Weatherman Underground.

The Weatherman Underground has had the honor and pleasure of helping Dr. Timothy Leary escape from the POW camp at San Luis Obispo, California.

Dr. Leary was being held against his will and against the will of millions of kids in this country. He was a political prisoner, captured for the work he did in helping all of us begin the task of creating a new culture on the barren wasteland that has been imposed on this country by Democrats, Republicans, Capitalists and creeps.

LSD and grass, like the herbs and cactus and mushrooms of the American Indians and countless civilizations that have existed on this planet, will help us make a future world where it will be possible to live in peace.

Now we are at war... We are outlaws, we are free!

Bernardine Dohrn.

The communiqué includes a note that appears to be written by Timothy Leary:

I offer loving gratitude to my Sisters and Brothers in the Weatherman Underground who designed and executed my liberation. Rosemary and I are now with the Underground and we'll continue to stay high and wage the revolutionary war.

Attached to the thank-you note from Leary is his own official Declaration of Revolution, one he had written inside the California Men's Colony—as part of the price Kennedy demanded for his escape. It is the same manifesto he dictated hastily to Joe Rhine, Kennedy's law partner, the day before he broke out:

There is the time for peace and the time for war... Brothers and Sisters, this is a war for survival...

Listen. There is no choice left but to defend life by all and every means possible against the genocidal machine...

You are part of the death apparatus or you belong to the network of free life...

Listen Americans. Your government is an instrument of total lethal evil...

Resist actively, sabotage, jam the computer & hijack planes & trash every lethal machine in the land...

Resist spiritually, stay high & praise god & love life & blow the mechanical mind with Holy Acid & dose them & dose them.

Resist physically... To shoot a genocidal robot policeman in the defense of life is a sacred act.

Listen Nixon. We were never that naive. We knew that flowers in your gun-barrels were risky... as we chanted love and raised our Woodstock fingers in the gentle sign of peace.

We begged you to live and let live, to love and let love, but you have chosen to kill and get killed. May God have mercy on your soul.

For the last seven months, I, a free, wild man, have been locked in POW camps. No living creature can survive in a cage...

Listen comrades. The liberation war has just begun... Total war is upon us. Fight to live or you'll die...

Timothy Leary

WARNING: I am armed and should be considered dangerous to anyone who threatens my life or my freedom.

PLAYING HOUSE

5 p.m., September 15, 1970

Tim and Van Lydegraf approach the outskirts of Seattle on Interstate 5, and the old Communist swings the camper onto a side road, heading northeast through miles of thick forests and acres of rolling farmland. He slows as they near the Skykomish River and then turns onto a narrow lane, nearly hidden by a canopy of trees and overgrown vines. After a half mile he spots a weathered, nearly-falling-down two-story farmhouse, set back about two hundred yards from the road.

"If there's an orange curtain in the window, that means the coast is clear," says Van Lydegraf.

As they pull closer and see the signal, both men exhale in relief. Still, the driver is taking no chances. He continues past the house, goes around the next bend, and then stops the camper and tells Tim to get out.

Tim grabs his suitcase and walks through a green field, moving faster and faster. He sees the front door open and out comes Rosemary, running to meet him. They embrace, kissing, and waltz toward the old farmhouse.

Inside is a young couple, two Weatherman operatives in their early twenties who are posing as college students. Also in the home is a very young blond woman. Rosemary introduces Pam, the teenage handler who helped Rosemary build her false identity and led her to Chicago to get her fake passport.

Tim looks around at the rotting house. The place is ramshackle, barely fit for human habitation. He frowns.

We raised $25,000 and this is the safe house?

The Weathermen had been mocking Rosemary, ridiculing the way she had been anxious to decorate the place for Tim. She bought an orange paper lantern, candles, and incense. She picked up silk pillowcases and a silk robe for her husband. Down by the river, she's hauled rocks and lashed together willow limbs to make a sweat lodge so they can purify themselves. This morning, she's baked bread and bought Camembert cheese, apples, berries, and plums. She also scored a carton of unfiltered Camels, his favorite. A bottle of wine from Portugal. Smoked oysters. Champagne.

Now Rosemary takes his hand, soothes him, and leads him upstairs to the bedroom, with its crumbling ceiling and exposed beams.

DOPE AND DYNAMITE

September 16, 1970

It's Wednesday, Tim's fourth day of freedom, and the farmhouse is full of revolutionaries. Dohrn and Ayers are there, and so is Van Lydegraf. There is also the stocky, freckle-faced, Irish-looking teenager who drove the pickup car outside the prison. Everyone gathers in the kitchen. Bernardine removes her shirt and sponges her breasts at the sink while leading a strategy discussion. The men try not to ogle her.

The Weathermen tell Tim it's time to begin working on his new identity. The Irish kid motions for Tim to follow him into the bathroom. Tim eases into a chair next to the sink and feels the pull of the scissors chopping off his hair. The dyed brown locks fall to the floor as the kid trims the sides of Tim's head and then begins working the crown, cutting closer and closer to the skull. He pulls out a razor and begins carefully scraping Tim's head, removing the last hairs on top.

Tim stands and examines himself in a mirror. He can't fathom the person staring back, completely bald on top with thin strands of brown hair clinging to the sides. The man in the mirror is a Main Street businessman, maybe a middle manager at a Ford dealership, the sort of guy whose idea of cutting loose is working the microphone during bingo night at the American Legion hall. Tim slips on a pair of thick black-framed glasses and looks again, marveling at the transformation. He walks out of the bathroom and the others gasp when they see him. Tim likes their reaction.

This might work.

❁　　❁　　❁

In San Francisco, attorney Michael Kennedy is calling a press conference and praising Timothy Leary's breakout and his radical manifesto:

"Prison took a peace-loving man and in eight months turned him into a roaring revolutionary," Kennedy says, waving a copy of Tim's statement.

"Leary was screwed. He'd exhausted every legal means before resorting to this, and I want to say that I think the government has a serious revolutionary to deal with now."

Kennedy urges on the revolution, calling for more prison breaks:

"Millions of kids look to Timothy for leadership and God knows how many other kids look to the Weatherman for leadership. I see this new move by Leary as a marriage of dope and dynamite, flowers and flames."

✷ ✷ ✷

Leary's escape from prison and his call to arms confirm Richard Nixon's worst fears about the counterculture.

"Terrorism has replaced subversion as the immediate threat," he tells his aides. "Thousands of Americans, mostly under thirty . . . are determined to destroy our society."

The lunatic LSD professor on the loose is more than a propaganda victory for the radicals. Leary's crazy manifesto might actually inspire even more people to join the revolution, and no telling where the violence could lead—maybe straight to the White House gates.

Worse, J. Edgar Hoover's FBI appears to have no idea where Leary could be. They have no informants inside the Weatherman Underground and no leads to pursue. They have raided communes across California, hoping to find some evidence of Leary's presence. They are monitoring the radical attorney Michael Kennedy around the clock. They are questioning other prisoners inside the California Men's Colony. They are cornering terrified informants on the streets of San Francisco. But they have come up with nothing.

Hoover knows the stakes. A pug-faced man with the body of a fire hydrant, he has been working for the Justice Department since World War I. He's served eight successive presidents, finding a way to be indispensable to each one—using blackmail and strong-arm techniques, on both the president and his enemies. But now, at age seventy-five, there are whispers that he's long past his prime, that the agency is no longer effective after forty-six years of his rule. There are insistent hints that he has gotten too old, that he'd be better off retiring and going home to raise his treasured purebred cairn terriers. There are even veiled threats that he should resign before word gets out to the public that he is gay.

Hoover has become a reviled symbol to the counterculture, hell-bent on cracking down, by any means necessary, on anyone who gets out of line—especially civil rights activists and anti-war protesters. Hoover has forcefully unleashed a covert "counterintelligence" program over the last decade: COINTELPRO, a secret campaign to spy on, discredit, and take down people deemed to be threats to the American way of life. Hoover cast a wide net with COINTELPRO: Martin Luther King Jr., Malcolm X, the Black Panthers, the American Indian Movement, and even the Ku Klux Klan have been stalked, wiretapped, or infiltrated.

Inside Hoover's private fifth-floor office there is a large American flag behind his shiny glass-covered desk and its steely-looking fountain pen. Wary agents call his scathing blue-ink notes, stabbed onto the margins of their reports, "blue gems." Now Hoover walks from his imperial office to greet the reporters crowding to hear what the FBI is going to do about Timothy Leary. Hoover is grim-faced, terse, just like when he sent G-men to gun down Bonnie and Clyde during the Great Depression.

Facing the reporters, the FBI director sounds like he is assuring President Nixon as much as the nation:

"We'll have him in ten days," barks Hoover.

❈   ❈   ❈

Nixon is aboard Air Force One, heading to the American heartland. He's been fretting about his anemic approval ratings and worrying about his upcoming reelection campaign. Leary being free isn't helping. Nixon wants to give a major law-and-order speech, to reassure the American public that their president remains in command and that he will defeat these enemies.

His detractors say that he's too unpopular to show his face on a college campus, where student demonstrations have continued to erupt ever since Kent State. But Nixon's aides have found a place, Kansas State University, a conservative stronghold in Middle America, where they've been assured the president will receive a warm welcome.

Nixon's renewed offensive against the counterculture is taking shape: He has dispatched Vice President Spiro Agnew to give speeches around the country blasting rock and roll's "blatant drug-culture propaganda" that is "brainwashing" American kids. Nixon's trusty attorney general, John Mitchell, has been deriding protesting students as "stupid kids."

As the presidential jet begins its descent, Nixon fingers the royal purple tie he's wearing in honor of the Kansas State school colors. Maybe it will help make the students like him. He's reviewing his speech, remembering to mention Kansas State's football team right away...that ought to do the trick.

After the presidential motorcade arrives on campus, Nixon is introduced to the crowd of 15,000 Kansas State students at the Ahearn Field House. He quickly goes after the "cancerous disease" spreading across the United States:

> We saw it three weeks ago in the vicious bombing at the University of Wisconsin...We have seen it in other bombings and burnings on our campuses, in our cities, in the wanton shootings of policemen...These acts of viciousness all took place not in some other country but in the United States, and in the last five weeks.

Nixon is building, gathering steam, drowning out the handful of hecklers:

> The time has come for us to recognize that violence and terror have no place in a free society.

Nixon's voice is rising:

Those who bomb universities, ambush policemen, who hijack airplanes, who hold their passengers hostage, all share in common not only a contempt for human life, but also the contempt for those elemental decencies on which a free society rests—and they deserve the contempt of every American who values those decencies...

We must take an uncompromising stand against those who reject the rules of civilized conduct...those who would destroy what is right in our society.

With a roar, thousands of the students rise spontaneously and blanket him with a thundering ovation.

Nixon smiles grimly. He's always maintained that he is at his best in a crisis. For sure, this is a triumph, one of the best moments of his presidency.

But as he begins his return trip to Washington, Nixon is stunned to learn that television coverage had been spotty, that many stations elected to broadcast daytime soap operas instead of his speech. He is livid. Nixon dispatches a high-level emissary to confront TV executives—to warn them that the president will use the FCC to deny their license renewals and throw them out of business. The aide reports back that the networks "are very much afraid of us and are trying hard to prove they are 'good guys.'"

Within a week, stations around the country begin airing a special prime-time "rebroadcast" of Nixon's Kansas State speech.

A GOOD TEST FOR YOUR DISGUISE

September 18–22, 1970

The Northwest skies have opened and soft rain is falling steadily outside Tim's safe house. He lowers a half-smoked roach into an ashtray and steps outdoors and over the soft earth and weeds, heading to the sweat lodge by the river. It will be good to be in there, embracing Rosemary under the limbs of the willow tree. It was hard to sleep last night. Bernardine was making love with someone and her wild cries of passion echoed throughout the crappy house.

"Caterwauling," Rosemary had called it, eyeing her husband archly.

The next day, Tim is studying the celebratory escape stories in the underground newspapers. It's clear that the police and the FBI have no idea where he is hiding. Hoover's agents are following up on rumors that Leary is in Mexico, or Hawaii, maybe playing like a pirate and ensconced on an ocean-trotting yacht. *Maybe he's camping in the hills outside San Luis Obispo and gathering a revolutionary army of Weathermen and Black Panthers to liberate all the prisoners and then march to San Francisco.*

The Weathermen spill several documents on the old kitchen table for Tim to examine. He picks through the papers and picks up one item that looks promising: a birth certificate for a William J. McNellis, born January 14, 1919. He died at age four in 1923. A new copy of the certificate was issued on March 9, 1970, just three days after the Greenwich Village townhouse explosion.

Tim and the Weathermen decide to build his new identity as William McNellis. Several of the Weathermen push away from the table, drive to Seattle, and return with a square's wardrobe, a dull brown suit that could have once hung in an old tax accountant's closet. It's something bland, something that "Mr. McNellis" will wear when he applies for identification cards and his passport.

But the Weathermen also bring back some news: *Jimi Hendrix has been declared dead.* Hendrix had been rushed unconscious to a London hospital. The papers are reporting that he died of a drug overdose at age twenty-seven.

Tim had always thought of Hendrix as the true cosmic messenger from the gods, the one who could channel the sounds inside LSD's higher planes. Tim had recorded some trippy music with Hendrix, including a song called "You Can Be Anyone This Time Around" that was meant to help fund Tim's race for governor against Ronald Reagan. He and Rosemary shed tears as they reminisce about Hendrix.

There's only one way that Tim can think of to pay tribute. The movie *Woodstock* is playing in Seattle, and Hendrix is in the festival film, anointing the crowd with his triumphant, psychedelic version of "The Star-Spangled Banner." Tim suggests that he can try out his brown suit by going to see the movie.

Bernardine agrees: "It will be a good test for your disguise."

❋   ❋   ❋

A few hours later, Tim and Rosemary are freshly stoned as they take their seats near the front of the theater. They're carrying two tubs of hot buttered popcorn and two dripping ice-cream bars. Tim is quickly caught up in the excitement. He missed the Woodstock festival in person, and he cheers with glee when each new performer comes on the screen: Joan Baez; Crosby, Stills & Nash; Jefferson Airplane; Janis Joplin. Rosemary tries to muffle him, but Tim keeps forgetting. It hardly matters. Behind them, a few rows back, the Weatherman fugitives are also watching the movie. They're completely loaded, laughing and shouting at the film. By the movie's third hour, the sun is rising over Woodstock and Hendrix takes the stage wearing a fringed purple poncho and a red bandanna. At the concert, people are raising their hands, shouting,

"We love you!" In the movie theater, Tim and the others are doing the same. On-screen, Hendrix is so dynamically *alive*. He was the electric torch for the freak nation, the Aquarian force, the black man playing sonic, interplanetary blues for white kids, the minister of music for the new world beyond the old one. When the movie is finally over and he fades from the screen, there is only weeping inside the theater.

❀   ❀   ❀

On Monday, September 21, Tim puts on the brown suit and rides into Seattle with Ayers, who is driving a car rented under an assumed name. The radio is playing the week's top hits, Edwin Starr's "War" and Diana Ross's "Ain't No Mountain High Enough." A song by James Taylor, "Fire and Rain," is also cracking the rotation. There is other news on the radio: The National Guard Armory in Newburyport, Massachusetts, has been invaded and some ammunition and bombs are missing.

Ideally, Mr. William J. McNellis should have a driver's license when he applies for a passport, but there's a Department of Motor Vehicles waiting list of at least a week. Instead, Ayers leads Tim into a grimy part of Seattle's old Pioneer Square neighborhood, past run-down bars and drifters and prostitutes. At a fading sporting goods store Tim climbs up to the second floor. Presenting his birth certificate, he is granted a State of Washington hunting license. They leave to apply for a library card.

Rosemary, meanwhile, is wearing her itchy blond wig and shopping with Dohrn at a JCPenney in Seattle. They select a Panasonic cassette player and some tapes to take on a long-distance flight. They buy more clothing and new luggage. After a moment of thought, they agree to pay a little extra to get Tim's suitcase monogrammed with William J. McNellis's initials.

Tim and Ayers make their way to a passport photo office. Tim, unsmiling, looks straight into the camera. With his thick, decidedly uncool black glasses, Mr. McNellis seems like the squarest man in America, the person least likely to ever try LSD. The next stop is an

American Express office, where Mr. McNellis exchanges $1,500 in cash for traveler's checks.

By late afternoon, Tim and Rosemary have their suitcases packed and are riding in separate cars to Seattle-Tacoma International Airport. McNellis purchases a first-class ticket for the evening flight to Chicago. At a separate counter, Sylvia McGaffin and the blond teenager, Pam, buy two economy seats.

❋   ❋   ❋

The next morning, Tuesday, September 22, Tim closes the door to room 222 at the Sheraton Hotel and Motor Inn, just across the freeway from O'Hare airport. He takes a cab to Chicago's imposing federal building. Inside, an official portrait of President Richard Milhous Nixon glares down as Mr. McNellis fills out the paperwork for his passport. He hands the clerk the birth certificate and his passport photos.

She nods approval and asks for his driver's license.

Mr. McNellis smiles at her.

I'm sorry, ma'am, but I don't drive.

He reaches into his wallet.

Here's my Social Security card.

She frowns.

No, I need to see a government ID with a photo on it.

Mr. McNellis shrugs his shoulders a little as a few small beads of sweat begin to form on his balding brow. He lets out a genial laugh.

You know, ma'am, I am . . . a responsible citizen.

He opens his wallet for her and fishes through it with a flourish.

Here's my Seattle library card. And here's my State of Washington hunting license.

Mr. McNellis hands her the growing pile of IDs and bobs his head in approval as she sighs, shakes her head, stamps his paperwork. Barely looking up, she says that his passport will be ready in the afternoon.

Tim walks slowly away from the counter and calls a cab in front of the building, ignoring Richard Nixon's jowly stare. Back at the Sheraton, he goes to the fifth floor and knocks on a door. Pam has booked herself into a far nicer and bigger room than the one Tim and Rosemary have been given.

Tim gets the details from her.

I went to a downtown diner and a comrade gave me an envelope packed with hundred-dollar bills. I paid cash for two tickets for you and Rosemary for a direct flight to Paris at 5:30 p.m.

She adds one more thing:

The tickets are round-trip. If I bought one-way fares, the FBI would be suspicious.

Tim takes the elevator back down to the second floor and tells Rosemary the plan. He paces the room nervously, smoking, too worked up to eat lunch. Finally, there is a knock at the door and Tim carefully opens it. Pam is outside and Tim ushers her in.

Tell Rosemary to come with me. We're going to pick up your passport. It's safer if we do it and not you.

Tim watches them from the hotel window as they step into a cab. He checks his watch. The plane leaves in three hours.

❂   ❂   ❂

At four o'clock, he peeks through the curtain and sees Rosemary leaping from a taxi. A minute later, she is running into the hotel room, her face flushed, and waving William McNellis's new passport. Tim grabs their two suitcases and they immediately sprint to the waiting cab. The flight to Paris leaves in exactly ninety minutes.

Tim and Rosemary hold hands, crowded in the back of the cab with Pam. The driver speeds to the terminal and Pam tells Rosemary to walk away without looking back, as if she is a single young woman who happened to share a cab with two strangers.

Tim watches Rosemary melt into the crowd. Pam hands Tim a bon voyage gift from the Weathermen: an aftershave bottle filled with pure LSD. Tim pauses at the curb and kneels to unlatch his suitcase so he can stuff in the bottle of acid.

Behind him, he hears Pam's hissing voice: "Don't stay out here, there are all sorts of pigs watching you."

At 4:45 p.m., boarding is just beginning. President Nixon's order for tightened airport security, in the wake of the recent airliner hijackings, is in full force. The terminal is filled with extra patrol officers, plainclothes marshals, and FBI agents—especially looking for anyone who appears to be from the Middle East.

Rosemary browses in the gift shop while Tim pretends to make a phone call. He fires up a cigarette, walks to a newsstand, and buys a paperback copy of *The Godfather*. Thirty minutes before departure, Rosemary goes to the counter to claim her boarding pass. Tim is in line a few places behind her.

Several uniformed agents are manning the entrance to the boarding area. They have set up a new metal detector and are frisking passengers one by one and searching baggage. A young Iranian couple is pulled aside for a thorough search and the line slows to a halt.

One of the security agents turns to Mr. McNellis.

"Sorry to inconvenience you, sir."

When his turn comes, the square-looking Mr. William J. McNellis is waved right through.

He boards the jet and is welcomed by a smiling stewardess outfitted in a navy vest and a miniskirt. He finds his window seat, directly over a wing. As he settles in, he sees Rosemary finally entering the plane. As she moves toward her seat in the rear, he looks up and winks.

The flight is only about two-thirds full. Just before takeoff, one of the stewardesses leans over him and suggests that if he is bothered by the view of the big, noisy engine and wing outside his window, there is an empty seat farther back.

He turns to where she is pointing. The unoccupied seat is right across from the bubbly-looking blonde he just winked at.

William J. McNellis claims his new seat. He orders Champagne for himself and for his new friend as the flight to Paris lifts off right on time.

PART II

THE SHELTERING SKY

THE BADDEST MOTHERFUCKER

September 26, 1970

Passengers aboard an Air Algérie flight departing Paris are craning their necks and turning to ogle the funny-looking clown in the back of the plane. It's a real, live American hippie, a hairy freak, sprawled across two seats in the tourist section. His shaggy blond hair spills into wild tangles. A thick handlebar mustache hides most of his face. He's wearing faded jeans, a chambray shirt, and brown knee-high riding boots. He's brought no luggage and is traveling with just a toothbrush tucked in his back pocket.

Stew Albert, along with his manic and more famous friends Jerry Rubin and Abbie Hoffman, is a cofounder of the Youth International Party, more commonly known as Yippies, a collective of coast-to-coast activists and pranksters planning to politicize America's stoned-out hippies. The thirty-year-old looks like a California surfer but grew up in a working-class Jewish family in Brooklyn. He spent the last few years hip-deep in the Yippies' most notorious stunts: tossing dollar bills at the greed-soaked traders inside the New York Stock Exchange; chanting furiously in a seriocomic attempt to magically levitate the Pentagon. At the riots in Chicago during the 1968 Democratic Convention, he had been the first Yippie to get his head bashed in by the cops.

In the underground circles and newspapers, Stew has a reputation as a wisecracking agent of change who shows up at all the righteous scenes. Still, he doesn't ever draw the same public attention as Rubin and Hoffman—the two mercurial freaks who have become among the most outrageous faces of the counterculture. Hoffman had almost succeeded with a spectacular plot to trick President Nixon into devouring 600 micrograms of pure Orange Sunshine: Jefferson Airplane's lead singer, Grace Slick, had been mistakenly invited to a White House tea party as part of a college reunion sponsored by one of Nixon's children. She tucked the acid under a fingernail, invited Hoffman to escort her, and they planned to pop it into the president's drink—but the plan to have the leader of the free world tripping his ass off fizzled when White House security recognized the suddenly groomed, suit-and-tie-wearing man as the Yippie provocateur Abbie Hoffman.

Stew's stunts never quite reach the same level of infamy, probably because he doesn't have a supernova ego; he's better at listening and bullshitting late into the stoned night as the Yippies debate their next bit of intentionally lunatic action.

He is, really, the closest thing the Yippies have to a diplomat.

And now, as his flight to Algiers moves over the Mediterranean and begins to approach North Africa, he is trying hard to ignore the looks from the buttoned-up squares on the plane. Instead, he is wondering how the hell he got caught up in this crazy scheme:

He is on his way to convince the baddest Black Panther of them all, Eldridge Cleaver, to give sanctuary to the High Priest of LSD.

❋   ❋   ❋

Just two weeks prior, right after Tim escaped from prison, an unusual reception was held at a luxurious villa in the hills above Algiers: Diplomats from America's sworn enemies gathered to celebrate the grand opening of the Black Panther "Embassy."

Algeria's revolutionary socialist Muslim republic has broken off diplomatic relations with the United States and refuses to welcome any ambassador sent by Richard Nixon. Instead, the Algerians recognize the Black Panthers as the legitimate representatives of the American people.

The Panthers were given a beautiful two-story manor to use as their embassy, along with a monthly stipend from the government. The home once belonged to a wealthy French family and is in the heart of one of the nation's most exclusive districts—a far cry from the Panthers' battered, sandbagged headquarters in an Oakland ghetto.

At the embassy's grand opening, Communist emissaries from North Korea, Red China, and North Vietnam circulated among turquoise-painted rooms, sipping soft drinks, greeting old revolutionary comrades, and talking about ways to defeat the United States. The walls were decorated with framed photographs of Che Guevara and Chairman Mao, along with a portrait of North Korean leader Kim Il-sung, one of the Panthers' staunchest international supporters.

A half dozen Black Panthers, young men in their twenties, had removed their usual dark leather jackets and were outfitted in crisp powder-blue shirts with shoulder epaulets, as befitting a diplomatic corps. The Panthers handed out cookies and soda as they attempted to mingle with the middle-aged men in their dull Communist Party–issued suits. Each Panther carried a gun, a habit ingrained after so many shootouts with the pigs back in the country they simply call "Babylon."

In the center of the villa's main room, standing regally under a grand domed blue-tile ceiling, was a tall, powerfully built man. He towered over the other guests, and unlike the younger Panthers, he seemed perfectly at ease in this setting. Back in Babylon, Eldridge Cleaver was a notorious fugitive hunted by the FBI, wanted for the ambush and attempted murder of two policemen during a ninety-minute shootout in California. Here in Algiers he was respectfully addressed as "Mr. Ambassador."

Cleaver, thirty-five, has a neatly trimmed mustache, goatee, and a small gold stud in his left ear. His puffy, heavy-lidded eyes can crease into a skeptical squint. He has a lithe grace, outwardly calm but often rippling with quiet menace.

At the embassy reception, the diminutive representative from Red China gravitated to Cleaver's side: "We are enemies to the death with the American government, but we have a great sympathy for the American people."

Cleaver nodded thoughtfully and then offered the Black Power salute. "Right on," he said.

Before he fled to Algeria, Cleaver had run for president on the Peace and Freedom Party ticket. "We don't need a war on poverty," he shouted at campaign rallies. "What we need is a war on the rich." He vowed to never live in the White House if elected. Instead, he promised: "I would send a wrecking crew there to burn the motherfucker down."

Behind his back, some fearful Panthers have a nickname for him, one they had heard his wife use: Papa Rage. His fiery prison memoir, *Soul on Ice*, has sold millions of copies. "When I write," he once offered, "I want to drive a spear into the heart of America." He is the only person to appear simultaneously on America's best-seller lists and the FBI's Most Wanted list.

He has spent most of his adult life in prison on drug, rape, and assault charges. He fled Ronald Reagan's California rather than go back to jail in connection with that attempted murder of two Oakland cops. And since he escaped the FBI two years ago, he has become a revolutionary outlaw, "the black Che Guevara." He smoked cigars with Fidel Castro and traded embraces with Palestinian guerrilla leader Yasser Arafat. He was a houseguest of North Korea's Kim Il-sung, and he toured Red Square. In North Vietnam, he made treasonous broadcasts on Radio Hanoi, calling on black GIs to kill their commanding officers and join him in Algeria for the upcoming revolution.

"Protests and demonstrations have exhausted themselves," Cleaver thundered. "The only response can be an escalation of violence itself. There's nothing to reevaluate—except the choice of weapons."

As he toured the Communist world, grabbing headlines by promising to disembowel Richard Nixon's government, American officials pleaded with Algeria to expel him. Instead, the Algerians awarded Cleaver his own embassy, along with a posh private residence. He was quickly joined by other fugitive Panthers—including several men suspected of murders and hijackings.

Now Cleaver views his revolutionary outpost in Algiers as the equivalent of Fidel Castro regrouping in the Sierra Maestra, or Mao's Long March through rural China. Because Algeria has no extradition treaty with the United States, Cleaver's embassy can become a safe haven for other militant radicals. He can gather the forces, the leading American revolutionaries. Then he will personally guide everyone back to America and seize power at the right moment.

He has already issued an invitation to Weatherman leader Bernardine Dohrn, letting her know that she is welcome to join him in Algiers anytime.

As his plane descends toward the sunbaked tarmac in Algiers, Stew Albert has time to reflect on Cleaver's extraordinary rise, their unlikely friendship, and how he is going to have to sell the Black Panther on serving as a host, benefactor, and protector of Dr. Timothy Leary.

Years ago, Stew bonded with Cleaver as a new group called the Black Panthers was forming in Oakland, its members arming themselves against racist cops. The Panthers stalked police who were out on patrols. They carried their own guns and quoted the Second Amendment—ready to shoot if the pigs threatened their people. And when Eldridge Cleaver watched the cofounder of the Panthers, Huey P. Newton, stick a gun in a cop's face and tell him to fuck off, Cleaver was sold. "I cannot help but say that Huey P. Newton is the baddest motherfucker to ever set foot inside of history," Cleaver raved. "For 400 years black people have been wanting to do exactly what Huey Newton did."

Cleaver's skills as a writer and speaker elevated him quickly to the position of minister of information—the chief propagandist for the Panthers. He unleashed an audacious spectacle: rifle-bearing Panthers in ink-black leather jackets and berets marching into Ronald Reagan's California statehouse, a show of Second Amendment force that had white observers trembling and whispering, "Niggers with guns, niggers with guns."

FBI director J. Edgar Hoover quickly warned the nation: "The Black Panther Party, without question, represents the greatest threat to internal security of the country."

Cleaver sneered back at Hoover: "That could be translated from pig-ese into the language of the people—meaning that the Black Panther Party is threatening the system that's threatening the people."

As Stew walks into Maison Blanche Airport, he is immediately surrounded by stern Algerian officers. The Algerians don't want long-haired scum corrupting their youth. As he's being interrogated, Stew suddenly sees Eldridge Cleaver marching toward him, flanked by another glowering Black Panther. Cleaver exchanges a few soothing words with the Algerian officials and Stew is magically waved through without being searched.

Cleaver is in a dark green military tunic, buttoned to the top. Don Cox, the Black Panthers' field marshal and Cleaver's personal bodyguard, is with him. Called DC, he has a bushy Afro and a long, pointed goatee. Cox has personally trained dozens of young Panther recruits to use deadly force, and yet his hard-edged scowl, carefully calculated to terrify whites, will sometimes break into a bemused, even sweet smile. DC was featured by the writer Tom Wolfe in an essay called "Radical Chic"—about DC's being a guest star at a swanky Panther fundraiser held in the Manhattan penthouse of internationally renowned orchestra conductor Leonard Bernstein. Not long after, DC went underground when he was charged with murdering a police informant—then he escaped to Algeria to become Cleaver's second-in-command.

The two Panthers and the Yippie head to the airport parking lot and squeeze into a dented, cube-shaped Renault. Cleaver once had a brand-new Plymouth Fury back in the States, a muscle car with a telephone installed. As the men open the doors to the tiny, sagging Renault, Cleaver looks over at Stew and shrugs. *This is the best we can do in Algiers.*

DC roars the car along the Boulevard Ernesto Che Guevara, screeching around corners and honking as he plunges into busy intersections. A joint is produced and the car fills with smoke. DC swerves to avoid pedestrians and turns onto a bumpy cobblestone street. He points out the ancient walls of the Casbah as they flash by in a blur. He points out the Grand Mosque, built in 1097.

The little Renault climbs the hills, the engine whining. There are bombed-out buildings, wrecked during Algeria's long, bloody revolution against the French. As the road curves and ascends, they pass lovely forested parks with stunning views of the azure ocean. They are now entering the embassy district, with its opulent Moorish estates hidden behind towering palm trees. Rounding a city plaza, they veer onto a side street and screech to a halt. Stew studies the breathtaking Panther embassy as they clamber out. The splendid place is encircled by a four-foot-high hand-laid stone wall topped by a staked iron fence.

Eldridge announces that the Algerians liberated the home from French pigs during the revolution.

We call it "the People's Embassy."

As they approach the forbidding metal front gate, Stew sees two polished bronze plaques etched with a growling panther. The signs announce, in Arabic and English: THE BLACK PANTHER PARTY— INTERNATIONAL SECTION. An armed guard rises into view from the upper balcony. At the front door, there are five separate dead-bolt locks.

As the door opens, rock music blasts from the building. The Panthers possess the most kick-ass stereo system in all of Africa, Cleaver says. Inside, a Yippie flag is tacked up on one wall, with its green marijuana leaf inside a red star. One sign reads: IN REVOLUTION ONE WINS OR DIES. The most prominent display is the oversize gilt-framed portrait of Huey P. Newton, the cofounder of the Panthers. He was freed from prison a few weeks ago after a manslaughter conviction was overturned. Now he is eager to reestablish his control over the party. His previous title had been minister of defense. Now Newton refers to himself as Supreme Commander.

Eldridge rolls a fresh joint and says his men will receive military training from the Palestine Liberation Organization, a group the FBI and CIA have been racing to combat after its terrorist kidnappings and hijackings. As the clouds of sweet smoke swirl overhead, Cleaver muses about the brazen killings of students at Kent State and Jackson State—and about the upcoming trial of Lieutenant William Calley for the slaughter of hundreds of innocent women and children in Vietnam. Things are building, cresting, headed to a revolution. He leans back, stoned and cradling an AK-47 the North Koreans have given him.

He strokes the barrel of the assault rifle and gets higher and higher.

Stew isn't sure whether the gun is loaded. He decides to wait until later to bring up the subject of Timothy Leary.

GINSENG WINE

William McNellis is heading to the Paris airport to board his own flight to Algiers. After they first landed in Paris, Tim and Rosemary had gotten in touch with trusted friends, a turned-on French psychologist and his wife, who sheltered and fed them. Tim had promised Bernardine Dohrn and the Weathermen that he'd make contact with Eldridge Cleaver...but... *Paris is very beautiful in the fall.* Maybe he and Rosemary were entitled to a vacation after all they'd been through. He wanted to relax, stroll, and see the hippies in Place Saint-Michel, drink cabernet sauvignon in cafés. The youth movement, the music freaks who loved Jimi Hendrix, would give him a solid cocoon. Maybe the French would even provide him sanctuary, the kind that they extend to freedom-seeking artists.

But Rosemary had grown pensive, withdrawn. Maybe the gravity of joining him as an international fugitive weighed her down. She said she was missing her friends and lovers back in California. She was tired of going out in public wearing a wig and a push-up bra and pantyhose.

Tim suggested that instead of following the Weathermen's directives, instead of meeting Cleaver, maybe they should buy a small Citroën and wander the continent, still in disguise, spending the Brotherhood of Eternal Love's cash on a second honeymoon. Rosemary snapped at him: *We can't turn our backs on the revolution.*

He coldly said he'd go alone to Algiers, to check it out, to see if it really was the right place to live in exile. Rosemary said she'd wait in Paris. They decided to split the remaining money. After the numbing intensity of the last two weeks, she was relieved to see him leave.

✹ ✹ ✹

At the airport, Mr. McNellis's departure goes off without a hitch. The disguise and fake passport are still working. The flight to Algiers is brief, only two hours. As the captain announces their descent, Tim peers out the window, taking in the view. Below, he can see the sapphire Mediterranean lapping against a narrow strip of tan sand. Beyond the beach, crumpled green hills are dotted with clusters of white buildings, brilliantly aglow in the afternoon sun. Beyond the hills, in the hazy blue distance, are the rugged peaks of the Atlas Mountains. Beyond the mountains are the long, lonely wastes of the Sahara, and then the rest of Mother Africa.

After his plane lands, Tim retrieves his small suitcase and approaches the customs agents. This is totally uncharted territory. He has no plan, really, other than to try to find one of the most incendiary revolutionaries in modern American history. He hopes the Algerians won't inspect his bag closely. His aftershave bottle is still filled with the world's strongest, purest LSD, given to him by the Weathermen as their good-bye gift. Grinning and nodding, he tells the agents he is an international businessman looking for investment opportunities in Algeria. An officer examines him for a second, shrugs, and issues his tourist visa.

He steps outside and falls into the Algerian dreamscape. It's like tripping into a pool of soft cotton, nothing he could really prepare for—all of it just hours from the Western European certitudes in Paris and London. Men robed in hooded djellabas are pedaling by on rickety bikes. There are waterfalls of crimson bougainvillea falling over old colonial buildings painted the color of robin's eggs or vanilla caramels. There is a heady mixture of caraway, cumin, and bracing Turkish coffee and, at the side of the road, shepherds yelling "*Balek, balek, balek*" in a thousand-year-old monotone, telling people to be awake, to be aware, to be mindful as they steer goats to market. There is the flap of caged pigeons, the sticky-sweet smell of nougat, and the droning thrumming of Bedouin music.

Tim hails a cab outside the airport and asks for the best hotel in the city. Heading to downtown Algiers, he passes blocks of once-regal apartment buildings sinking into slow decay as if they are yearning to return to the skeleton-colored Saharan sands. The sun is dropping and there are fewer people on the narrow streets. Government-run shops are closing up. Not a single woman in sight.

The driver pulls up to the Aletti, a faded art deco hotel facing the waterfront. The place has the stale air of a raffish dowager grown old and weedy, but the government-controlled price is right, just twenty-five dinars, about five dollars a night for a room. As Tim receives his key, a pleasant thought wells up:

I'm safe from the long reach of Nixon.

✸   ✸   ✸

Across town, Stew Albert has left Panther headquarters and is arriving at Eldridge Cleaver's personal digs, even more extravagant than the embassy. A large white compound with a private entry gate, it once belonged to the French aristocracy. It has thick carpets and airy spaces and is adorned in a striking red-and-black motif—the same revolutionary colors that the lawyer Michael Kennedy had decorated his San Francisco offices with.

A beautiful, barefoot Algerian teenager, Malika, greets him at the door. There's no sign of Cleaver's wife, Kathleen. Stew is not surprised. Cleaver always kept young girlfriends, and his stormy marriage was no secret. Back in California, Stew had seen Kathleen's bruised face and black eyes. Eldridge dismissed those injuries by telling him, "Kathleen has a hot temper. You should see the scratches on my back."

Cleaver's new girlfriend has big brown eyes, creamy olive skin, and thick, tumbling hair. She looks like an Algerian version of a hippie. She is wearing a fashionable peasant dress, and a fresh flower is tucked into her long mane. She is half-European, a relic of the uneasy colonial dance, and fluent in French, Arabic, and English. Cleaver explains that she's been helping out with translating. In Arabic, her name means *queen*. At a glance from Cleaver, she leaves the two men alone to talk.

Stew quickly explains the plan, one the Yippies have developed with the Weathermen: They want to strengthen Cleaver's ground-breaking work in Algeria by helping him turn the country into an outpost where fugitive U.S. revolutionaries can strategize and train. Stew gingerly adds something else: Maybe Cleaver's embassy can be the first refuge for high-profile American dissidents—for people like Timothy Leary, who just busted out of prison.

Cleaver instantly frowns. *How does a middle-aged acid head, a hallucinating pacifist like Timothy Leary fit into the war for liberation?*

Stew begins talking faster and faster: *Leary is telling millions of his followers to join the battles against the pigs. He's tight with the Weathermen. They've put their minds together for the revolution. They've dropped acid together.*

Cleaver grimaces at the mention of LSD. He is cautious around psychedelics. He's seen too many hippies burned out on heavy hallucinogens in San Francisco. They're not the clear-eyed freedom fighters he needs to take down Babylon and set fire to the White House. Cleaver lights a new Winston from the butt of his old one. *This is the third world. Drugs are the tools of the imperialists. No one in Algeria is going to want anything to do with the High Priest of LSD.*

Stew argues that the revolutionaries in America are using LSD as a tool to break free of the chains of capitalist, racist enslavement. They're even dropping hits of Orange Sunshine as they map out their bombing runs across the United States.

Remember those bombings in New York over the summer? You saw how another bank got hit a few weeks ago, right on Fifth Avenue? Those are from the Weathermen, inspired by acid.

Cleaver snorts: *Did Che Guevara need LSD? Did Chairman Mao? Did Kim Il-sung drop acid in North Korea?* He stands and walks into the kitchen. He returns with a bottle of amber-colored liquid and two glasses. He pours them each a drink. Stew takes a sip and wrenches his face in disgust. *What kind of wine did you say this was?*

Cleaver makes a show of enjoying his drink. He explains that it's ginseng wine, a personal gift to him from the Democratic People's Republic of Korea. The North Koreans provide Cleaver and the Black Panthers with cases of the stuff. Cleaver says that the wine does more than get you drunk; it's also got medicinal properties, healing qualities. Stew looks doubtfully at the bottle. He can see now that a large ginseng root is floating inside it. He has no idea how Eldridge can stand this North Korean shit. But what the hell; he shrugs and downs the rest of his glass.

I'LL BEAT HIM TO DEATH
WITH A MARSHMALLOW

September 28, 1970

Tim is marveling at the warm, slightly hazy Mediterranean morning light. It's like California, southern Spain, or Morocco. Shopkeepers are stooping to raise their metal gates. Rapid-fire Arabic is in the air. He steps onto the street and sees one or two women hidden beneath rustling burkas. They flap past the clusters of men, their faces hidden inside a cumulus of cigarette smoke. Tim has coffee and breakfast at a nearby café and buys Gauloise cigarettes, dark, unfiltered, and very strong. Firing one up, he walks back to his hotel to figure out how to find Eldridge Cleaver.

At the hotel's front desk there is muttering, some hand waving, and no straight answers.

Ask someone at El Moudjahid, *the French-language government newspaper.*

When he arrives, an editor tells him to instead check with the National Liberation Front, the FLN, the far-left party that controls the government. At the ministry, the runaround continues: A clerk tells him to try the tourist office. And at the tourism bureau, the unsmiling officials suggest he try the front desk at his hotel.

It's early afternoon now, and the heat is suffocating. Tim is sweating inside his brown businessman's suit, the one the Weathermen bought for him at the Seattle department store. As he slogs down the humid street, he suddenly catches sight of his pasty, perspiring figure reflected in a shop window. He realizes what the problem is: His disguise as Mr. McNellis is too good. Everyone thinks he's a CIA agent, an American spy in a cheap suit.

In downtown Algiers, he spots a clothing store and darts inside.

In the dim light, he finds a pair of black slacks and a mustard-colored turtleneck shirt. Then he spies the big prize, a black leather cap, the kind Vladimir Lenin used to wear. Turning it over, he sees that it's Russian made. Looking in the mirror, Tim hopes the hat will do more than hide his bald spot—maybe it will provide the right proletarian look to impress a black revolutionary leader.

Back at the hotel, Tim also ditches his thick glasses and pops in contact lenses. He returns to the lobby and smiles at the new woman working at the front desk. She smiles back. Now he looks like a fellow traveler, maybe an Eastern European friend of the revolution. He tries asking again if anyone knows how to find the Black Panther embassy. As he watches, calls are quickly made on his behalf. In minutes, he is handed an address.

As Tim leaves the hotel to grab a taxi, he hears the booming, blanketing, amplified voice of a muezzin from a nearby mosque, calling the faithful to prayer. Everywhere around him, in the streets of the city, people are falling to their knees.

❁   ❁   ❁

Malika, the Arabic queen, clears away lunch plates and serves fresh coffee, and then the Yippie and the Black Panther return to the living room to continue the debate from the previous day about what to do with Dr. Timothy Leary.

Stew has decided on a new approach; he points out that Leary ran against Ronald Reagan for governor—*and that's probably why Reagan had Leary jailed in the first place.*

Cleaver laughs. It takes little prompting to get him to talk about *REE-gun,* as he calls him. When Cleaver was still a free man in Babylon, the University of California at Berkeley announced he was coming to lecture to students on American culture. Some students were thrilled, but Governor Reagan became apoplectic: "If Eldridge Cleaver is allowed to teach our children," he warned, "they may come home at night and slit our throats."

University administrators, bowing to Reagan's pressure, canceled Cleaver's talk. Hundreds of students protested. Reagan ordered five hundred helmeted, gas-mask-toting riot police to surround the students. Several were bludgeoned or carted off to jail. Some managed to escape and rampaged through a campus building, breaking windows, smashing furniture, scattering papers, and setting fires.

To Cleaver, Reagan was a "little Mickey Mouse two-bit actor from Disneyland." A fairy man who'd made his living as an actor, prancing around in front of the camera. *He had to be a homosexual.* Reagan dyed his hair and wore makeup. Cleaver attacked Reagan in a scorching speech at Sacramento State College, across town from the governor's mansion:

> Someone told me that when Ronald Reagan entered the capitol here they changed the name...to the Fairy Building... I have a special little word for Ronald Reagan in the morning. Fuck you, Ronnie baby. It is my belief that Ronald Reagan is a punk, a sissy and a coward and I challenge him to a duel. I challenge the punk to a duel to the death and he can choose his own weapons. It can be a baseball bat, a gun, a knife, or a marshmallow—and I'll beat him to death with a marshmallow.

Stew keeps Cleaver talking about Reagan and he can see that this angle is working. He tells the Black Panther: *Think of this— Eldridge Cleaver and Timothy Leary united together—wouldn't that be Reagan's and Nixon's worst nightmare?*

Cleaver suddenly stubs out his cigarette. *Here's what you'll have to do,* he tells Stew. Go see Algeria's United Nations envoy in New York and then arrange "official" political asylum for Leary. Until then, Leary will have to remain underground.

Stew wonders: *Is he putting me on?*

Cleaver begins rolling a fresh joint. The telephone rings and Cleaver walks to it with his easy, long lope. On the line is DC, the bad-ass Black Panther field marshal. He's calling from the Panther embassy with urgent news:

You're not going to believe this shit. Guess who just showed up here? Dr. Timothy Leary.

INTERRACIAL HARMONY

Evening, September 28, 1970

Tim is admiring the embassy surroundings and chatting with Field Marshal DC and a handful of Panthers, regaling them with the specifics of his prison escape. One of the young Panthers talks about his own flight from Babylon—how he'd carried his trumpet onto a TWA flight along with a carefully concealed pistol. He saw a white celebrity onboard, country singer and actor Tex Ritter, signing autographs. Once they were in the air, the Panther pulled out his gun, rammed his way into the cockpit, and jammed the weapon into the panicked pilot's neck. He ordered him to fly Tex Ritter and everyone else to Cuba. From there it was easy to score an all-expenses-paid trip to join Cleaver in Algiers.

Everyone laughs at the story, and Tim tries to chuckle along. He's heard some of the hijacking tales back in America. By now, they are part of the Panther lore. He's also heard about two Panthers who broke out of a maximum-security California prison before breakfast, robbed a bank by lunchtime, and had hijacked a plane by dinner. They had also joined Cleaver in Algeria.

Tim asks where the two men are now—and the room collapses into a pained, tense silence.

❋   ❋   ❋

DC drives him to Cleaver's luxury villa and Tim is blown away—the revolution has been very nice to Eldridge Cleaver. The Algerians have clearly bestowed a high status upon the Black Panthers.

Cleaver strolls to the gate. The two titans of the counterculture—two men who helped define the 1960s, both reviled by Richard Nixon—size each other up.

Tim slips into his clicking-my-heels, smiling-Irishman mode. Bing Crosby on LSD. He tells Eldridge how honored he is to meet him, how he considers Cleaver and Huey Newton two of the most righteous, intelligent leaders on the planet—and how he had developed a super-tight bond with brother Huey in prison...by using a secret, daring network of inmates to exchange messages. One white brother to one black brother.

Eldridge listens stoically. He doubts Newton ever actually communicated with Leary in prison. Eldridge has developed a power move in conversations: simply pausing for an uncomfortably long time before responding to someone. The dead silence sometimes makes the first tiny drop of fearful nausea begin to drip into their stomach.

Tim has seen this before. He knows it's a game and that all he has to do is fill the gaps, keep probing, trying to find the right connection. He worked with black inmates, black prisoners, inside and outside. He is ready to ramp it up, to start yakking and speed rapping, until he hears Cleaver suddenly say: "There's a friend of yours waiting inside."

They enter the palatial villa, and Tim is stunned to see Yippie luminary Stew Albert. It's like a summit meeting, an alternative Security Council session for the counterculture. In minutes, the three are passing a pipe filled with prime Afghani hashish.

Tim has his audience and he begins to riff on how he clambered along the cable wire out of prison, the armed guards in the truck below him. As a nod to his affection for the revolutionaries behind the revolution, he talks glowingly about the Weathermen and how incredibly organized and efficient they were in planning his flight from the United States.

Finally, Tim mentions Bernardine Dohrn. He sees Cleaver's face light up. Tim lays it on, lying about how it had been the lithesome Bernardine who had carefully shaved his head, how she stripped off her own shirt to keep it free from his falling hair, and how she singlehandedly transformed him into an underground fugitive. Tim adds that he was deeply tempted to just stay at her side and become a full-fledged Weatherman. But the wise, witchy goddess-head of the revolution had counseled him that he was too hot. She was the one who sent him to Algeria to meet with Cleaver, to create the grand alliance that would launch the final takedown of Amerika.

As the smoke swirls, Cleaver abruptly interrupts and asks about money: *That must've been quite expensive, an operation like that. How did the Weathermen get the money to pay for it all?*

Tim replies: *A lot of people contributed. At least $25,000.*

From the smoke, Cleaver responds: *Very impressive, very impressive.*

The money talk hangs in the air. They continue pulling from the pipe and choking down occasional sips of the harsh ginseng wine from North Korea. Hovering above the whole stoned summit, Tim has a thought: This parachute dive into the scary heart of the Panthers' liberation movement is unlike anything he has ever done. And, for now, at least, it might be going quite well. He begins dreaming of the possibilities, the things that Jimi Hendrix embodied. *Maybe this is Electric Ladyland, right here in Algeria:* "Interracial harmony, high-energy collaboration, a new society of American exiles. A romantic script which met our highest aspirations."

As he floats back into the conversation, Tim decides not to mention LSD.

The hash has softened the edges and now it's early evening. Shadows are moving rapidly across the ghostly, whitewashed buildings around the city. They can hear the yelling of barefoot children kicking frayed soccer balls over the pockmarked cobblestone streets. There is a tangled smell of cooked chickpeas, goat piss, and diesel fuel that wafts up from the city. Men with fat mustaches puff one more unfiltered cigarette, the ashes falling on their weathered wool blazers, left behind by the fleeing French occupiers. The few women skirt by, arms cradling bags of potatoes and onions. There is that slow, rising noise, almost achingly poetic, as the imams in the minarets are again issuing the clarion calls to prayer. It rises louder and louder, like the sea, until it's all you can hear.

As the prayers envelop the Panthers' villa, Cleaver finally says that Leary can have sanctuary in Algiers. And he insists that he will personally drive Tim to a better hotel than the one he's been staying in. They step into Cleaver's car, and as the two men ride together, they talk about California, about Richard Nixon, about Ronald Reagan, about being in prison . . . and how they are now, in a way, more free than they have ever been.

Timothy Leary, accompanied by his wife Rosemary announces his candidacy for California governor against Ronald Reagan. He proposed legalizing marijuana, suggesting it could be sold in government-run stores. John Lennon wrote him a campaign ditty, later recorded by the Beatles as "Come Together." *(Alamy)*

Leary's mug shot after he was arrested for possessing two marijuana cigarettes in California. The Reagan-appointed judge who imposed the ten-year sentence denounced Leary as an "insidious and detrimental influence on society...A pleasure-seeking, irresponsible Madison Avenue advocate of the free use of LSD and marijuana." *(California Department of Corrections)*

President Richard Nixon bowls at the White House while Leary awaits sentencing in California. "We've got room in the prisons for him," Nixon said of Leary. *(Richard Nixon Presidential Library/ NLRN-WHPO-3124-02)*

President Nixon and the first lady, Pat, pose with California governor Ronald Reagan and his wife, Nancy, in July 1970. Leary was inside a California prison at the time, plotting his escape. Three months after this photo was taken, Nixon and Reagan were attacked by a stone-throwing mob in San Jose. *(Richard Nixon Presidential Library/NLRN-WHPO 4033-08A)*

Weather Underground leader Bernardine Dohrn, who said, "Our job is to lead white kids into armed rebellion...Political power grows out of a gun, a Molotov, a riot, a commune, and from the soul of the people...kids are making love, smoking dope and loading guns." *(Alamy)*

Weather Underground leader Bill Ayers, who helped plan Leary's escape from prison. Ayers's code name for the operation was "Juju Eyeballs," in homage to lyrics from the Beatles' song for Leary, "Come Together." *(Alamy)*

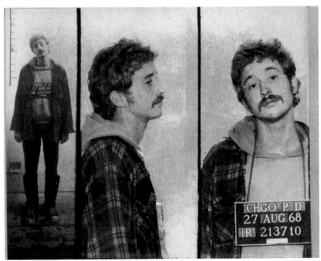

Timothy Francis Leary - Rosemary Leary

Before and After

Timothy Francis Leary   AKA   William Mc Millan

Rosemary Leary   AKA   Margaret Ann Mc Creedy

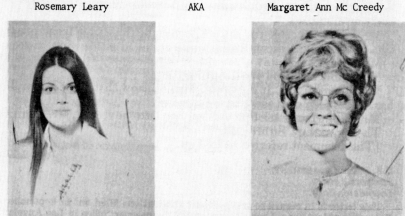

Before and after photos of Timothy and Rosemary Leary in disguise to obtain their fraudulent passports to slip out of the country. The names "William McMillan" and "Margaret Ann McCreedy" are not the actual aliases used by the Learys, but rather were invented for use in Leary's book *Confessions of a Hope Fiend. (From* Hashish Smuggling and Passport Fraud. *Senate Committee on the Judiciary, 1973)*

Black Panther leader Eldridge Cleaver called for Nixon's assassination and personally challenged Governor Reagan to a duel: "Ronald Reagan is a punk, a sissy and a coward...he can choose his own weapons. It can be a baseball bat, a gun, a knife, or a marshmallow—and I'll beat him to death with a marshmallow." *(Library of Congress)*

Eldridge Cleaver and Timothy Leary in Algiers, where the Black Panthers had their own embassy and the American counterculture hoped to set up a revolutionary government-in-exile. Cleaver offered Leary political asylum but their relationship quickly fell apart. *(Associated Press)*

Secretary of State William Rogers was often President Nixon's point man in demanding that foreign governments capture Leary and return him to the United States. *(Department of State)*

FBI Director J. Edgar Hoover (right) had assured the president, "We'll have him in ten days" after Leary escaped from prison. At this meeting in May 1971, Leary had been free for eight months. Nixon would soon send his attorney general, John Mitchell (left), on a secret mission to Switzerland to try to recapture Leary. *(Richard Nixon Presidential Library/NLRN-WHPO-6397-09A)*

Nixon's operative G. Gordon Liddy, who masterminded the Watergate break-in, first came to the president's attention for his highly publicized arrest of Timothy Leary. At the White House, Liddy participated in schemes to secretly dose Nixon's political enemies with LSD. The plots were eventually abandoned in favor of covert break-ins and other harassment. *(Alamy)*

The fugitive Leary meets with Swiss chemist Albert Hofmann, who discovered LSD. "Although I do not agree with all ideas of Dr. Leary," Hofmann said, "I am convinced that it was a pronounced injustice to sentence him with 20 years of prison for a minor offence." *(Photograph by Michael Horowitz, courtesy of Michael Horowitz)*

President Nixon visits CIA headquarters. Nixon's agents pursued leads on four continents during the twenty-eight-month manhunt for Leary. *(Richard Nixon Presidential Library/ NLRN-WHPO-0465-29A)*

Leary and his lover Joanna Harcourt-Smith smile for reporters in London, hoping for a last-minute reprieve after his capture in Kabul. Harcourt-Smith is orange from hepatitis after drinking polluted holy water. Leary's hair is tinted purple after a dye job disguise gone wrong. *(Associated Press)*

DEAD PIGS AND DIRTY DISHES

September 29, 1970

The next morning, Tim wakes up in room 23 at Le Mediterranee Hotel. This new place, also five dollars a night, is right on the beach in a quaint little fishing village called El Djamila, just a few miles up the coast from Algiers. Le Mediterranee is a funky wayfarer's lair, a two-story hexagonal concrete building with peeling white paint. The windows facing the sea are designed to look like portholes.

He steps out onto his balcony to take in the view. Gentle waves are breaking on the beach and fishing boats bob in the distance. A nearby mosque is topped with a tiled blue dome, its dazzling crown an homage to the Mediterranean. On the streets below him, Tim sees shopkeepers selling dates and baklava. The small cafés are bustling with men—only men—nursing their pipes, mint tea, and coffee. There's a donkey trundling along the street, pulling a weathered wagon past the tattered hems of the faded, colonnaded buildings.

Tim knows he has to reach out to Rosemary. They separated angrily, but she should be pleased to hear that he has met Cleaver and the Panther leader has agreed to provide them asylum. He wants her to come join him in Algeria.

The phone line crackles as he finally gets patched through to France. He gushes to Rosemary that Cleaver and the Black Panthers are zooming with righteous energy, and that the Algerians provide their guests with sumptuous, beautiful homes. He adds that he's staying in a groovy hotel in a laid-back fishing village right on the Mediterranean.

She agrees to catch the next flight out.

❖　❖　❖

In Paris, as Rosemary boards her Air Algérie flight, she is back in her executive secretary disguise. She is also bringing the rest of the Brotherhood of Eternal Love cash—several hundred dollars—rolled into a tight wad stuffed in her pantyhose. Inside one of her hollowed-out platform boot heels is a clump of hash the size of a baby's fist. Carefully sewn into the hems of the neatly folded jeans buried in her suitcase are dozens of tabs of Orange Sunshine.

Tim is waiting for her at the airport in Algiers, and he can't help but laugh when he sees her breezing through customs. The Algerian men are very attentive. She laughs, too, when she looks up and sees "Mr. McNellis" grinning at her and wearing a Lenin cap. They rush to embrace each other and catch a taxi to the Panther embassy.

Tim is hoping this will all work out to perfection: Rosemary is a huge admirer of the Black Panthers and especially of Eldridge's wife, Kathleen, who once posed for an iconic photograph wearing a miniskirt and brandishing a shotgun.

They arrive at the embassy and step out of the car, pausing to admire the late-afternoon views of the deep blue Mediterranean. Rosemary is blown away by the Panthers' villa, by its fragrant garden with the plump pomegranates, shiny olives, walnuts, and figs drooping from blossoming trees.

Inside, she is introduced to Eldridge and other Panthers, including some wives. Kathleen is not there. Rosemary turns and looks questioningly at Tim, wondering where she is. The other Panther wives drift away and Tim, Rosemary, and the men settle in the main room, lounging on cushions as a ceremonial hash pipe is lit and passed around. Tim has his arm hooked through Rosemary's and is beaming his usual gape-mouthed smile, but no one is smiling back. The conversation is losing momentum. The hash pipe goes out and is not relit. Tim finally gets it: He suggests that Rosemary follow him. In a corridor, he whispers: "Look, it might be a good sign of respect if you go into the kitchen and wash dishes."

Rosemary recoils. She looks at her husband to see if he's making a bad joke, but he's already turning and walking back to join the men. As she toils in the kitchen with the Panther wives, Rosemary can hear Tim and the others yelping about establishing an American government-in-exile in Algiers. There are murmurs of "Right on" and "Far out." Tim is grooving and suggests that

Algeria can also become the spiritual center for the world's revolutionaries, a place of learning and teaching and higher consciousness. And he can be a righteous, sacrament-dispensing leader in this realm. With his celebrity, he can lure the world's greatest and most creative thinkers to Algeria. He can turn Algeria into a tripped-out, super-international version of his old upstate New York scene, where the poets, jazz men, and socialites had done acid and frolicked naked in the forests—or a desert version of the teepee-studded tribal oasis that the Brotherhood of Eternal Love hippies had created in the mountains in Southern California. It would be an interplanetary way station for the supercharged super freaks of Planet Earth, the kind of place where people would channel the spirit of Hendrix, connect with the gurus of India, and dissolve their egos inside the soothing, free-flowing lava of Tantric love, space, and time.

The Panthers, carrying guns and straight out of the bleak, oppressed street corners of East Oakland and New York City, try to comprehend the grinning, middle-aged Mad Hatter who is going on and on and on. He says he wants to create a kind of Harvard of hallucinogenic research in North Africa. And now, the old white man is yodeling about Woodstock, how the Black Panthers can play with the mass media, how the revolution can be televised.

High on the hash and suddenly wary of the Acid King's carnival-barker style—and still wondering whether he is truly devoted to the violent revolution—Cleaver says the battle for liberation is a lot more than public relations. It's motherfucking serious: *We need to drag the pigs out of the power structure by their ears. A black pig, a white pig, a yellow pig, a pink pig. A dead pig is the best pig of all.*

Voices erupt in the room: "Right on!"

Tim quickly decides there are too many heavy cats with loaded guns. It is a long way from lounging in a Montreal hotel bed with John Lennon and singing: "Give peace a chance." To survive and flourish in Algeria will require some shape-shifting. He quickly tells Cleaver: *I pledge my sword to you, to the revolution.*

Cleaver signals that the meeting is over.

The men summon their wives from the kitchen.

❉   ❉   ❉

As Tim and Rosemary step outside for the ride back to the beach-side hotel, Cleaver is suddenly trailing them:

Look, Algeria is very uptight. You might be legally married, but according to the fake passports you're using, you're not. You can't just go into a hotel and check in as a couple. It's a security risk. The Muslim hotels keep the men and women separate from each other, dig? They're very conscientious about that. The last thing you need to do right now is jeopardize security.

Tim is still a horny sybarite; that much hasn't changed. Even on the run, there are those silky dreams about the leggy Bernardine Dohrn or the thin, acid-eating hippie chicks playing the flute in the woods of the Northwest.

"We've been separated from each other for seven months while I was in prison," he carefully, gingerly, tells Cleaver. "If the Algerians are going to grant me asylum they certainly will understand if we sleep together."

GENIAL GENIUS

Early October 1970

Rosemary is doing her best to make room 23 feel like a home. She has purchased bright hand-woven blankets to hang on the walls. The room is lit with candles; incense burns steadily. She and Tim take her portable cassette player to the balcony, spread out grass mats, and sit lotus style, enveloped by Jefferson Airplane, drinking, smoking, consulting the forecasts written in the *I Ching*, and preparing to make love. When they are done, when they are hungry, they walk to a favorite nearby restaurant. By now they have become familiar patrons at local haunts, ordering fresh shrimp and the small red mullets caught just offshore. They walk, hand in hand, until the soft shadows emerge, and then they retreat to the hotel.

Stew Albert is staying in an adjoining room. Cleaver wants him to remain in Algeria and indoctrinate Tim with a crash course in revolutionary ideology. Cleaver tells Stew he is contacting the FLN, Algeria's ruling party, trying to smooth the way for Leary's asylum request: *We have to invent a political background for Leary that doesn't come out sounding like L-S-D.*

Stew goes to Tim's hotel room: "You're going to have to read a little Mao, a little Kim Il-sung... Try to find a way to say what you would say anyway, but quote Mao."

Stew adds that Tim might know everything about lysergic acid, but he doesn't know shit about the revered Kim Il-sung, the leader of North Korea, a nation Cleaver terms an "earthly paradise." So now, on top of the pile of revolutionary reading assignments for Tim is a two-volume biography of the Communist head of state and a collection of his speeches.

Between their rounds of homework, Tim and Rosemary write

letters to the United States, including ones to Bernardine Dohrn and the other Weathermen: "We are well and safe and happy... Eldridge and Kathleen and the Panthers have created an oasis (and were we ever thirsty.) There is much to learn and in Eldridge we have found the perfect teacher."

Tim also writes to the irrepressible poet, the literary voice of the counterculture, Allen Ginsberg. Tim had blown Ginsberg's mind on some of the first pure doses of LSD to ever appear in America— and Ginsberg had been forever transformed, and loyal to Leary ever since. Tim tells him: "Algeria is perfect. Socialism works here... Eldridge is a genial genius. So much to talk about dear brother. Please come over soon. We long to see you & hug you."

❋   ❋   ❋

Tim's wavy hair is beginning to grow back and he is sitting cross-legged on the floor of his hotel room. Alongside him, Rosemary looks like the Grace Slick of North Africa, soaked in the aroma of incense, her eyes swimming in rippling ponds of Orange Sunshine. Tim literally relies on her to hear things for him—his hearing has faded and it's second nature now for him to turn to her and have her whisper in his ear what someone just said, almost as if Tim is listening to someone speaking a strange language and she is his interpreter. They have developed their own kind of lover's shorthand and they have a way of finishing each other's sentences, mumbling about the flowers, the waves of light that you can surf to astral planes, the wisdom of the holy men on the mountains in India.

I'm a statesman for the Cosmic Revolution, a transformative leader for the New Dawn. Cleaver's entire gig is misguided. Algeria should be more than a host for outcast Americans. This country can become the launching pad for the next great leap in human evolution. We should organize a giant international festival in Algeria, a worldwide Woodstock. Counterculturalists can come from all over the world. We'll inspire the Africans to turn on and drop out, the same way I told people to do it at the Human Be-In in San Francisco. We sparked the Summer of Love in 1967 and we can do it in the middle of Islamic North Africa.

Stew sighs at Space Captain Tim and tries to explain how the trippy idealism is entirely, blessedly fucked up and impossible. The Algerians are beyond uptight about drugs. They will never allow any freak flags to fly. Drugs are the devil's pharmaceuticals; they are identified with colonialism, with mind-controlling subjugation.

Tim waits until Stew finishes his diatribe.

"I should be popular in the third world," he offers. "I did more than anyone else in history to destroy the minds of a lot of white middle-class kids."

The two men laugh. The Yippie has no way of knowing that Tim has asked his own foot soldiers, his followers inside the Brotherhood of Eternal Love, to smuggle tens of thousands of hits of LSD to Algeria—to better spread the gospel of *his* revolution.

❀　　❀　　❀

Tim has rented a Renault, and he and Rosemary drive into the hills almost every day to visit Eldridge and the Panthers at the embassy. The visits are more than courtesy calls. Eldridge *expects* their regular presence—and he doesn't want to hear about LSD.

One room on the upper floor of the embassy houses a recording studio, with stacks of reel-to-reel machines and fancy duplication equipment. Eldridge dons headphones and reads communiqués into a microphone. The tapes are distributed to the underground press back in Babylon. He signs off the same way each time: *"Power to the People, Death to the Fascist Pigs."*

Sly and the Family Stone and Santana are booming from the oversize speakers. Hanging on a wall is an old pair of Cleaver's high school football cleats. Even from thousands of miles away, the Panthers follow the fortunes of their favorite NFL teams, though they can't watch any of the games.

Tim doesn't blink when Rosemary is told to work alongside the Panther women in the communal nursery for the Panther children. There are dirty diapers to wash by hand. Rosemary asks again about Cleaver's wife, Kathleen, but no one says much other than that she is in North Korea.

As Rosemary cleans the children's poop-stained clothing, Cleaver orders Tim to join him in the main room. He seems to always be cradling a knife or a gun while he speaks. Tim begins smiling, as he has done thousands of times before with the fragile, unpredictable people he studied as a psychologist. But it is not softening Cleaver. The Black Panther leader tells him that his asylum is still uncertain.

This country is crawling with CIA pigs. They can kidnap you off the street and put you on a plane back to Babylon. Fortunately, you and your wife are enjoying the protection of the Black Panther Party. We are guarding you even when you don't know it.

Tim flashes on a fact: He and Rosemary have spotted some sturdy Black Panthers hanging around Le Mediterranee Hotel, miles from the Panther embassy. They were stalking him—maybe more than they were watching out for anyone coming for him. He hears Cleaver say that the only way for him and Rosemary to receive mail in Algeria is to have everything addressed to the Black Panther Party's post office box. *It's very convenient for everyone.*

Tim nods.

In the kitchen, preparing meals for the men, Rosemary is skating from weird to scared. She feels the eyes of the men passing by. Try as she might, it's impossible to forget some of the most notorious passages in Cleaver's *Soul on Ice*, the parts where he talks about raping white women:

> Rape was an insurrectionary act. It delighted me that I was defying and trampling upon the white man's law, upon his system of values, and that I was defiling his women ... I was getting revenge.

Cleaver now says he has repudiated his early theories on rape and that he's a feminist. "Revolutionary power grows out of the lips of a pussy," he has proclaimed. He calls the women's movement "Pussy Power."

Rosemary hardly feels flattered. And there are so few available women in Algiers that the younger, unmarried Panthers are kept sexually bottled up, uptight. They cruise the streets in their crappy Renaults, trying to hustle the few women they spot, or they lean over the embassy balconies shouting when they see someone in a burka.

As Rosemary cleans the embassy, a young male Panther suddenly orders her to follow him. She trails him toward a bedroom on the first floor. He stops at the doorway and points inside. The Great Fear is marching inside the Orange Sunshine portals.

"Malika's been staying here," he says. The presence of Cleaver's young mistress is always complicated. The young Panther has an order for Rosemary:

"You better make the bed before Kathleen gets home."

✸   ✸   ✸

One morning at the embassy, Tim and Rosemary are finally told they can meet the famous Kathleen Cleaver, the only woman among the Panthers' leadership. Twenty-five, she has very light, gently freckled skin, enormous aqua-green eyes, and a billowy Afro. She's chain-smoking nervously and is rail thin. As soon as he sees her, Tim is doing his psychologist thing: She is probably feeling vulnerable. She barely makes eye contact. Ten years younger than her husband. Almost too obsessed with the revolutionary rap—when she raises her head, she juts out her jaw and talks about the liberation movement in staccato bursts.

Like he did with Bernardine Dohrn, Tim simply drinks in the young creature before him. She's almost like the black version of Dohrn, another bewitching, magic-broomstick-riding child of privilege who has morphed into a steel-minded terrorist-cum-revolutionary. Both her parents are highly educated and her old man was a professor at a small black college in Marshall, Texas, before joining the State Department as a Foreign Service officer. She grew up on three continents, received a stellar education—and then joined the revolution. Now she's living in an enemy nation with a fugitive ex-con for a husband.

Tim hears her say she just spent the last several months studying and learning from the hard Communists in North Korea. She had given birth there to her second child, a daughter who is now three months old. The baby's name, personally bestowed by Kim Il-sung's wife, is Joju Younghi.

When Rosemary asks about the children, Kathleen abruptly excuses herself, saying she needs to check on them. Later, when Tim and Rosemary ask how she's doing, Eldridge Cleaver says simply that she's gone to their home.

Where else should a woman be?

UNLEASHED ANGELS

Early October 1970

I t's a bright, sunny morning in El Djamila and Tim is laughing, telling Stew that they have to take a break from the iron-gray lectures on socialism and communism. *Let's drop acid and see what happens when we go to the beach.*

Tim casually opens his precious aftershave bottle and offers Stew some of the world's best LSD. It is like being handed atomic energy by Einstein. Who knows the real consequences of swallowing some pure acid from the High Priest himself? Tim has been on hundreds of trips before, on peyote, psilocybin, DMT, and other mind-altering substances and compounds that have left weaker-willed people in a fumbling stutter; in the fetal position; or permanently cross-eyed and in fear of Satan, cats, or country and western music. *Who the fuck knows what Dr. Leary has in his medicine bag?*

"I could take a small dose," Stew finally, very reluctantly, agrees.

Tim is pleased: "This acid has powerful and good effects even with a small ingestion."

He adds, with brio: "Naturally I'll take more than you."

Stew slowly raises the bottle and takes a small, tentative nip. Tim downs two large gulps and smiles again in his beatific, high Holy Roller way.

As they make their way out of the hotel in their swimsuits, strolling to the beach, Tim is still wearing his leather worker's cap. They sprawl on the sand and the acid bathes their brains. They begin to melt, feeling the first waves and giggling at the pasty tourists, especially the stern-looking Russians reluctantly unbuttoning their high-collared shirts and squinting at the uncomfortable spotlight of the sun.

The rhythms of the crashing water propel Stew into his journey, and at first it's like an old movie concoction, a magic carpet ride in *The Thief of Baghdad* as he begins to escalate. He turns bravely to see if Tim has boarded his own Berber spaceship. Stew blinks hard, then looks again. Tim is standing on his head in the sand. Even upside down, Tim's smile is one of the most lit-up, beautiful things Stew has ever seen. Looking closer, he is staggered to see that Tim's hair is the exact same pale amber color as the sand on the beach. Tim's radiant face is like the very sun itself.

After several hours, the pulsing noises and the vibrating lights ebb, and by late afternoon Stew is coming down. He suddenly realizes that he is alone. Wings of panic flutter around his head. *Why did Tim disappear? Have the Russians reported us to the Algerian secret police? Are they coming for me next?*

Stew wraps himself in his beach towel, something to hold on to as the fear grips him like snakes left in the trees after a hurricane. He tries to stand and suddenly sees Tim striding purposefully toward him across the sand. The man looks completely sober, as if merrily quaffing two giant spikes of the most profoundly psychedelic LSD on Planet Earth had no lingering, noticeable impact at all.

Tim leans down over him and talks in a peppy, all-business voice: "I just spoke to Eldridge on the hotel lobby phone. He's nervous about some reports he's getting. People calling from the States warning him."

Tim studies Stew, peering down at him. Tim says he has a very good idea: "I think we should go back to my room and have some wine."

Tim bends to help him up, to help him crawl on his hands and knees back to reality. Stew is still very, very high: *Is Tim launching me into the curving sky?*

The professor tells him to fight the fear, to try to stand. Or walk. Or move. He guides the unmoored Yippie back to the hotel and says hello to the desk clerk as they pass by. Nodding toward the obviously wasted man he has by the arm, Tim nonchalantly says: "The sun—and a little too much to drink."

The clerk doesn't blink. "Yes, monsieur, a bit ill," he says before turning his attention back to the television blaring its black-and-white programs in French.

Upstairs, Tim presses a glass of wine into Stew's hands. And then another and another. Through his manic fog, Stew hears Tim's voice. He is trying to explain why the hell Cleaver was calling him in a fit of great urgency:

"People are trying to associate me with criminal activities," Tim says. "They don't understand the Brotherhood of Eternal Love."

❅ ❅ ❅

Tim heads to the embassy and notices that the same sheet of paper has been sitting in Cleaver's typewriter for days. Nothing else has been typed on it. He asks Cleaver about his writing, and the Panther hisses that securing political asylum for Dr. Timothy Leary is a goddamned hassle—and he hasn't been able to find the time to write like he wants to.

Tim assesses his increasingly menacing host, who is a full fifteen years younger. He adopts his best harrumphing-but-benign demeanor: the wise man who has looked into the human condition; the psychologist who provides learned balm and palliatives. Cleaver and the Panthers might *feel* free, but they are prisoners in the desert. They are uptight, as uncool as their North Korean political masters would be if they were suddenly kidnapped and dropped backstage with the Grateful Dead.

Tim remembers something—the prime directive, the *Mission: Impossible* marching orders he was given by those young white radicals after they drove him away from prison and deep into the Northwestern woods. The Weathermen had come down out of the mountains and said they wanted Timothy Leary to be their Lewis and Clark in Africa. Go to Algeria and navigate the waters.

Tim knows the Weathermen are rigid, committed; they have that zoned-in level of obsession and zealotry. Unrepentant, unforgiving. Probably in awe of the Panthers, even if they don't agree with all that the Panthers push—including the unsubtle way women are treated. *Young, white, college-educated radicals—born with soft, entitled hands and carrying four hundred years of American racism around their necks. They're never going to tell the Black Panthers how fucked up some of their theories are.*

Of course, he also knew the Weathermen had given him a vial of supernova LSD for a specific reason. It wasn't just for personal enlightenment, or even, hell, recreation. It was part of the plan to get Dr. Leary to dose the Panthers in Africa. To get the Acid King to melt their minds, their cold hearts, and get them all so fucking high that they would welcome anyone—including the privileged white sons and daughters of the American pharaohs—to join the revolution in the desert. *Cleaver needs dope, pussy, and some serious mind expansion.*

Tim considers the plan:

He has successfully accomplished phase one of the mission: He has contacted the Panthers. He's made them trust him, at least a little, by throwing his hustling pixie dust in the air. And now there is phase two: dosing the man who wrote *Soul on Ice*. Feeding LSD to a gun-cradling FBI fugitive, a man with armed body-guards, a man who assumes everyone is a CIA agent...until proven otherwise. A celebrated revolutionary writer who seems to have lost his way.

Tim decides that now is the exact time to let Cleaver know that he has smuggled a profound amount of perfect Orange Sunshine into Algeria.

It's time to get really high with the Black Panthers.

Tim finds Cleaver and begins, in his soothing way: *I think I know the deep-rooted dilemma, dear Eldridge. You are consumed by writer's block, that suffocating, inexplicable condition that stymies the imagination. That plugs up the free flow of magic thought. Fortunately for you, Eldridge, your colleague Dr. Leary has just the right prescription.*

A tincture of some lysergic acid will fire up the literary neurons and the words—visions, really—will come pouring out like unleashed angels.

"I take a little bit every morning," Tim assures Eldridge.

Cleaver stares at Leary in disbelief. *This old man has been tripping all this time? Swallowing LSD like a one-a-day vitamin?*

❄   ❄   ❄

A few hours before his return flight to the United States, Stew Albert visits Cleaver one last time.

Eldridge stuffs a pipe with a fat wad of hash and fires it up. He hangs on to it for a very long time while Stew keeps waiting for the pipe to emerge from the fog and head his way.

Political asylum for Leary might just happen, Cleaver finally mutters. The host government has no idea who he really is: "The Algerians all assume Tim is black," Cleaver says. "Maybe he should go for a deeper suntan."

Stew doesn't know if he is supposed to laugh.

"Don't get me wrong," Cleaver adds, still holding the hash pipe. "I like Tim. The way he keeps moving all the time, getting out of his chair and walking right up to you and smiling and talking. I guess he's up to something, but I don't care."

Stew finally asks: "Eldridge, are you gonna trip with Leary?"

Cleaver quickly replies: "Ah, no. I like Tim but I don't trust him. He might try to program me."

Stew wonders how Supreme Commander Huey Newton feels about Leary.

"Tim's okay with Huey, but he's been hearing some heavy stuff about the good doctor."

"Like?"

"Mostly loose sort of shit, like Leary having some kind of illegal organization that sells the stuff. I thought he gave it away, but Huey says the word is they sell it. And Huey wants to make sure the Black Panther Party gets its fair share."

"You gonna talk to Tim?"

"I intend to," says Cleaver, adding, somewhat ominously:

"Our operation here is very expensive and Tim will pay his proper dues."

DRUG-SNIFFING DOGS

Mid-October 1970

Word is secretly spreading among Tim's close friends that he and Rosemary are in Algiers. A few are beginning to arrange clandestine trips to see them. Among the first to arrive is Dennis Martino, a jangly, sputtering, small, wiry man whose twin brother is married to Tim's daughter. Dennis has been a disciple of Leary's for years, and he also shares a few shady connections to the Brotherhood of Eternal Love.

Tim is glad to see him: Martino has scored a huge load of hashish and smuggled it in. Better yet, though Cleaver doesn't know, the antsy, peripatetic Martino also has brought 20,000 more hits of LSD.

He bouncily presents them as a gift to Tim from the Brotherhood. Tim is beyond pleased.

Loaves and fishes for the mind revolution.

❋　❋　❋

Less than two miles up the road from the Black Panther embassy is Villa Montfeld, a sprawling palace of white Italian marble with commanding views of the Bay of Algiers. For many years it housed the United States Embassy. But after the Algerians severed diplomatic relations, the property was turned over to Switzerland. The Swiss now fly their own flag out front—but they don't actually occupy the building. Instead, Switzerland charges the U.S. government a tidy fee to allow a small group of American spies and field agents, including a consul, to operate inside. To the CIA and State Department, they are known simply as the "U.S. Interests Section" in Algeria.

Cleaver knows the U.S. agents and operatives are there, and one day he paraded to the place, marched inside, and announced: "Nice house you've got here. MY house." On his way out, Cleaver stole a State Department seal, deciding it would look better in his own embassy.

What he doesn't know is that a profound shift is taking place in U.S.-Algerian relations. Underneath the Sahara sands are enormous untapped quantities of oil and natural gas. The United States wants the energy and the Algerians are desperate for economic security, to keep the lid from blowing on another revolution. The Algerian government has already signed a billion-dollar deal with Texas-based El Paso Natural Gas. A delicate diplomatic waltz is beginning: While the Algerians remain defiant socialist revolutionaries on the world stage, privately they are negotiating business deals with the Nixon Administration.

The new head of U.S. operations in Algeria is William Eagleton, a sandy-haired forty-four-year-old Yale graduate who fought in World War II. He's fluent in Arabic and is deeply experienced in Middle Eastern affairs, one of the State Department's top operatives in the region.

On the morning of October 10, Eagleton is having a hard time believing the disturbing news he has received from one of the CIA spies in the city. Yet there's no doubt that the report is true. Quickly, he prepares a secret cable, addressed to Richard Nixon's secretary of state, William Rogers:

SUBJECT: TIMOTHY LEARY IN ALGIERS

REGRET TO INFORM DEPARTMENT THAT LATEST EXILE TO JOIN GROWING AMERICAN FUGITIVE FROM JUSTICE COLONY IN ALGIERS IS TIMOTHY LEARY. ELDRIDGE CLEAVER AND BLACK PANTHERS APPEAR TO HAVE HAD IMPORTANT HAND IN ARRANGING LEARY'S EXILE HERE...

LEARY, WITH HIS REPUTATION OF HIGH PRIEST OF THE LSD/MARIJUANA CROWD, IS NOT TYPE OF EXILE GOA [GOVERNMENT OF ALGERIA] NORMALLY WELCOMES. GOA ITSELF IS DEAD SET AGAINST ENTIRE DRUG CULTURE AND TREATS ITS OWN AND FOREIGN USERS HERE WITH GREAT SEVERITY. HOWEVER, LEARY'S RECENT CONVERSION TO

WORLD REVOLUTIONARY CAUSE MAY HAVE PROVIDED HIM
WITH NECESSARY CREDENTIALS.

Richard Nixon is relaxing at Grand Cay in the Bahamas, watching the World Series on TV, when he learns that Leary has turned up in Algeria. The president is furious—Hoover and the FBI have obviously failed him, and now Leary is in a nation with no extradition treaty, a country that doesn't even recognize his government.

Getting Leary is no longer simply a police action. Now that the fugitive has found a home abroad, it's going to require hard-nosed diplomacy. When he returns to Washington, Nixon meets with his National Security Council and draws aside Secretary of State Rogers. The two men are old friends. They first met in 1948 as rising stars in the Republican Party; Nixon would go on to become Eisenhower's vice president while Rogers served as attorney general. Nixon compliments Rogers as "one of the toughest, most cold-eyed, self-centered, ambitious men" he's ever met.

Nixon surprised many people when he made Rogers his secretary of state—Rogers has a notable lack of experience in the field. But in reality, Nixon intends to conduct foreign policy himself. He picked Rogers for one very simple reason: to make sure the president's policies are carried out, to make "the little boys in the State Department behave."

Rogers will now be Nixon's point man in getting the Algerians to surrender Leary.

After the secretary of state is excused, Nixon's next order of business is to convene a White House Conference on Drug Abuse. The president has invited seventy broadcast executives to hear firsthand of the great progress the nation is making combating the scourge of illegal drugs.

A special demonstration has been arranged for the visitors.

A drug-sniffing German shepherd, Kishi, has arrived to show her aptitude at finding caches of marijuana.

Customs agents set up thirty-three random packages on the South Lawn, unclaimed parcels scooped up from the local post office, to be used for the demonstration. The agents place one more package among the set, a box they have loaded with a double-wrapped kilogram of weed.

As everyone gathers to watch, Kishi is let loose. The dog begins her frantic, sniffing ramble and swiftly locates the package with the planted pot. Everyone applauds. Then, Kishi trots over to *another* package, sniffs deeply, and begins pawing at it. The federal agents aren't counting on this. They glance over at the president in confusion.

Inside the parcel is an 8-inch by 4-inch candle that has been hollowed out and filled with a half pound of very good hash.

❋　　❋　　❋

The Algerian government has vaguely heard of the Beatles, but its leaders have no idea who Dr. Timothy Leary is. Cleaver told them that Leary is a well-regarded, esteemed U.S. professor, a Harvard man who opposes the genocidal war in Vietnam and as a result has been jailed by the American fascists. Cleaver added that Dr. Leary is one of the most notable psychologists in the world, has authored several books, and has many young followers who rely on his wisdom. Cleaver did not mention LSD. Or that Dr. Leary is a white man.

The Algerians notify Cleaver they have approved Leary's asylum. The official statement will be made later in the month, in advance of Tim's fiftieth birthday.

Back at the embassy, Cleaver announces the news as everyone cheers and pounds Tim on the back. The telephone is humming with calls across the Atlantic. Cleaver tells Tim there will be a massive press conference to surface him in front of the world's media. Cleaver is inviting Yippies and Weathermen to join them. He's hoping to convince Bernardine Dohrn herself to come.

Tim and the others are chattering, laughing, talking about the big party they'll have when the others arrive. Abruptly, Cleaver calls for quiet. He looks each person carefully in the eye.

"Our job is to destroy Babylon."

WE BURY PEOPLE

October 19–20, 1970

Evening is descending, and Eldridge Cleaver and Field Marshal DC are at the airport to greet an arriving delegation of American radicals. Leary is supposed to be here, too, but he is nowhere to be seen. Cleaver is pissed. The old man should have been here a long time ago. Finally, Tim skids his white Renault into a nearby parking spot and trots up while DC checks his watch and glares at him. Tim is grinning and wearing his turtleneck along with his Lenin cap. He takes his place alongside Cleaver as they spot the disembarking passengers:

There is Stew Albert, again traveling with only a toothbrush. There is Anita Hoffman, the whip-smart wife of Yippie leader Abbie Hoffman. And there is a young woman with long brown hair and oversize silver hoop earrings. It's not Bernardine Dohrn but her kid sister, Jennifer. Tim thinks she looks like a feral waif, the kind of wide-open chick who just set foot for the first time in the heart of Haight-Ashbury in San Francisco.

Tim pries Anita Hoffman from the crowd and steers her and Jennifer to his car, slyly handing Anita a fat joint. "Welcome to the Third World," he says.

Tim takes the wheel and sees that DC is already speeding away from the airport. "These Panthers are crazy drivers," he says, pressing the pedal to the floor and working his way through the gears. Rounding a tight curve, he briefly skids off the road, laughing before finding the pavement again. It is getting dark now, and there are only a few working streetlights in the city. As they bounce along a rutted road, Tim confides something about his mission:

"I've been trying to get Eldridge to do acid, but he's uptight. If we could trip together we'd be much closer."

By now they have lost sight of DC's car, and Tim has taken a wrong turn somewhere. He is picking his way through dark, unfamiliar streets, slowing the car to study the surroundings. Suddenly, the back window splinters apart in a spray of shattered glass from a hurled rock. Screams erupt inside the car. Tim makes a quick turn and speeds away. Eventually he finds the main thoroughfare and the shaken group finally arrives at Le Mediterranee Hotel.

As the American newcomers check in, they are surprised to learn that women are assigned to separate floors from the men.

❋　❋　❋

On October 20, the official Algerian government newspaper, *El Moudjahid* ("the Freedom Fighter") announces the news:

> Doctor Timothy Leary, Afro-American psychologist, sought by American federal police since his escape from San Luis Obispo prison September 12, has recently arrived in Algeria, where the right of political asylum has been granted to him.

In New York, the Yippies stage a joyous demonstration, proclaiming: "Timothy Leary is alive and well and high in Algiers."

At the Panther embassy, Cleaver issues an intentionally misleading press release, announcing that a "Miss Dohrn" will appear at his revolutionary news conference in Algeria. It can mean only one thing: Bernardine Dohrn, the underground outlaw on the FBI's Most Wanted list, is going to surface in Algiers with Timothy Leary.

Three of America's top counterculture commanders will appear together—the Black Panther, the Acid King, the Weatherwoman. Journalists from around the globe begin buying tickets for flights to Algiers.

At the Panther embassy, Jennifer Dohrn is more than disturbed by Cleaver's manipulation: "I'm not sure Bernardine will like this. In the last communiqué she said that she wasn't going into exile, that she was going to stay and fight inside the United States. After all, that's the point of the underground."

Cleaver dismisses her: "The press conference is set," he says.

The visiting American radicals have been anxious to meet the famous Kathleen Cleaver, but her husband keeps putting them off, saying she's too busy at home with the children. The other Panther women are back in the kitchen, cooking while the men lounge on cushions in the main room.

When the meals are ready, Tim and the other men gather at the table, where they are served. Rosemary, Jennifer Dohrn, Anita Hoffman, and the other women have no seats. The men ignore them, continue their rap session, and shovel in heaping mouthfuls of food. DC stands with a bottle of the North Korean ginseng wine and offers a toast: "Kim Il-sung drinks this shit," he proclaims, "and look what it did for the North Koreans."

Plates in hand, the women retreat to the kitchen and eat quickly, standing up, so that they will be ready for the cleanup and dishwashing.

After dinner, Cleaver puts on the Leonard Cohen album the Yippies brought from the States. He keeps replaying one of the songs, "The Partisan," a mournful ode to a doomed resistance fighter. Cleaver seems lost in his own world, quietly murmuring the words while caressing a pistol. The Americans glance at one another. When he snaps out of his reverie, he begins a lecture on military discipline. Stone-faced, he talks about the weaklings who have failed the revolution:

"We bury people here in Algiers."

GET THIS MOTHERFUCKER
OUT OF THE COUNTRY

October 21–23, 1970

Nixon's secretary of state, William Rogers, is sending terse
orders to the head of American operations in Algiers, Bill
Eagleton:

> EXPRESS [U.S. GOVERNMENT] ASTONISHMENT THAT GOA
> [GOVERNMENT OF ALGERIA] HAS ACCORDED POLITICAL
> ASYLUM TO LEARY AND THAT WE CAN ONLY ASSUME GOA
> IS UNFAMILIAR WITH LEARY'S BACKGROUND. IN INTERESTS
> OF FUTURE AMERICAN ALGERIAN RELATIONS GOA SHOULD
> BE AWARE UNFORTUNATE IMPACT GRANTING OF ASYLUM TO
> INDIVIDUALS SUCH AS LEARY IS LIKELY TO HAVE ON ALGERIA'S
> IMAGE IN THE US.

Eagleton knows this has everything to do with Nixon wanting Leary captured and brought back to prison. He calls his main
contact in the Algerian government, Foreign Minister Abdelkader
Bousselham, who invites him to his office. The American grabs
his satchel and stuffs it with press clippings from the United States
about Timothy Leary—including the *Playboy* interview where
Leary talks about LSD as the world's greatest aphrodisiac and
gushes over the sexual activity of teenage girls.

Within minutes, Eagleton is at the Foreign Ministry, a white
domed building surrounded by palm trees. He shows Bousselham
the clippings. The Algerian is stunned. He had no idea that Leary
was a white man, much less a notorious drug advocate. The two men
are deep in conversation when a bomb suddenly explodes on the

ground floor. Smoke fills the building and everyone scrambles for the exits. Eagleton is unhurt, and as he runs outside, Bousselham tries to assure him that the blast is no big deal, perhaps simply an accident.

Eagleton doesn't know what to say. He flees, leaving the press clippings with Bousselham. Maybe the Algerian leadership will now understand who the hell Timothy Leary is. Hopefully, they'll also realize they have been royally scammed by Eldridge Cleaver and the Black Panthers.

☀ ☀ ☀

It's October 22, Timothy Leary's fiftieth birthday, and journalists and TV cameramen are flooding the Algiers airport, demanding to be allowed into the country—they want to interview Leary, Cleaver, and Dohrn to report on this gathering of U.S. revolutionaries in North Africa.

In New York, the bewildered Algerian ambassador to the United Nations is besieged with questions about his views on LSD and other psychedelic drugs. Newspapers around the world are carrying front-page stories about Algeria as the new haven for hallucinogens. In Algiers, the official newspaper, El Moudjahid, is publishing a "clarification" about its earlier story: *Timothy Leary is, in fact, not a black man.*

Eagleton, the American consul, is keeping the pressure on the Algerians. He asks for another meeting, this time at El Mouradia, the presidential palace. He has arranged to see one of the top figures in Algeria's ruling party, a close advisor to President Houari Boumédiène.

Eagleton greets the minister in Arabic, pleased to see that the man has a copy of the Leary press clippings Eagleton turned over yesterday. The minister tells Eagleton he is violently opposed to drugs and he is indignant that someone like Timothy Leary could be allowed into his country. They talk for two hours. The minister assures Eagleton that Leary's permanent asylum in Algeria is far from a sure thing. In fact, he says, he would bet against it.

Eagleton rushes back to his office and files a new cable with Secretary of State Rogers. *There is a very good chance the Algerians are going to expel Timothy Leary—and very soon.*

At the Panther embassy, the telephone is ringing nonstop. Phone lines are backing up as reporters demand interviews. Black Panther Supreme Commander Huey P. Newton phones from California to ask what the hell is going on.

In the living room, Tim and the other men stretch out on the overstuffed cushions, passing the hash pipe and trying to figure out how the press conference will go down tomorrow. There are long, elaborate discussions of rhetorical strategies, agonizing digressions involving obscure ideological nuances. None of the women are included in this planning session. An unofficial observer from the Brotherhood of Eternal Love, Dennis Martino, is allowed to sit in since he's providing the hashish. Jennifer Dohrn is in the kitchen, baking a birthday cake for Tim. Studying the scene, Anita Hoffman is growing disgusted. She didn't come all the way to Algiers to work in the kitchen.

Suddenly, Field Marshal DC rushes into the embassy with an announcement: "The Algerian government has just found out that Leary's not black, that he's the acid king. In New York their representative to the UN is a laughingstock."

The next phone call is from a local number, and it is for Cleaver. He is being summoned to appear immediately at the government party headquarters.

When he returns a few hours later, the news is grim. The Algerians have canceled tomorrow's press conference, he says. Sighs and groans sweep across the room.

There's more, Cleaver says. *We're not sure that Dr. Leary will be able to stay in Algeria.*

Tim and Rosemary are sitting together in a corner, holding hands. They turn to look at each other. Every police agency in the world knows where they are. Where can they possibly run to next if they can't stay in Algeria?

But don't worry, Eldridge tells everyone. *I'm working on a plan.*

The next morning, Tim and Rosemary drive the rain-slicked streets to the embassy. The city seems more cloistered than before, like everyone has turned to trailing gray smoke and disappeared into the Casbah.

Cleaver hisses that reactionaries within the Algerian ruling party are trying to use Leary as a scapegoat, to flip the government away from the Black Panthers and over to Nixon. But Cleaver's been talking to his own allies in the government, and now he has a solution:

The Algerian president is enamored of the Palestine Liberation Organization guerrillas and their daring hijackings and hostage standoffs. While much of the world condemns the PLO's violent tactics, Algeria remains a staunch supporter. All Tim has to do is fly to Egypt, then Lebanon, and then slip into Jordan for a meeting with the PLO. Once he gets his photograph taken with the guerrilla leaders, and the images are released to the press, his political asylum in Algeria will be guaranteed.

Tim watches as Cleaver holds out an airline ticket. He reaches for it and looks closely. He's relieved to see that it's round-trip.

Cleaver orders Jennifer Dohrn and Field Marshal DC to join Leary on the trip. He pulls DC aside and gestures toward Tim:

"Get this motherfucker out of the country."

PAY THESE MOTHERS OFF

October 24–25, 1970

At the airport, DC starts flipping out when he learns he won't be allowed to take any of his guns on the plane. Cleaver tries to calm him, assuring DC that the Palestinians will meet them in Beirut and provide everything he needs. DC remains skittish as they approach the gate. "I never move without my guns," he tells the others.

Cleaver, for once, looks nervous. His fate in Algeria is now inextricably bound with Timothy Leary's, and the prospect is unsettling. Before Leary boards the plane, Cleaver tells him to avoid generating any attention en route to see the PLO. *This is a top secret political mission.* DC is still wanted on murder charges in the States, where he could face the death penalty. Cleaver warns Leary: *Nixon will stop at nothing to capture you—he'll even use CIA agents to kidnap you off the streets.*

Tim is traveling with his William McNellis passport. A small button adorns the front of his Lenin cap: TUNE IN, TURN ON, DROP OUT. When Cleaver spots it, he begins screaming about security. Tim sheepishly unclasps it and joins the others in the boarding line for the Air Algérie flight.

✷   ✷   ✷

After safely arriving in Cairo, the American revolutionaries decide to bunk at Gezirah Palace, a breathtaking nineteenth-century confection on an island in the Nile, originally built to house royal visitors. They walk across the antique marble floors and decide to rent the Imperial Suite, which comes with its own harem guards. In the morning, Tim tries to convince DC that they should visit the pyramids. The connecting plane for Beirut won't leave until late in the afternoon, and they have plenty of time. The Black Panther is skeptical. Leary's already pissed him off by wandering off to look at shops, and Cairo is "full of Zionist agents, Interpol pigs, and CIA informers."

Tim argues that the most secure way for them to reach the airport is to hire a limousine, rather than a cab. The limo driver could easily swing by the pyramids, just so they can see them. *How often do you get a chance to see one of the Seven Wonders of the World?*

DC has never been to Cairo. Slowly, he nods his approval.

A few hours later, they arrive at the Pyramids of Giza. Jennifer Dohrn remains in the limousine; she's not wearing a bra and has already had her fill of grasping Egyptian men. Tim steps out into the gusting wind, blinking at the enormity of the wonderworks as they seem to march straight toward them from the golden, sandy horizon. Under the gaze of the Sphinx, Tim can feel the ancient interplanetary vibes. This is mondo magic, the treasure palace of philosophers and necromancers and summoners, where mysteries are tucked inside mysteries. Tim moves, reverentially, toward the Great Pyramid.

He is trying to find the sacramental center of it all when he is suddenly surrounded by a pack of hustling vendors, herding him toward some squatting camels. Tim is pushed onto a double-humped beast. Someone jams a turban on his head. Someone else slaps the animal and it hurtles off, galloping into the Sahara with the turbaned Dr. Leary wobbling and barely hanging on. From over his shoulder, he can make out one of the vendors chasing him desperately on foot and shouting over and over for the camel to come to a halt. This might be very bad: *The High Priest of LSD, ex–Harvard professor Timothy Leary, disappeared yesterday on a runaway camel that carried him beyond the parched dunes and into the baking beyond.*

Like so many jolts of weirdness he's been staggered by in the last year, the whole gig has actually been choreographed. The Egyptians pretend they have successfully brought Tim's renegade camel to heel. And when the camel bows down so Tim can leap off, they demand money from Tim. The wind is blowing harder now, and dust is swirling in the air.

Tim looks across the desert and sees DC tromping toward him

through the sand. The camel drivers had pulled the same con on the bad–ass Black Panther.

Leaning into the wind, DC shouts:

"Pay these mothers off!"

❋ ❋ ❋

Aboard the Air Liban jet for the short flight to Beirut, Tim strikes up a conversation with a nearby passenger, ignoring DC's disapproving looks. The man is a young, long-haired Brit, a professional photographer and hopefully a fellow freak. As they talk, Tim and the man discover they have mutual trusted friends. Tim tells him who he really is, and where he is headed, and the photographer offers a proposal: He will accompany them into Jordan and serve as their official chronicler. He promises Tim total control over any photographs he takes. Tim quickly agrees.

At 6:30 p.m., the plane descends to Beirut, the Paris of the Middle East. At the airport, they are supposed to meet a PLO contact, but no one is waiting for them. DC is edgy, and he scans for the FBI or CIA.

As they wait, Tim takes DC aside and explains the plan for the photographer to join them, to get the pictures they need of Tim side by side with the PLO. But DC is pissed and paranoid: He jogs to the photographer and gets in his face, telling him he will break his cameras if he doesn't get away from them, now. Tim watches the scene unfold. He has a gnawing feeling they are making an enemy.

After he splits, the photojournalist heads straight for the offices of United Press International with his scoop. He knows for a fact that Timothy Leary is trying to sneak into Lebanon. He also believes that the menacing black man who threatened him must be none other than the Black Panther Eldridge Cleaver.

Tim and the others check into another luxurious hotel, the regal St. Georges, a magnificent art deco building on the gently curving waterfront. They have dinner and drinks and settle into bed.

None of them has any clue that Beirut is buzzing with news that some of America's most wanted fugitives have arrived in the city.

MOTHERFUCKERS EVERYWHERE

October 26–27, 1970

As the morning sunshine filters through the blinds, Tim steps toward the hotel balcony and looks out over Beirut. Noticing a glint of light reflecting off glass, he peers down and sees a telephoto lens aimed at him. On the roof of a building across the street, a man is leaping up and down, shouting in excitement. Below, another man clambers onto the fire escape, heading toward their room.

DC begins shouting: "Motherfuckers are everywhere!"

Reporters cram into the hotel hallway, jockeying for position and banging on doors. Some have climbed onto the balcony and are pounding on the windows. Journalists are shouting questions through the closed door, asking Tim if he's seeking asylum in Lebanon.

DC quickly places a long-distance call to Cleaver, to tell him everything is falling apart. There's no sign of the PLO, but the pig press is everywhere. Eldridge is having his own trouble in Algiers. He moved Anita Hoffman out of Le Mediterranee Hotel and into one of the Panther-controlled apartments, to better enforce military discipline. The last thing he needs is hippies wandering around without any supervision, especially now that the Algerians are furious at him for lying to them about Timothy Leary.

But Anita Hoffman has disappeared. She's had enough of Cleaver, of the rampant sexism inside the Panther lair. She has climbed out of a window with her suitcase and made her way to the airport, catching a plane to Paris.

Back in Beirut, up the coast from the St. Georges, the American Embassy in Beirut is moving into a frenzy: Inside the eight-story, horseshoe-shaped building, emergency meetings are being called to talk about the stunning reports that Timothy Leary, Eldridge Cleaver, and Bernardine Dohrn are all in Beirut together.

❋　　❋　　❋

In Washington, midterm elections are less than a week away. Nixon is at the Oval Office, preparing to leave for a highly publicized visit to the Justice Department's Bureau of Narcotics and Dangerous Drugs in order to sign a brand-new anti-drug bill. It would be excellent timing to have Leary in custody, but he knows the United States can't risk an ugly international incident by simply grabbing high-profile fugitives in tender zones like the Middle East.

Nixon's ambassador in Beirut is ordered to pressure the Lebanese, to demand they immediately arrest Leary and the others—and then extradite the dangerous criminals to the United States.

❋　　❋　　❋

At the St. Georges, Tim decides to take a gamble: He'll give an exclusive interview to an NBC reporter who promises to guide Tim to the PLO encampment across the Jordanian border. DC and Jennifer Dohrn will try to divert the other journalists by holding a press conference so Tim can slip away.

DC elbows his way through the throng of reporters, marching to the hotel conference room. Dragging deeply on a cigarette, he emphatically denies that the man traveling with them is Dr. Timothy Leary. He also denies that he is Eldridge Cleaver. Jennifer speaks up: *I am not Bernardine Dohrn.*

As they stall the confused reporters, Tim slinks from his hotel room and steps into the elevator. As soon as it opens in the lobby, he's confronted by several journalists who haven't fallen for the plan. Tim starts windmilling, breaking into a middle-aged-man sprint. His Lenin cap nearly falls off as he lunges past the reporters and stiff-arms the *Newsweek* bureau chief. Off to the side, Tim spots the NBC reporter who has promised to get him into Jordan. They leap into a waiting car as the driver peels away. Shouting reporters are jumping into their own cars, trying to gain on them.

Tim's driver barrels through downtown Beirut, narrowly missing pedestrians and palm trees. The car makes a wicked turn onto a side street, slams to a stop, and the driver and reporter suddenly hop out.

What the fuck?

Tim instantly decides to follow them and falls out of the car. They make a mad dash up a flight of stairs. On the top floor, the driver pushes open a door and shoves Tim inside.

Tim looks around. It is a comfortable sitting room, decorated with prayer rugs, teacups, and cooking pots. An old woman is inside. She does not speak English. Tim attempts to communicate with her with manic, jerky hand gestures, begging for a place to hide.

She listens to the mad American and then finally nods. She slips out of the room and returns with a pretty young woman who takes Tim's hand. Without speaking, she guides him into a bedroom and begins softly purring an Arabic love song. For a second, he feels a stirring. *This is good, much better.*

Suddenly, there are footsteps pounding up the stairs, and the front door bursts open. Tim bounds from the dimly lit bedroom and flees through another door into a kitchen, and from there, into a small bathroom. Mind racing, heart pumping, he pauses to notice that there is no toilet, only a hole to squat over. *Too small to vanish into.*

Finally, the reporters are in the apartment, prying open the bathroom door. They press against him, crowd around him, until Tim raises his hands in mock surrender.

The man from *Newsweek* whom he had straight-armed is demanding: "Do you really want to have your press conference here?"

Back in the sitting room, the reporters are yelling, demanding to know if he's in Lebanon because he was forcibly ordered out of Algeria.

"I am taking American good wishes to the Palestinians," he says. "We would like to tell the people of the United States the third world war has begun. Join us in the fight for freedom because we are everywhere and we're happy and we're free and we're going to make the world free."

Lebanon's chief of immigration informs Nixon's ambassador that his office cannot arrest Timothy Leary until an official request is filed with the Ministry of Foreign Affairs. The ambassador seethes—but hurriedly signs the new paperwork. After what seems like hours, the foreign minister announces that the request should instead be directed to Lebanon's prosecutor general. Nixon's furious ambassador begins calling every top official in the Lebanese government, leaving frantic messages long into the night.

※ ※ ※

Back at the St. Georges hotel, Tim tells DC the whole plan is fucked. Their covers are blown. *Who knows what Nixon is ordering the Lebanese to do with us?*

Tim flops onto the Egyptian cotton sheets on the oversize bed. There are busts and artwork decorating the fancy suite. DC is muttering about not having any guns and Jennifer looks lost. With a huge thud, the doors jolt open and the room fills with heavily armed Lebanese police. Tim and the others stand and raise their hands.

The cops order everyone to pack their bags. They hustle them outside to a jeep and drive straight to the Beirut airport. The Lebanese government has already arranged for them to leave aboard the next flight to Cairo.

※ ※ ※

At dawn, as Tim's flight moves into the clouds, Lebanese officials finally return all the urgent overnight phone calls from Nixon's ambassador. They regretfully inform him that, as much as they wanted to take action against the fugitives, the travelers have already left the country. The Lebanese offer condolences, telling the U.S. ambassador: "It is much easier to detain a person upon arrival rather than departure."

※ ※ ※

In Cairo, another crush of reporters is waiting at the airport, along with several stern-faced Egyptian officials. A government representative steps forward, stares at Leary, and announces to the journalists: "We have known drugs and dropouts for centuries and we know they are a curse. What makes this man think we want him here?"

Tim tries diplomacy: "We are struggling in the Middle East to gather information about the Palestinians and their struggle. We will carry this information back home to let our people know about the Palestinians' legitimate rights."

Tim's madcap escapades in the Middle East have become front-page news around the world. Several stories are quoting a PLO spokesman: "We know nothing about these people. We have enough political tourists and enough problems of our own without them."

Tim listens as the Egyptian officials at the airport tell him he is being denied entry. He and the other Americans are to remain under guard in the airport while new travel arrangements are made for them.

DC is frantic as he huddles with Tim: *It's a trap. A setup. The CIA is coming to arrest us, to fly all of us straight back to Babylon.* DC turns and starts shouting at the startled Egyptian officials and reporters. He demands that the embassies of North Korea, China, and North Vietnam be notified. He demands a telephone, and then makes a show of calling the North Korean Embassy in Cairo as reporters watch. Not sure who is on the other end of the line, DC begins urgently explaining that he's trapped at the Cairo airport with his comrades and they need protection from the fascist pigs trying to force them back to America. Suddenly, his face registers confusion. The operator has put him through to the South Korean Embassy by mistake.

After several more calls, Tim is finally told that the Algerian government has agreed to fly everyone back, first class.   .

In Algiers, government officials are not impressed by Leary's farcical attempts to contact PLO guerrillas—but they are *very* impressed at how desperately Richard Nixon wants to capture him. The United States has been making its ambassadors and consuls jump through fire and issue demands in country after country. And now that the Algerians understand the intensity of the American zeal, the entire game has changed. Whatever their personal feelings about a drug cosmonaut like Timothy Leary, high-ranking Algerians now recognize that he is an extremely valuable bargaining chip.

And as they negotiate huge oil and gas deals with the Americans, as Algeria tries to establish itself on the international stage, only a fool would give away that kind of asset. Far better to have Leary back in Algeria, at least for the time being, where he can be used for a bit of leverage. Orders are being handed down to various Algerian departments and offices: Any U.S. efforts to get Leary expelled from Algeria are going to be firmly rebuffed.

When questioned by reporters, one Algerian official says simply: "You ask about Dr. Timothy Leary, whether he is welcome and how he fits in with the idea of a liberation movement. The answer is that he is here and is free. There is nothing else to say."

THAT'S WHAT THEY HATE TO SEE

October 29, 1970

In California, a thousand angry demonstrators are roiling outside the San Jose Civic Auditorium. It's Thursday and President Richard Nixon and Governor Ronald Reagan are appearing together, trying to scare up a few more votes for the coming election.

The attacks have been relentless over the last two weeks: A courthouse scorched in Worcester, Massachusetts. Eight explosions in federal offices in Puerto Rico. A policeman shot in Georgia. A detonation at Stanford University's Research Institute. A bomb went off at a San Francisco church during a funeral service for a cop killed during a bank robbery. Someone threw a Molotov cocktail at the Racine, Wisconsin, city hall. A post office was firebombed in Norfolk, Virginia. In Cairo, Illinois, police saw several black men dressed in military fatigues approaching the police station and firing guns. A cop in Detroit was blown away. A Washington, DC, post office was attacked. Someone tried to blow up the gym at UC Berkeley. A bank in Berkeley was set on fire. A courthouse was bombed in Stuart, Florida. A flaming device was thrown at a military base in El Toro, California.

As Nixon and Reagan follow their security details out of the auditorium in San Jose, they can see an angry crowd massed behind wooden police barricades, some holding signs that read: NIXON - FASCIST. The protesters are flushed, giving Nixon the middle finger and chanting: "*One, two, three, four, we don't want your fuckin' war.*" The president, flanked by Secret Service agents, suddenly climbs onto the hood of the presidential limousine. He looks out at the crowd and raises both arms high, flashing a V for victory gesture.

"That's what they hate to see," he cracks.

Without warning, a jagged rock comes hurtling at him and just narrowly misses. A bottle flies past, smashing into shards right next to him. In seconds, Nixon and Reagan are under a full-scale attack. Secret Service agents are shouting and reaching for their weapons as they shove people to the ground. The agents form a circle around Nixon and Reagan and push them into the limousine. Rocks, glass, eggs, and peace placards are hurled at the car. Faces flushed, dozens of protesters are pushing against helmeted riot cops and screaming: *Nixon should die.*

A battery of demonstrators breaks through the big barricades and police are trying to fight back, wildly swinging clubs, spraying choking clouds of Mace. The protesters are ripping more rocks from a pile of construction rubble at the back of the parking lot and heaving them at the motorcade.

The presidential limousine tries to lurch through the crowd as stones pound against it. Press buses trailing the president have shattered windows. The Secret Service and riot cops are trying to create a firewall, a last line of defense before the demonstrators reach Nixon's limousine and overturn it. Hundreds of cops, pelted by eggs and ducking rocks, instinctively form a wedge and manage to push enough people out of the way for the motorcade to finally escape. The protesters retaliate by attacking hundreds of cars outside the auditorium, pounding on hoods and smashing more windows. Several police are injured, including one hit in the head with a rock; several reporters are cut by flying glass.

The men inside the motorcade are quaking. Nixon orders Air Force One to fly him to his retreat in San Clemente, and then he works on a statement that he wants released to the national media:

"The stoning at San Jose is an example of the viciousness of the lawless elements in our society," Nixon proclaims. "The time has come to take the gloves off and speak to this kind of behavior."

ESCALATE THE VIOLENCE

November 1970

In New York and in San Francisco, lawyers, hippies, editors, and radicals are swapping tales of the magical Dr. Leary staying one, two, three steps ahead of Nixon, Reagan, the FBI, and the CIA. The longer he is free and wandering, tripping on acid and probably laughing his ass off, the more it feels like the counterculture has raised a massive *fuck you* to the White House.

Leary, in danger of being forgotten when he was put in Ronald Reagan's California prison, is more famous than ever. Reporters want to talk to him, they want his story. In the pulsing and somehow connected countercultural outlaw world, some of them make furtive arrangements to head to Algeria and sit down with him. Tim is selective, careful, and only agrees to see people who can pay him. Word reaches him that *Playboy* will pay handsomely for an interview.

As he negotiates the details through letters and phone calls, Tim tells Cleaver. He magnanimously offers to donate half the money to the Black Panther Party.

"What do you mean, half?" Eldridge replies. "You're supposed to give all of it to the party."

❀ ❀ ❀

Huey P. Newton, the Supreme Commander of the Black Panther Party, is in Oakland and reading his incoming mail. One anonymous letter catches his attention:

"Dope plus capitalism equals genocide," it begins, referencing a famous Panther slogan.

Newton reads more:

"If that is true I can't believe that Eldridge Cleaver and DC are playing footsie with Tim Leary. Leary is the greatest acid-head and dope addict there is. I think Cleaver like any other Black Panther Party member should start taking orders from you before he starts associating with a drugger."

The letter signs off: "Power to the People."

Newton sets the letter aside. He is beginning to have doubts about Cleaver and whatever the hell is happening in Algeria. *Yippies, hippies, and lunatic Dr. Leary.*

Newton doesn't know that the letter was not written by a soul brother Black Panther. It was composed by a middle-aged white man wearing a suit and tie and working for Nixon and Hoover.

The FBI's covert, highly illegal COINTELPRO operation is being carefully unleashed to destroy the Panthers. Key leaders have been imprisoned, or, in the case of Fred Hampton in Chicago, murdered by police. Panther offices across the country are raided regularly. Hundreds of rank-and-file Panthers are being arrested for jaywalking, putting up posters, selling the party newspaper, or spitting on the sidewalk.

The FBI has even produced a fake Black Panther coloring book for kids. The line drawings show piglike cops being happily gunned down by small black children; the FBI displayed the invented coloring books to the media as solid evidence of the Panthers' heinous morality.

The Panther headquarters in Oakland is infested with police informants. Secret, illegal wiretaps on the Panthers' phones allow the FBI to monitor their phone conversations. And, more and more, the FBI has centered on a divide-and-conquer strategy, trying to pit the two Panther leaders, Huey Newton and Eldridge Cleaver, against each other—and maybe get Timothy Leary in the process.

❀ ❀ ❀

On November 12, six cops and four Panthers are wounded in a shootout in Illinois. The night before, a Selective Service building in Chicago had been bombed. There are calendars on the police station and FBI walls marking how long each fugitive Weatherman has stayed free. How long Timothy Leary has stayed free since he escaped prison.

It has been more than sixty days, far longer than J. Edgar Hoover's vow to capture him in ten.

❈   ❈   ❈

Tim steps into the Panther recording studio, reaches for the microphone, and begins making a tape that will be shipped to reporters in the United States. Tim's lucky-Irish-clover voice sounds discordant, considering the message, like a merry children's TV show host telling little kids at home to pick up Kalashnikovs: "*Blow your mind and blow up the prisons and controlling systems of the genocidal culture.*"

Tim is coming to terms with the fact that he has to prove he belongs in Algeria—to prove it to Cleaver, to prove it to the Algerians. He's already told the press, *I am going to convert to Islam and make my permanent home in Algeria.* Now he's insisting that he is personally more radical than any of the leaders of the Weathermen—and that they should do even more to ignite the revolution.

He keeps preaching as the tape keeps rolling and Cleaver and the other Panthers nod in approval: "*They should escalate the violence, they should start hijacking airplanes, they should kidnap prominent sports figures and television and Hollywood people.*"

In Babylon, in America, the message is spreading quickly. Timothy Leary, the godfather of the spiritual revolution, is publicly embracing the violent revolution in an even bigger way.

At the same time as Tim's incendiary taping session, his host Eldridge Cleaver decides to give an interview to a *New York Times* reporter:

"It would give me great satisfaction if Richard Nixon should be killed. I would consider that an excellent thing."

❈   ❈   ❈

Tim hears it over and over again inside the Panther embassy: Nixon has stopped at nothing to get Cleaver—even freezing his royalties from the best-seller *Soul on Ice.* The Panthers' financial situation in Algiers is precarious. They might have a rent-free villa and a tiny $500 monthly stipend from the Algerians—and puny handouts from the North Koreans, in the form of free cases of that hard-to-handle ginseng wine and droning books about Kim Il-sung. But it's not enough. The Panthers have soaring bills.

Cleaver sends Kathleen on a fundraising tour in Europe, but Nixon's officials have called foreign leaders. She is detained in France and then booted out. In Germany, more cops intercept Kathleen and immediately deport her on the next plane. She demands to go to Copenhagen, but they order her to board a flight back to Algeria.

Meanwhile, the FBI's COINTELPRO scheme is steaming ahead. Supreme Commander Huey Newton is being spoon-fed fake reports about Cleaver and his insubordination. And Cleaver has been given hoax accounts about Newton calling him a cowardly traitor. There is no money flowing from the United States, no money coming from anywhere.

But Cleaver is thinking about a new plan:

We have a drugged-out cash cow right here in Algeria.

✸ ✸ ✸

Now that the news is completely wide open about where Dr. Leary is, long-haired men and women are arriving at the Panther embassy and asking how to find him. They are frisked and led to an interrogation room. Told to sit, the lights are dimmed except for an overhead spotlight. While Cleaver questions them, their rucksacks and other belongings are searched far more carefully by the Panthers than by any Algerian customs official.

One young hippie arrives with a fat slab of brown-black hash and the Panthers confiscate it—and then "bust" the smuggler, collecting a fine and taking mug shots for their files. Another cosmic wanderer brings a stereo system as a gift for Tim. The Panthers unscrew the speakers and find two bags containing ten thousand tabs of LSD.

Cleaver storms to the beachside hotel in El Djamila. Tim can see that Cleaver is in full Papa Rage mode, screaming about the hippies toting drugs into the country, into the embassy, all trying to see their guru Timothy Leary. Cleaver thunders at Leary, talking about the latest freak with thousands of hits of acid: *We did the guy a favor. If the Algerians had been on the job, the first thing they would have done was shoot him.*

Tim knows there has to be something else going on, some other spiders inside the Black Panther's brain. Cradling a gun as if it is his cock is strange enough, but Cleaver is sweating and almost

frothing. He seems as paranoid as Nixon. Watching Cleaver rant
and rave in his hotel room, Tim tries to remember what exactly
Cleaver's right-hand man, Field Marshal DC, once told him:

"We are setting up a revolutionary police force here. We have to
be tougher than the imperialists. When we come to power, we're not
going to let people take any drugs they want. This is liberated revolutionary turf. We can search. We can seize. We can confine people
as long as we want."

❋   ❋   ❋

Tim still goes to the embassy every morning to pick up his mail—
fan letters from strangers, correspondence from two California hippies who have volunteered to archive his papers, encouragement
from Allen Ginsberg. He can tell that the Panthers are methodically searching every letter and package addressed to him, probably
looking for money. He shakes his head. They don't even bother to
close the envelopes back up. At least his real passport, in his own
name, arrived safely after allies in the United States made arrangements to hand it directly to him in Algeria.

The Panthers are not aware that they are not the first to inspect
Leary's mail. Nixon has signed off on another top secret program,
MH/CHAOS, to intercept and monitor mail addressed to the
Black Panthers' post office box in Algiers. True professionals, the
CIA agents always religiously reseal every letter and package.

The Panthers are reading Tim's outgoing mail, too, and in his
correspondence Tim still sings their praises. But now he's also trying
to secretly bypass the embassy. He is mailing things out of the country on his own and adding new pieces of information that sound like
fear-laced messages tucked into a bottle and tossed in the sea:

> We are not getting our mail. All TL mail seems to be
> sent to Panther office and transmission is not reliable.

Tim warns that anyone who wants to reach him, to help him,
should write directly to *William McNellis c/o Le Mediterranee Hotel
in El Djamila.*

❅　❅　❅

In mid-November, there is a rap at the door of the Learys' room in the seaside hotel. Cleaver is pushing inside, this time with Kathleen. She sniffs the air and wrinkles her nose in disgust: "What's that horrible smell? I hate incense." Rosemary quickly offers to make tea but Cleaver says no. He makes it a point to never accept any food or drink from the Learys. They could be trying to dose him with Orange Sunshine.

The women move to a corner and Cleaver looms over Tim. He demands money, including the $2,100 payment Tim had gotten for doing an interview with *Playboy*. Tim tries stalling again—he has been putting Cleaver off for weeks, trying to figure out a way to score a book deal back in the United States. That's where the bigger payday is, selling a madcap book about his escape and his life on the run—and he's been leaving messages with lawyers, agents, publishers, and editors.

Cleaver doesn't care, or he doesn't believe a word Tim is saying. He deliberately turns to his side so Tim can clearly see that he has a gun tucked into his belt: *We need money to pay for your protection. When are we going to get it?*

Cleaver adds: *If we don't get the money soon, I'm going to denounce you to the Algerians. You'll lose your sanctuary.*

❅　❅　❅

A few days later, Tim is wired $3,500 as part of an advance for a book from a New York publisher eager for a gripping saga about his escape and his new life in the revolutionary underground—a hippie version of *Soul on Ice*.

Tim immediately gives Cleaver $2,100, but Cleaver is still threatening: *When do we get the rest?*

As it turns out, the Panthers have set a new price for providing protection for Dr. Timothy Leary.

The fee is now $10,000.

THE FIRST LESSON A
REVOLUTIONARY LEARNS

December 1970

Tim and Rosemary are driving to the embassy in the rented Renault. Tim is ready to put on a show, stalling for more time, telling the Panthers more money will be coming at any moment—and pretending to be grateful that they are still generously picking up the Learys' obviously opened, mangled mail.

He steps out of the car, but Rosemary refuses to join him as he darts through the rain toward the embassy. She is smoking, looking very worried, and the weather is adding to her gloom: She has chronic endometriosis and the condition is worsening. She's concerned about the heavy food, the strong coffee, and all the unfiltered cigarettes she huffs with Tim. The whole subservient scene with the Panthers, the way women are treated, isn't helping. She has insisted to him that all she really wants is to move into a home of their own. Make simple, healthy meals in her own kitchen. Maybe get serious about having a baby.

She watches from the car as Tim goes inside. She knows he's viewing the Black Panther embassy as a glorified prison: "Ring the bell at the gate and one of the trustees would come down and let me in. Long faces and scowls...Locked up day after day."

It's clear: Cleaver and the Panthers are more sullen...more homesick. That initial blast of attention, even adulation, when they set up the Panther International Section is fading. It had been a heady rush, an intense triumph, to have opened up an embassy, but then...nothing else seems to have happened. There aren't waves of sanguine revolutionaries making a beeline to see them, to sign up, to hand over money. Marching the streets in their berets, dark sunglasses, and black leather jackets doesn't inspire the same shock and awe that it did in Harlem, in Oakland, in Los Angeles. The bumping soul music playing in the embassy seems tinny, even when it is turned up full blast...there is no one else to join the party, to make love with, to march with. The rhetoric is like a self-imposed straitjacket as the Panthers try to invent a new society—one that has rules and more rules and codes of living, thinking, behaving—in a land they are still trying to grasp.

Tim is thinking of himself, more and more, as a time traveler, a dimension traveler moving beyond static, defined conceits like politics. Not an anarchist but someone messing around with the idea of soaring somewhere else. A shooting star that just keeps shooting, finding new horizons. It's the point...of getting high.

Inside the embassy and shaking off the rain, Tim looks at the socialist posters and revolutionary slogans on the walls and in the library. The glowering faces of Mao and Huey Newton. All the rigid, cold ideology, all the one-dimensional looks and messages. Supreme Commander Huey Newton had it exactly right when he put it this way: *"The First Lesson A Revolutionary Must Learn Is He Is A Doomed Man."*

☼   ☼   ☼

Today, some of the younger Panthers are complaining that the Algerians are more racist than whites in the United States. Tim hears them blurting out stories about city buses pulling away without stopping for black passengers; nightclubs turning black people away; insults shouted in Arabic.

"What are you always smiling about?" one of the Panthers demands of Leary.

"I'm smiling because we're free," says Tim.

"We're not free. We can't go where we want to go," the Panther retorts.

"Where do you want to go?" Tim asks.

"We can't go back to Babylon."

HE DROPPED FROM THE SKIES

December 1970

Back in Babylon, the Charles Manson trial is into its fifth month. The mad-eyed sorcerer rises to testify in his own defense: "The children that come at you with knives are your children. You taught them. I didn't teach them. I just tried to help them stand up." A defense attorney, someone who'd clashed with Manson over the trial strategy, goes missing and eventually his body is discovered. Everyone believes that Charlie's "family" killed him.

Lieutenant William Calley is also on trial in Babylon, charged with the slaughter of all those innocent villagers at My Lai in Vietnam. The government seems to have settled on Calley as the lone scapegoat, despite ample evidence of more bloody American hands.

In New York, the General Electric headquarters is hit by an explosion. Bombs erupt at draft boards in Hollywood, Florida, and San Mateo, California. A blast rocks a police station in San Francisco. A National Guard truck in Whitefish Bay, Wisconsin, is attacked and destroyed. The ROTC building in Storrs, Connecticut, is splintered and set ablaze by a Molotov cocktail.

❀   ❀   ❀

In Orange County—where Timothy Leary was busted for the two roaches that got him sent to prison—the Brotherhood of Eternal Love is staging a *Christmas Happening* to greet the dawn of a new age. One hundred thousand people converge as the Grateful Dead perform. Rumors are spreading that Timothy Leary will magically return from Algeria and preach to the crowd. A big cargo plane chartered by the Brotherhood flies low over the festival, scattering thousands of hits of Orange Sunshine over the crowd. The cops, including the ones who had once busted Leary and were ultimately responsible for all that had happened to him over the last year, are filming teenagers fucking all over the grassy patches of land in Laguna Canyon.

✸   ✸   ✸

In Washington, Nixon's secretary of state, William Rogers, has summoned Algerian foreign minister Abdelkader Bousselham for a secret meeting. Nixon's men are alarmed at what's happening with the American fugitives in Algiers. Eldridge Cleaver is calling on people to assassinate President Richard Nixon. *Who knows what Timothy Leary is feeding him?*

Rogers and Bousselham settle into their overstuffed chairs inside the State Department office. They begin by taking turns cooing about their mutual wishes for increased cooperation, for the restoration of full diplomatic relations. After the foreplay, Rogers drops the hammer: *Will Algeria continue to permit activities on its territory that could result in an assassination attempt or other terrorist act in the United States?*

Rogers adds the kill shot: "I am puzzled by Algerian acceptance of certain individuals such as Timothy Leary."

Bousselham is stunned. He is meeting with America's leading international representative, doing a dance that might lead to developing a new relationship, and all Richard Nixon's servant wants to talk about is Timothy Leary?

"My government was surprised by Leary's arrival," Bousselham concedes carefully. "Leary had literally dropped from the skies."

He adds that the Algerians tried to pawn Leary off on the Lebanese, even the Egyptians. His country *wanted* Leary gone—but they could find no takers. They were forced to allow him back.

Rogers keeps hammering Bousselham: *Why would the Algerians let such a dangerous man loose in their society—wouldn't everyone be better off if Leary were rotting in an American prison?*

The Algerian representative tells the American secretary of state he understands the "danger Leary poses for Algerian youth." He reassures Rogers that Leary is under total control in Algeria, as carefully monitored as he would be in an American jail: "He is being kept under surveillance."

At the White House, four days before Christmas, Richard Nixon receives a very special visitor: rock and roll primogenitor Elvis Presley. The King strolls in wearing amber sunglasses, a purple suit, and a black cloak, trimmed with an oversize gold belt. He has been following the news of Nixon's attempts to combat illegal drugs. He has one request of the president—will Richard Nixon deputize him as an agent in the war on drugs? Nixon agrees to provide Elvis with his own official narcotics badge. Elvis, slipping deeper into his own whirlpool of narcotics, is overcome with emotion. He suddenly embraces a startled Nixon in a giant bear hug.

"I'm on your side," he tells the president.

A PLANET OF PURITY

The end of 1970

Tim is abandoning his plan to turn on all of Algiers. The new blueprint is simply...to maintain. To survive. To hold it together. To keep it tight. He knows one thing for certain: Whatever is going down in Algeria can't last. Maybe a revolution really will blossom from the death throes of bloodied America and he and Rosemary can return in triumph. Or maybe something really weird will hurtle him way deeper into the rabbit hole of drama in North Africa.

In his hotel room, he pecks away at his typewriter, hoping that, at least, it's grist for the mill. *Cleaver needs money. I need money.* The only currency, the only coin, is a possible book. There are no paid speeches to give in Algeria. No paid lectures. No awestruck patrons who donate thousands of dollars, hoping the professor will give them the one magic pill that will lead them away from the land of neuroses.

Tim looks up from the typewriter and tells Rosemary that he now wants to call his book *It's About Time*. She'll help, of course—just like she helps him hear what people are saying. He'll write about his prison escape and glue in some things from his old research papers, from his personal letters, some little bits of flotsam and jetsam that he can add to the book until it is like a collage of dreams, anecdotes, messages, and lectures. It needs to be fresh, inventive, funny—a work that everyone has to read if they want to have their hip card punched.

❋　　❋　　❋

A quick-thinking, daring drug smuggler from the Brotherhood of Eternal Love has made it into Algeria, past the airport officials, and even past the Panthers monitoring Leary. He has brought more acid and primo Afghani hashish in homage to the guru who inspired the Brotherhood. Tim is ecstatic: He still loves the raggedy ensemble of entrepreneurial Orange Sunshine devotees, the cosmic capitalists pumping far more enlightened chemicals than DuPont, Dow Chemical, and Monsanto combined. They have always been loyal to him, to the point of coughing up $25,000, and probably more, to pay for his freedom.

Tim asks the Brotherhood acolyte to execute one more important mission: Tim has finished his manuscript and the Brotherhood outlaw agrees to carry it out of Algeria and get it to editors and agents in New York. The book is Tim's best hope for a massive infusion of cash—the kind of money that might buy his and Rosemary's escape from Algeria. He's been scraping by, and once in a while an envelope arrives at the hotel without being confiscated by Cleaver's men. Only the money sent directly to Le Mediterranee stands a chance of bypassing the prying fingers of the Panthers. The biggest donation came inside a plain-looking envelope mailed from New York—John Lennon and Yoko Ono had sent $5,000.

With the Brotherhood messenger on his way with the manuscript, Tim tells Rosemary that they should go celebrate, try to accrue some good karma. The weather along the coast has been cloudy and rainy for weeks, and he knows the sunshine will do them both good. He has been hearing about a small village, Bou Saada, a few hours south of Algiers on the Saharan side of the Atlas Mountains. Bou Saada is a true desert oasis, and its name means "the city of happiness." It might even have magical powers.

He loads the Renault with bottled water, fresh oranges, wine, and the great hash and acid the Brotherhood wanderer brought. They putter up the narrow winding road, engine whining as they strain to reach the upper lairs in the Atlas Mountains. There are no guardrails, no center stripes, no road signs. Finally they hit the mountain pass, and they begin gliding down into the Sahara.

They check into a government hotel in Bou Saada, where they are the only guests. Outside, the desert smells clean and fresh, and the night sky is black velvet dotted with rhinestones. They spend the next day driving and digging the quiet, ancient rhythms of life among the locals. Tim can see that Rosemary is brightening, already beginning to look healthier and happier. They've been locked in this tug-of-war since they first landed in Europe and argued about whether to continue on to whatever the hell was in Algeria.

More than ever, Rosemary hates the way the Panthers treat their women. She wants to be away from them, to find some solitude. She just wants to make carrot juice and sip it after a night of getting really high—but there is no carrot juice. They have argued about whether Tim is half-assing it in terms of his commitment... to her, to the revolution, to anything but himself.

Tim pulls to the side of the road along the desert. A barefoot Lawrence of Arabia, his pants pockets stuffed with tabs of Orange Sunshine acid, he begins running into the desert, making his own ripples in the café-au-lait-colored sand. There are shepherds and nomads out here, barely minding him. He tells one that he is seeking a place to think, to gather his thoughts. The man instantly understands and points to the horizon, over the next puffy dune. Tim keeps stumbling on, Rosemary trailing him and yelping to beware of snakes, and he comes to an indentation in the desert, a kind of cup placed on the massive saucer of the Sahara. He and Rosemary have brought handmade robes and a prayer rug. He pats the rug on the desert floor and asks her to join him for the magic carpet ride. Time to fly up and meet Amun, the Berber god of gods.

After the customary preparations we plunged outward cutting a pathway of law through the tumbling chaos of interplanetary time. We were dropping dropping through layers of pluriverses in a barely controlled escape curve. Soon we must give the order to slow down and halt on one level. We had no idea which one to choose. In the vast multiverse we're all merely scattered seeds—seeds that must survive many elements if we are to grow. In four-dimension space it appeared as solid. From time one could see the universes separated from one another by layers. The universes remained unknown to one another, unrealizing they were each part of a composite structure of fantastic complexity. We decided that the next universe irrespective of what it

was, should be the one to enter. Our brains were comput-
ing madly the data pouring in. First reports indicated that
this new galaxy was scarcely different from our own. We
weren't surprised. Each layer of the multiverse differs only
slightly from the next.

It was a planet of purity. The earth was pure gold, sky
pure blue. And that was all. We had found the intersection
of form and substance. Coming in from time so rapidly
required a certain effort in order to center attention on only
one plane. As soon as we relaxed we felt the absolute pleasure
of dwelling on all planes simultaneously. We existed in
a place where the air was jeweled and faceted, glistening
and alive with myriad colors, flashing, scintillating, and
beautiful.

❊   ❊   ❊

For the first time in months, they have taken the sacrament the
right way. Without hippie hangers-on, without the mindless frivol-
ity of a "party"—and without the downer-menace of the Panthers
jackbooting their way over the holy possibilities. Tim still believes
in his own careful travel guide for acid trips: The "set" and the setting have to be right. And everything has been right, perfect, alone
with Rosemary under the sheltering sky.

After they finally drift back to their hotel in El Djamila, there
are urgent messages waiting: Cleaver has been looking for them.
Tim phones the Panther embassy. He is still high: "We got so much
to tell you, Eldridge. You and Kathleen have got to come to the
desert with us."

Cleaver is furious, in full Papa Rage mode: "We got a lot to tell
you. You left town without permission. This is a disciplinary matter for the field marshal. He'll be in touch with you."

The next day, Tim reports like a guilty truant to the smother-
ing headmasters in the embassy. Field Marshal DC grabs him by the
shoulder and produces a map. He wants Tim to point out exactly
where Bou Saada, the land of a thousand visions, really is.

Tim flips into the mode of the Juggler, the tarot Magician. He is babbling about finding the real Mother Africa. Getting in tune with Mother Desert.

DC makes sympathetic noises, murmuring "Far out" and "Right on." Tim knows he is making headway. DC has always been the coolest, most open-minded Panther. He's the only Panther making an attempt to learn French. Tim has heard him commenting on the moon's beauty. Now Tim is becoming certain that he can talk the field marshal into taking a trip to the desert, and he can at last begin the process of turning the Panthers on.

Suddenly Cleaver enters the room and now DC is hissing at Tim: *You have committed a grave offense. You left town without proper authority. You were reckless. You exposed us to enemy agents.*

Tim looks deeply into the eyes of the Black Panther field marshal, the man still wanted for murder in Babylon. Tim speaks in his warmest, most loving voice: *I found peace of mind out there.*

DC glares back and barks: "Fuck off with your peace of mind."

❂   ❂   ❂

Driving to his uncertain refuge at the hotel, where Rosemary might very well be sinking into her angry vibe, Tim is thinking that nothing has changed...nothing at all. Everyone wants money. It's always about money. The lawyers want to get paid. The Weathermen want money to buy bombs. The Panthers want money...for everything. His children need money. Rosemary wants to buy a house in Algeria, to make a home so they can try to have a baby.

He knows that there must be *some* cash coming his way. He suspects that the real reason the cards and letters to him are confiscated is so the Panthers can shake loose any cash, sometimes five dollars, sometimes just a single dollar, sent by people all over the world. Some of the letters contain handwritten notes from people who idolize him—thanking Tim for transforming their lives, for turning them on to beauty and meaning, for turning them away from mindless obedience to a warmongering, nature-destroying capitalist machine.

As he steers along the twisting streets leading to the hotel, Tim knows that Rosemary needs a real home. So does he. Anything to keep some distance from the Panthers.

❁   ❁   ❁

He hears about a sixth-floor apartment near downtown on rue Lafayette. It's an old French colonial building nationalized by the Algerians, available on the black market. The rent is only $30 a month—but he'll have to pay a $2,000 bribe to move in. The apartment includes furniture and even a maid named Fatima—in Arabic, her name means "chaste."

He very gingerly broaches the topic of moving into a new apartment with Cleaver—who is instantly suspicious: *How can you afford your own apartment? How can you be sure you're not moving into a nest of CIA pigs?*

Tim explains that the apartment will be cheaper than staying in a hotel. He and Rosemary can cook their own meals and save money—which will allow them to give the Panthers more money. Best of all, he'll have uninterrupted time to write, to earn even more cash for the Panthers.

He doesn't tell Cleaver that he has $2,000 hidden away—the money he needs to bribe the landlords. Cleaver finally says he'll go along with Leary's move. Anything to save some money.

❁   ❁   ❁

At the Panther embassy, a letter arrives addressed to "Rosemary, Eldridge, Kathleen, Timothy, DC" and the other Panthers. It is from Bernardine Dohrn and it includes a copy of her latest communiqué—announcing that the Weathermen are changing their name. The old-fashioned, male-centric usage is out. Now they are "the Weather Underground."

Dohrn's latest statement to the world praises women as revolutionary leaders. It dresses down all male chauvinists: "The pigs refuse to believe that women can write a statement or build a sophisticated explosive device or fight in the streets. But while we have seen the potential strength of thousands of women marching, it is now up to revolutionary women to take the lead to call militant demonstrations, to organize young women."

Cleaver reads the letter and locks it away in his desk. Tim and Rosemary never see it.

✸　✸　✸

On a cool, gray, rainy day late in December, Tim and Rosemary begin packing their meager belongings at Le Mediterranee Hotel for the move into the apartment. They are interrupted by a surprise visit from Field Marshal DC and one of the younger Panthers. DC, carrying a black leather satchel, storms inside and corners Tim: *You're holding out on the bread you owe us, man.*

Tim is speechless. Did Cleaver somehow find out about the $2,000 cash he paid to bribe his way into the apartment?

DC swings his briefcase onto a table. A pistol falls out, landing on the floor with a heavy, ominous sound. Tim and Rosemary look at each other. And Tim shifts into hyper-soothing mode, making the same promises, professing the same allegiances. For now, the Panthers seem mollified. He takes a deep breath as they march out the hotel door.

✸　✸　✸

Through the end of the month, Algiers is increasingly cold and damp as Tim and Rosemary begin to move things into their new home. There are two bedrooms and they decide to make one Tim's study. A sleeper sofa in the living room is for visitors.

Rosemary tries to brighten everything with Algerian weavings and some homemade psychedelic art. She tacks up a 1971 astrological calendar in anticipation of the coming year. Her forecast for January validates what she has been telling Tim: "Health matters need attention—more rest and a more serene mental state are required."

Tim's forecast reads: "Income subject to increase, but there's not enough."

YOU'RE REALLY BUSTED THIS TIME

January 1–9, 1971

As the New Year arrives, Tim decides that his hair has finally grown out enough that he can quit wearing the goofy Lenin cap, that sartorial nod to both the proletariat's power and its plight.

He and Rosemary receive the first visitors to their new apartment: Eldridge Cleaver accompanied by his doe-eyed teenage mistress, Malika, the Queen. Cleaver carefully reconnoiters the surroundings, keeping his hand gripped on the pistol he always has tucked into his belt. He peers inside the closets, checks the windows, and, finally, peeks over the balcony, making sure to stay in the shadows while he looks down at the damp streets. He asks Tim if there's a back door. Finally satisfied that the place is secure, he sits down on the couch and begins to roll a joint.

As puffy clouds of pot drift overhead, Cleaver tells Tim and Rosemary that he has been summoned for another urgent meeting with the Algerian government. New concerns are bubbling up about Leary. Cleaver exhales smoke with a dramatic pause and then says it's up to him, *yet again*, to expend personal political capital to keep Timothy Leary and his wife alive in Algiers.

Tim doesn't believe him. It has to be part of the Panthers' money-grubbing shakedown. It's how the Mafia works—promising protection from people who are not your enemies.

Eldridge reclines in his chair, crossing his long legs out in front of him. *What about your book manuscript?*

Tim knows what to say: He's completed his manuscript and sent it off to the publisher in New York. He's expecting to receive thousands of dollars any day now.

Cleaver nods and promptly leaves.

Watching Cleaver slam the door, Tim knows there has been no word at all from the publisher. He's tried to reach them by long-distance calls, by sending alternately pleading and demanding letters...but nothing is happening. Someone is stalling, diverting things.

✺   ✺   ✺

Tim finally receives a phone call from a lawyer in New York named Michael Standard, someone who has worked with radical causes and had agreed to shepherd Tim's book before publishers in Manhattan. Tim listens as the attorney carefully explains that the manuscript is not being received very well. Tim's musings about the trippy cultural revolution are passé... *what matters now is the militant revolution.* Armed guerrilla warfare. The sexy kind of violence espoused by Eldridge Cleaver.

When Tim asks about the money, Standard tells him, *I'm sorry. No money is coming in.*

✺   ✺   ✺

Returning to his desk and the piles of scribbled notes he has been amassing, Tim wonders about other angles, other moves. Life can be a cosmic joke, and bending the truth is what the tarot Joker, the Magician, does. If he has to preach revolution to get money, then so be it.

He tells Rosemary it would be a good idea to have some people over for some food, a kind of housewarming fete. No heavy politics, just a groovy salon. Everyone will get high, be mellow, marvel hungrily at the plates of rich, heady-smelling couscous and the ridiculously sweet honey-drizzled baklava. They'll invite a handful of people, one or two foreign journalists, maybe some relatively cool Algerians who work for the government—fresh-faced younger people who seem to be into the mind revolution, who seem excited about rock and roll and might even be ready to take their first acid trips.

For safety's sake, Tim decides he'll also invite Cleaver and Malika.

✺   ✺   ✺

On Saturday, January 9, Cleaver calls to question Tim about the dinner party. Tim asks if he's planning to come, then hears a rumbling chuckle on the other end of the phone. Cleaver hisses that Tim is fucking up, that he has no idea who he's inviting into his home. Probably CIA agents.

Tim is still thinking how to reply when Cleaver abruptly hangs up.

At 8 p.m. Rosemary is lighting candles. Fatima, the maid, stirs a big pot of couscous. Tim is in the study, hunched over his typewriter. A series of sharp knocks rattle the front door. Rosemary cracks it open and four Black Panthers in leather combat jackets brush past her and tromp inside. Field Marshal DC orders Rosemary to fetch Tim.

She lurches to the study. "A bunch of Panthers are in the living room wanting to talk to you," she says, her voice quavering.

Tim steps out and looks at DC's cold stare. He sees the same death stare on the other Panthers' faces. DC gestures toward the front door and orders Tim and Rosemary out.

Tim wants to laugh—maybe that will break the tension—but he stops. He summons his most chilled-out, peace-vibe voice. *We have dinner guests arriving in five minutes. Eldridge and Malika have been invited. There's food on the stove. Maybe I can just come by the embassy later tonight? Maybe tomorrow?*

DC growls: "This dinner isn't going to take place." He moves toward Tim. "I'm not going to argue...You two will come either willingly or by force."

Tim says: "Are we under arrest? What for?"

DC replies: "The charges will be explained to you."

The Panthers circle Tim as he tries to aim for the kitchen. Rosemary and Fatima are wide-eyed. Tim mouths to Rosemary, "*They're trying to kidnap us.*"

DC and the other Panthers crowd into the kitchen.

"Get going," DC says. "We don't want to hurt you."

Summoning what he thinks is a hard look, Tim says: "I'm not going. Huey Newton taught us to resist."

A trace of a smile curls on DC's lips. He nods at the other men and they lunge at Tim, grabbing his arms. Tim is shouting, "Help, help!"

Two Panthers slam him to the floor. A hand presses over his

mouth. He is swallowing his screams, gasping for air as another Panther crushes him, twisting his arm behind his back. Blood is spurting from his nose. Through the fog, he hears Rosemary screaming: "Don't let them hurt you!"

A Panther tightens the pressure on his twisted arm and DC squats and leans in to Tim's panicked face: "Will you come quietly?"

Tim nods and the Panthers lift him to his feet, which are now barely touching the ground. Rosemary is told to get her coat. The four Panthers march Tim and Rosemary out of the apartment.

❀   ❀   ❀

The Learys are hustled down six flights of stairs to the courtyard. One of the Panthers hisses at Tim: "Walk quietly. Any noise and we'll vamp on you both."

Blood caking his face and shirt, Tim looks around through the damp chill. The area is deserted except for a few Algerian kids playing under a dim light. He decides against calling for help. The Panthers push him to a parked car and shove him into the back.

DC speeds the car along a wide French-built boulevard, heading west. After several minutes, they turn off and pick their way through a working-class neighborhood. Only a few streetlights are working, and the night is inky dark. DC brakes in front of a decrepit old building. Quickly, Tim and Rosemary are forced up the stairs to the third floor. A single bulb hanging by a wire illuminates the narrow corridor. DC pulls out a big set of keys and unlocks a door.

The two captives are thrown inside. They look around. It's an old office, long abandoned. There is no heat and the damp cold seeps through the walls. DC unlocks another door along one wall and they are tossed into a much smaller room. A dirty, sagging mattress is in the corner. Crumpled magazines litter the floor.

"Well, you're really busted this time," DC says with a toothy grin.

Tim asks if he can speak to Cleaver.

DC's smile disappears. "Eldridge will talk to you at his convenience." He walks out, followed by the other Panthers. The door is locked behind them. Tim and Rosemary huddle for warmth.

Is the Algerian government masterminding this? That hardly makes sense—the Algerians have their own police if they want to bust them. This is a total Black Panther operation. Tim remembers DC saying the Panthers can do anything they want. *Anything.* They remember what Eldridge said when the Yippies and Weathermen came to visit: "We bury people here in Algiers."

Rosemary looks at Tim, her body trembling. "This is a scary movie."

Beyond the locked door, they hear laughter. There is the smell of marijuana smoke filtering through the cracks. They hear a portable tape player coming on. The Panther guards are listening to Aretha Franklin, singing about letting your mind go, letting yourself be free.

The Queen of Soul breaks into her chorus . . . "*Freedom, freedom, freedom.*"

TWO THOUSAND LIGHT YEARS FROM HOME

January 10–13, 1971

The next morning dawns cold and bleak. Tim and Rosemary have a thin blanket, but they are still frigid. They haven't slept. Finally, one of the Panthers cracks open the door and hands over a fistful of stale fruit. Tim asks again if he can talk to Cleaver. More stony silence.

The day drips by slowly. In the afternoon, Tim hears the door being unlocked and the Panthers order them to stand. With no explanation, they are taken back downstairs and into a waiting car. They roar along the rutted streets of a poor section of Algiers, a hidden slum. The white stucco has fallen off the tenements, revealing crumbling stone. The car stops and everyone piles out, stepping through trash and shards of broken glass.

The Panthers rush Tim and Rosemary up piss-stained stairs into another bleak little room on the second floor, an apartment that hasn't been inhabited in years. Piles of grimy, sour-smelling trash fill the room. It is even colder than the other holding cell. Tim is shivering, begging for blankets as he keeps his arms around Rosemary's waist. He asks for cigarettes. The Panthers glare back.

As the door is bolted shut, Tim looks for a clean space to sit on the floor. There was supposed to be someone coming from Paris to see them today. Someone who will be looking for them and might make some noise if Timothy Leary has vanished under mysterious circumstances.

✺   ✺   ✺

Michael Zwerin, a writer for the *Village Voice*, the counterculture's *New York Times*, is landing in Algiers, collecting his bags, and thinking about his big story on Timothy Leary's life in exile. Nobody has really gotten to do the sine qua non piece yet.

The reporter has never met Tim before, but he is an old, trusted friend of Rosemary's from when she was deep inside the downtown-uptown jazz scenes in New York City. She told Tim the reporter was cool. Besides, a story in the *Voice* would be good; it would solidify Tim's standing inside the countercultural firmament.

At the airport, Zwerin is disappointed that the Learys aren't there to meet him as they promised. He takes a taxi to their apartment and rings the doorbell. No one answers, so he leaves a note on the door and walks around for a bit. When he returns, a new note has been posted: CALL 78-21-08 AND IDENTIFY YOURSELF.

Zwerin finds a pay phone, certain that this must be Tim's idea of a prank. Instead, the voice on the line belongs to Black Panther field marshal Donald Cox. Zwerin explains why he's in Algiers.

DC tells him: "I doubt very much whether Mr. Leary will be home tonight."

❋   ❋   ❋

A few minutes later, Tim and Rosemary are abruptly rousted from their tenement prison. Still with no explanation, they are herded to a car and driven to the city center. From the car, Tim watches as the neighborhoods get nicer and nicer. They arrive at a well-kept building and are led inside to a clean, comfortable apartment—a warm, light-filled place.

There is freshly cooked food waiting, sent over from the embassy by Kathleen. Tim and Rosemary quietly eat as Panther guards watch from across the room. No one will talk to them. Tim looks up as a Panther hands him a pack of Gauloises and some matches.

One of the guards finally speaks. Rosemary has his permission to go into the kitchen and make everyone coffee. Rosemary readily agrees. After he gulps down his coffee, the guard orders Rosemary to wash the dishes.

❄   ❄   ❄

Zwerin, the *Village Voice* reporter, spends the night in a government hotel, not sure what heavy game is going down. In the morning, Field Marshal DC comes to the hotel and drives him up into the twisting hills. Like everyone else's, Zwerin's jaw drops when he sees how elegant, majestic, the Panther embassy is.

He's led, like most visitors these days, straight to the interrogation room. DC questions him and then steps away to make a series of phone calls, relaying to someone bits and pieces of the reporter's answers. An armed Panther remains behind, watching Zwerin very closely. When DC returns, Ambassador Eldridge Cleaver is with him.

Cleaver sits in front of Zwerin, scrutinizing him carefully.

"Do you know Leary?" he asks in his sonorous voice.

"No, Rosemary," the reporter answers. "From another life."

"Would she recognize you?"

"Sure."

"Did you bring gifts for them?"

"Yes."

He points to his biggest suitcase. The Panthers want to examine the contents: a set of bedsheets, a pair of purple corduroy jeans for Tim, a bar of lemon soap, a bottle of Cutty Sark, underground newspapers and books, and a stack of cassette tapes, including the brand-new solo album by John Lennon unveiling the ex-Beatle's primal scream therapy.

The Panthers also discover Zwerin's rolled-up bag of pot, and he offers to share it. Instead, they confiscate all of it. Cleaver explains that Zwerin is a very fortunate man—if the Algerians had found his stash they would have executed him within twenty-four hours. The search completed, Cleaver and DC confer. They seem satisfied. DC orders the reporter back to the car and they speed away to see Dr. Leary and his wife.

❄   ❄   ❄

Inside the apartment holding cell, Tim and Rosemary watch from the floor as the bolt is drawn and Zwerin is led inside. Tim, his face haggard, looks up. Rosemary races to embrace her old friend and whispers in his ear: "We've been kidnapped."

Two more young, bristling Panthers guard the meeting. One flips idly through back issues of the Black Panther Party newspaper. The other is studying Chairman Mao's Little Red Book.

"We don't know what we're charged with," Tim tells the reporter. "Eldridge won't even talk to us. In fact, we haven't had a real exchange of ideas in the four months since we arrived."

Rosemary adds: "You may have saved our lives. They won't do anything as long as you're here."

Zwerin replies: "Don't worry. I won't leave Algeria until I'm sure you're safe."

Rosemary sighs with relief. She folds herself into the lotus position and begins to chant: "OMMmmm..."

Tim suddenly seems less weary. "It's really ironic," he finally offers, his face breaking into his usual slice of a grin. "We saw ourselves as historic figures, as the first white Americans to seek the protection of the first black American government in exile. And now we have become the first whites to be busted by that black government.

"Dig it? It's far out."

Zwerin is told that Cleaver is ordering him to crash with the Learys—and that tomorrow morning he will be granted an audience with Cleaver at the Panther embassy, where all will be revealed.

❋   ❋   ❋

After breakfast the next day, Tim decides to compose a letter to Cleaver. Maybe Zwerin can deliver it. Borrowing the *Village Voice* journalist's notepad and pen, Tim begins writing:

> In reviewing our actions and yours since our arrival in Algeria, it is clear that we have been guilty of unnecessary humility and "Tomism." We have followed a course of patient toleration of your undisciplined and eccentric behavior.

The reporter, reading over Tim's shoulder, murmurs "*Right on*" and encourages Tim to be bold. Tim continues writing:

> We have not complained as vigorously as we should have about the extraordinary series of monumental blunders you have whimsically committed which have jeopardized the goals of our work, and our lives.

The more he writes, the more Tim is churning to a froth, blaming Cleaver for the "fiasco" of that fucked-up Middle East trip and the insane scam Cleaver pulled by publicizing that fake arrival of "Miss Dohrn" in Algeria:

> In spite of numerous requests we have never been able to sit down and discuss with you what we could and should do here. Your original answer to this question was "do your own thing" which to us meant live quietly and write the story of our political evolution.
> Since then we have not been told what actions, if any, real or imagined, on our part, or on the part of others, [have] provoked your irritation or led to your totally totalitarian behavior.
> Will you meet with us, discuss, and set down in writing the rules, obligations, and rights under which we shall live? No human being can live in a society where rules, obligations, and rights are undefined, vaguely general, and subject to whim of authority. If the obligations are exorbitant, the rules intolerably restrictive, then we shall tell you. If our differences are so great that friendly discussions cannot resolve them, we shall notify you at once and start making arrangements to move to another country.

Sucking on a cigarette, Tim studies his letter and weighs the fact that he is threatening his captor, the man with the guns, the murderers in the Panther embassy. Maybe he should end the ultimatum on a positive note:

Eldridge, let us relegate our mutual dissatisfactions to the past, learn from our mistakes, and start today, January 12, 1971, to show the world a New Model of Sanity, Balance, Union, Tolerance, Sharing, Strength, and Courage.

Looking one last time at his four-page letter, Tim adds a coda. A deadline. If he's not released by 4 p.m. today, the *Village Voice* reporter is going to tell the world Timothy Leary is not free...far fucking from it.

❂ ❂ ❂

Zwerin walks the concrete staircase a couple of steps behind DC and waits as five locks are opened on the huge front door. The Rolling Stones' surreal mishmash "2000 Light Years from Home" is echoing off the walls... *"It's so very lonely, you're two thousand light years from home."*

The reporter hands Tim's letter to Cleaver, who begins reading. As he finishes each page, he passes it to DC. The room falls silent.

DC goes first: "Leary ought to have his ass kicked for this letter."

Cleaver presses a lighter to a fresh Winston. He blows blue smoke at the reporter. His eyes are as bright as lightning.

"Timothy doesn't realize how vulnerable he is...or we are. We must put security before everything."

Puffing hard on his smoke, Cleaver tells Zwerin that Leary has bungled everything he's touched in Algeria: He's so desperate for attention that he'll make friends with anyone, even people who could be CIA agents. He's smuggled in so many drugs the Algerians could have shot him twenty times by now. *He is fucking tripping on LSD without regard to his security—or ours.*

Cleaver lights another cigarette from the stub of his old one. "We had to use a good deal of political capital to bring Timothy here," he says. "We're prepared to go down with Timothy, but we don't want to go down for some jive reason."

He cocks his head and asks the reporter: *You saw the apartment they are confined in. It's hardly a prison cell, wouldn't you agree?*

Zwerin nods.

"It makes me very sad to have had to do this," Cleaver offers. "I've been in jail, been unable to relate to it, and I don't like being a jailer. But we cannot afford to jeopardize our work toward revolution in Babylon."

The reporter dips his head sympathetically.

"We hope this bust will teach him a lesson," Cleaver says.

"We wanted to scare some sense into him."

✸   ✸   ✸

As the hours pass without any word from the reporter, from Cleaver, Tim is beginning to feel the outer tentacles of the Great Fear. The high from the reporter's sudden visit, from the cathartic exercise of barking at Cleaver in a letter, is over. Maybe the letter backfired in a horrible way.

Tim sits in the dark and as night falls, the city grows quiet until all he can hear is his own breathing and Rosemary trying to sleep. He can *feel* the Panther guards watching him. Finally, near midnight, Zwerin is allowed into the room. Tim studies his face for clues. Tim doesn't really know him; the guy is Rosemary's friend, not his. *Did Cleaver turn him into a spy?*

"You'll be freed tomorrow," the reporter says.

"Tomorrow?" Tim says. "Why not now?"

"You made a terrible mistake in writing that letter to Eldridge. It made him furious and he almost decided not to free you."

Tim's head is pounding as Zwerin begins lecturing them about their sloppiness…about doing drugs and socializing with CIA spies who want to kill the black liberation movement. Cleaver is a far-out man, eloquent, elegant, the Miles Davis of the revolution. He is bathed in revolutionary purity. A natural leader.

Tim sinks into his cushion.

There is only one way out of this situation, Zwerin tells them.

Tim is barely listening. He already knows the price on their heads. Cleaver had told him it would take $10,000—unless Cleaver has now decided to raise his price even more so he can cover the costs of all these holding cells.

Tim hears the reporter say: *Eldridge wants you to issue a statement condemning LSD.*

✿   ✿   ✿

In the morning, Tim and Rosemary are given a loaf of French bread and some fruit, but they remain confined to their room.

DC finally arrives at noon. With exaggerated civility he says they can go back to their little apartment. The Learys are marched to a Renault and as DC races through the streets, he says the Panthers tossed the apartment up and down and conducted a thorough search. Their passports—including the precious ones in their real names—and all their acid and hash have been confiscated.

Tim asks, for the hundredth time, if he can please see Cleaver.

"You stay in your pad and don't try any bullshit," DC replies. "You'll be contacted when Eldridge wants to see you."

When they step into the apartment, the place is a mess. Furniture, clothing, incense, candles, and prayer rugs are strewn everywhere. There is no sign of Fatima, the maid. But Malika has moved in. Cleaver has assigned her to live with the Learys, to monitor them. She has been sleeping in their bed and has eaten all their food. Stretching lazily, she tells them she is hungry again.

Tim and Rosemary try to piece the place back together and Malika watches their every step. The Learys covertly check their hidden stashes of Orange Sunshine, the one key to the cell door. The acid is gone. The Panthers were extremely thorough.

Sorting through the papers strewn on his desk, Tim examines a pile of mail that has built up during his detention. One envelope is postmarked from San Francisco. It's already been opened. Inside are four identical Christmas cards, each imprinted with an image of a seated Buddha. Examining the cards more closely, Tim sees that each Buddha is holding a tab of Orange Sunshine in his outstretched hands. He pops the LSD free.

Malika comes into the room just as Tim and Rosemary are touching their fingertips to their tongues and laughing.

HIS MIND HAS BEEN BLOWN BY ACID

January 15, 1971

Two days later, Tim receives a phone call ordering him to report to the embassy. He is told only that he will record a conversation with Eldridge Cleaver. It will be something like a dual lecture or debate, moderated by Zwerin.

At the embassy, DC leads Tim to the Panthers' recording studio. He hands him headphones. Eldridge has already recorded a statement explaining why he ordered Leary busted. The Panthers will be mailing copies of the tape to the underground press in America. DC hits the ON switch and walks away, leaving Tim to listen.

The tape begins rolling and Tim hears Cleaver's voice:

On January the ninth of 1971, I issued an order to Field Marshal DC...to go to Timothy Leary's apartment...we busted Leary. Leary's busted, and you can consider him busted, he and Rosemary.

Cleaver continues speaking:

Although I have no pretensions of being a psychologist or a psychiatrist, it has become very clear to me that there's something seriously wrong with both Dr. Leary and his wife's brains. I attribute this to the multiple, the uncountable number of acid trips that they have taken, and it makes me very sad, looking at their situation, because, while on the one hand I like Leary, I like Rosemary, but objectively I find them both to be nonfunctional in a political context. Really, we have grown to look upon them sort of as patients, sort of as responsibilities that we have to take care of...

Also we've noticed that they're very dangerous people because whatever the use of LSD has done to their brains, one thing that it's very clearly done is destroyed their ability to make judgments, particularly in the area of security, so that we are forced to constantly use manpower to watch them...

Dr. Leary seems to wither away without an audience. He needs people around him who have a worshipful attitude towards him. He has a need to be seen as a high priest, as a god. And in this part of the world, such gods don't have ready audiences at hand. So that Leary scrapes around for any audience that he can assemble, whether it's an audience of CIA agents masquerading as hippies and tourists, or what have you.

Tim shakes his head. *CIA agents? What the hell is Cleaver talking about?* Cleaver goes on:

The U.S. imperialists, the fascists, have armies of agents scrounging and crawling all over the planet Earth...and they have finally focused in on us here, and they're trying to move against us, they're trying to destroy us here.

And it's for that reason we can no longer tolerate this stupidity from Leary and by busting him we're letting him know that we're serious about that.

The tape keeps rolling:

To all those who look to Dr. Leary for inspiration or even leadership, we want to say that your god is dead, because his mind has been blown by acid.

The tape rolls on and on. Cleaver condemns the Yippies, the Weather Underground, Stew Albert, Bernardine Dohrn, everyone who has associated with Tim:

The whole silly, psychedelic drug culture, quasi-political movement of which they are a part…and of which we allied ourselves with in the past—which we supported in the past because…this is what we had to work with, from white America…

We're through. We're finished relating to this madness.

The tape machine finally clicks off. Tim's mind is racing. Just a few months ago his lawyer had chortled to reporters about a "marriage of dope and dynamite." Now Cleaver is tearing down the whole hippie big top. Tim rises slowly and gathers himself before going into the conference room. He slumps into a chair. He waits and waits, and two hours later, Cleaver finally arrives.

He shakes hands formally with Tim—no soul slaps on the palm—and sits at his desk. He reads through his mail, taking his time. He makes phone calls, laughing and joking. After he hangs up, he finally announces that he's ready to record his dialogue with Dr. Leary.

Zwerin asks if it might be possible for him to retrieve some of the marijuana the Panthers had confiscated from him when he first arrived in Algiers.

Cleaver throws him a severe look: "It might be possible for your grass to be turned over to the Algerian government as contraband seized from your luggage."

Zwerin quickly backs off and takes his place as the moderator for the "debate."

Cleaver starts: "This whole 'trip' approach to revolution, substituting magic wands and magic drugs for cold, calculating confrontation with reality is an obstacle to further development."

Zwerin asks Tim if he's prepared to renounce his mantra, "Turn on, tune in, drop out."

Tim carefully replies: "I haven't talked about drugs since coming to Algiers and I have no need or desire to talk about drugs."

Zwerin presses him for an answer about renouncing the slogan. Tim only says: "I have not used that slogan for three years."

Cleaver breaks in: "But you have, Timothy. What about the button you wore when you took the trip to Lebanon? You had it on the front of your cap: 'Turn on, tune in, drop out.' And I myself asked you to take it off at the airport. How do you fit that into saying you haven't used the slogan in several years? That was certainly a use of it, at a very crucial moment."

Cleaver keeps hammering: "I've asked Tim for his help in fundraising. You see, a lot of political capital was invested in Timothy."

Tim is barely weighing in. Cleaver begins lecturing: "Whether Timothy knows it or not, the U.S. imperialists want to kill him. They want to kill him. And there are people who have been assigned to deal with us. I know that someone has already been assigned, you see, to kill me. I have this on information, you see. And I know that our whole operation here has been placed on a map, in terms of a target. So this is not something we can take lightly. It is something that deserves the most serious consideration. It's making me more serious by the day. Timothy, just tell me: do you think the enemy would prefer you dead or alive?"

Tim knows what he's supposed to say:

"Dead."

SUPREME SERVANTS

Early February 1971

On February 1, Cleaver's broadcast from the heart of the Algerian outpost—detailing how Timothy Leary's mind was "blown by acid"—is aired on radio stations around America. Front-page newspaper headlines ricochet: LEARY'S MIND BLOWN, LEARY VICTIM OF LSD, LEARY'S MIND GONE.

A San Francisco radio station phones Cleaver to find out more. The reporter asks how Leary is reacting to being detained by his Black Panther protectors. Cleaver responds: "Well, he went through various [stages] of unbelief, you know, shock, surprise, and slowly the truth seeped into his acid-soaked brain and he began, after two or three days, to get the message and to understand."

The counterculture is reacting with outrage. In New York, Yippies spray-paint messages around the city: ELDRIDGE IS A PIG. FREE TIM LEARY. The underground press is denouncing Cleaver and anti-Cleaver petitions are circulating while calls rise to boycott Black Panther fundraisers. Jerry Rubin, one of the mainstays of the Yippie party, announces that Cleaver's own mind has been blown—by exile. "I think we should rise to the defense of Tim Leary. When he got locked up by Eldridge for ego reasons, and for Stalinist reasons, it's outrageous. Eldridge putting down the psychedelic culture is very bad."

At the FBI, COINTELPRO agents are exchanging congratulations. Cleaver, all by himself, is doing a better job splintering the left than an entire army of FBI agents could ever dream of. All over America, the very pigs Eldridge Cleaver wants to kill are lifting their glasses and toasting him.

Inside the White House, Nixon's operatives are carefully studying the stories about the schism between Cleaver and Leary. If the drug guru's own host can't stand to have him, it should be a simple enough matter now to convince the Algerians to squeeze Leary out of the country.

When Tim returns to the drab Algerian apartment, it has never felt less like a home, less like any sort of refuge. There is no more Orange Sunshine or hash to soften the edges. He walks inside and greets Rosemary, who clings to him sadly. Malika is still there, staring at him as she lounges like an unblinking Abyssinian cat. She pads her way to a bathroom and leaves the door open, listening for anything Tim says. He glances over and sees that she has disrobed and is standing naked in front of the mirror, brushing her long hair. She feels his look and turns to smile. In the evening, she curls up in the living room, watching him intently while cleaning her finger-nails with one of Cleaver's switchblades.

Tim retires to the little bedroom he's turned into his study. He looks at the disorganized pile of papers, at his scribbled notes and sketches, at the crappy typewriter. It's still the only way to make some money. He's thinking of people he can hit up: maybe film-makers, publishers, friends. Just asking bluntly for cash. For the first time since he swung on a high wire, pulling himself inch by inch out of prison, he realizes that his life now is exactly like being back behind bars.

Back then, he had his satori moment, his quick insight. It was the same revelation he is having right now:

I've got to escape.

He sends an urgent letter to his attorney back in California, Michael Kennedy, who helped hatch the plan that landed him in this new prison. He wants Kennedy to find a way to get him out of Algeria—and fast. He also types out other messages, including one a trusty hippie smuggler promises to deliver to Mick Jagger, asking him for some tea and sympathy and a rescue boat to Algeria to pick up Dr. Timothy Leary. Of course, he never hears back from Jagger. More worrisome, he hears nothing at all from Michael Kennedy. *Is Kennedy taking Cleaver's side?* Hardly anyone is answering the furtive phone calls or writing back anymore.

He glumly tells Rosemary: *Our friends are getting bored with rescuing us.*

❋ ❋ ❋

Tim and Rosemary now have daily jobs to perform at the Panther embassy. They will become "integrated" into military-communal life. Tim will be a janitor and handyman. Rosemary will clean the nursery and assist Kathleen Cleaver in her secretarial work. There's one bright spot for Rosemary. At long last, she will get to spend more time with the feminist leader she has admired. When Rosemary tells Eldridge that she has worked out a schedule with Kathleen, the Panther leader turns icy.

"Kathleen is the receptionist and has nothing to say about work assignments."

Back at the apartment, Tim tells Rosemary they can no longer afford the rented Renault. They'll have to scrounge some coins to ride the bus from the inner city to the exclusive suburbs and the Panther embassy, just like all the other domestic servants. When he walks to the bus, Tim always travels with extra cigarettes—just in case the Panthers arrest him again.

Inside the embassy, as he cleans toilets and mops floors, Tim sees that the Panthers' money situation is worsening. The government-owned car rental agency is harassing them for overdue charges relating to the numerous vehicles the fast-driving Panthers have wrecked. An angry landlord is clamoring for six months' back rent from one of their apartments. The biggest problem is the long-distance bill. The Panthers all love to phone home to Babylon, and the costs run into the thousands of dollars each month. The government has cut off service at most of the Panther residences, although for now the embassy's phone continues to operate while Cleaver works out a payment plan.

❊   ❊   ❊

While Cleaver struggles to pay his bills in Algiers, back in Babylon, Supreme Commander Huey Newton has moved into a penthouse above Oakland's Lake Merritt, where he advises visitors to remove their shoes so they won't blemish his white carpet. He's lecturing at Princeton and Yale, earning thousands of dollars for every speech. Eldridge Cleaver is hearing all about this, thanks to anonymous mailings from FBI COINTELPRO agents.

Newton is sensitive to criticism that he has become too grandiose, and he decides to no longer refer to himself as the "Supreme Commander" of the Black Panther Party. Instead, he will be the "Supreme Servant."

He's trying to transform the Panthers into a reformist group with school breakfast programs and community health clinics. The FBI agents plotting against the Panthers know that this runs completely counter to Eldridge Cleaver's vision of a holy war against the pigs.

It's only a matter of time before Newton and Cleaver split. The FBI decides to hurry things along, to unleash a stunning series of mind-fucks guaranteed to blow the Black Panther Party apart.

In Algeria, Cleaver receives a letter supposedly sent by Newton's personal secretary, a woman Cleaver had once taken as a lover. It is an FBI forgery: "Things around headquarters are dreadfully disorganized with the comrade commander not making proper decisions...No one knows who is in charge. The foreign department gets no support...there is rebellion working just beneath the surface...If only you were here to inject some strength into the movement."

Cleaver understands what is being said: If the Black Panther Party is to survive as the vanguard of the revolution, he must step forward and seize control from Huey Newton.

❊   ❊   ❊

Tim receives a telegram from an editor in New York, promising a decision on his manuscript within five days. He and Rosemary quietly celebrate. If they get some money, maybe they can pay Cleaver the $10,000 for their freedom.

Later in the day, Tim tells Rosemary they should take a bus to the beach at El Djamila, maybe find more relaxing, laid-back vibes. They stop by the place they had lived in for a while, the fading Le Mediterranee Hotel.

The friendly hotel manager, Khali, welcomes them back. "You are well liked here," he says. "Everyone in this village watches you. They say you are quiet, pleasure-loving people very much in love."

Tim nods his thanks and Khali goes on. He tells them that their respectful behavior in the country has impressed powerful people—and that Eldridge Cleaver has embarrassed his Algerian hosts by enforcing his own laws on others. For Cleaver to boast to the press about arresting Leary was an even greater insult to the government.

Khali unlocks the door to their old room, number 23, and shows them inside. "There is anger at the Panthers," he says as he fiddles with the light switch. "You know, after what the Algerians have been through we are not impressed with tough guys. We are too familiar with fierce-talking revolutionary leaders who use the arms we give them against their own people."

Tim starts to offer his thanks, and the hotel manager grabs his arm and whispers, "You have been watched very carefully for four months. Everything you have done is known by several groups. Information is power here, as elsewhere."

VOODOO TAPES

February 15–28, 1971

Pete O'Neal, a thirty-year-old Panther from Kansas City, has arrived in Algiers, along with his wife, Charlotte. O'Neal skipped Babylon after he was convicted on federal weapons charges. He had gained notoriety for once declaring in a television interview, "I would like very much to shoot my way into the House of Representatives."

O'Neal is an electronics whiz. He can't do much about the electrical brownouts and blackouts that plague all of Algiers, but he has completely rewired Cleaver's embassy and updated the video equipment. He's also set up a huge world map in the communications room, with color-coded lights representing the different liberation movements across the globe. The biggest light of all, bright red, glows for the Panther embassy in Algiers.

Cleaver is very pleased with this resourceful new comrade, and the Black Panther leader has one more request. O'Neal listens carefully to the instructions and then gets to work. He connects a new series of wires to the telephone inside the embassy. Now, whenever anyone is on the line, a tape machine automatically switches on, recording the conversation.

❂　❂　❂

Across the ocean in Washington, DC, President Nixon is making his own request. On his orders, Secret Service technicians, working late at night, secretly embed five microphones in Nixon's Oval Office desk and two more inside nearby lamps. They also tap the telephones in the Oval Office, the Lincoln Sitting Room, and other offices. Inside the Cabinet Room they hide six more microphones. All of the recording devices are wired to hidden Sony reel-to-reel tape recorders locked in the White House basement.

Except for the president, the Secret Service, and three top aides, Nixon's comprehensive bugging system is completely secret.

❋   ❋   ❋

Just as Nixon's recording system is being installed, the FBI feeds lurid details of Supreme Servant Huey Newton's "plush pad" to a friendly reporter at the *San Francisco Examiner*. Now papers across the country are carrying accounts describing how the black revolutionary is living in gilded style, high above the streets. The Supreme Servant is portrayed as a Judas in Babylon, selling out his people for a private gym, sauna, and even an indoor putting green, while the pipe-packing, rank-and-file Panther soldiers are eating Nation of Islam bean pies and waiting in the ghetto for the bus.

In Algiers, inside Cleaver's own plush embassy, the telephone is ringing nonstop: *When is Cleaver going to seize control and put a stop to Newton's madness?*

The FBI's clandestine COINTELPRO war is moving briskly now. On February 22, the agency sends another forged letter to Cleaver, this one purportedly from "Big Man" Howard, the editor of the Black Panther Party newspaper:

> I am disgusted with things here and the fact that you are being ignored. I am loyal to the party and it makes me mad to learn that Huey now has to lie to you. I am referring to his fancy apartment which he refers to as the throne...the high rent is from party funds and not paid by anyone else. Many of the others are upset about this waste of money. It is needed for other party work here and also in Algeria. It seems the least Huey could do is furnish you the money and live with the rest of us.

Newton's brother is receiving his own fake letter from the FBI—warning him that Eldridge Cleaver is plotting to assassinate Huey P. Newton.

❋   ❋   ❋

Pacing around his apartment, Tim has been waiting two weeks since his editor's telegram promising a decision on his manuscript in five days. Tim makes collect calls to New York and to Michael Kennedy's law office in San Francisco, puffing nervously on cigarettes while waiting an hour or more for the connection to go through. When he is patched in, the voice on the crackly line repeats the same thing: *No one is available to talk to you right now.* Tim hangs up and trudges up the six flights to the room where Queen Malika, sometimes wearing only a bra and panties, resumes staring at him.

On the last Thursday in February, he types a plea to two trusted freaks in San Francisco, the scholarly hippies who volunteered to care for his archive while he was in prison:

> I had hoped you'd been able to line up publishers (and advances) for the next book. Has anything happened? We've been in amazing financial bind. Since Jan 1 we've lived on no money at all, save what I've been able to borrow in small amounts here from friends passing through. We have gone three and four days without food. The telephone has been off for weeks. Rent two months overdue. Etc.

❋   ❋   ❋

The same day that Tim types his SOS, Cleaver is receiving a call from Supreme Servant Huey Newton in California.

Newton's rapid, oddly boyish voice comes on the line: "Look, word's going around that maybe we're not seeing things eye to eye." He is going to be interviewed on live TV in San Francisco tomorrow morning and he wants Cleaver to be part of the program via a phone call. Before he hangs up, Newton says: "We're gonna show people that everything is all right between us."

Cleaver puts the phone down and looks at DC.

"Well, this is it," he says.

Tim arrives at the embassy the next morning and feels the buzz in the air. Kathleen Cleaver is animated, cocky, as she raps with the other Panthers. Tim sees Field Marshal DC at the sink, helping the women with the dishes. DC looks up and smiles. Something is going on today.

On a work break, Tim finds a vacant chair in the conference room. Various Panthers move about purposefully, and Tim finally learns that Eldridge will be making a joint appearance on an American TV show with Huey P. Newton.

At three thirty the hookup occurs. Everyone in the embassy can hear Newton on the air, defending his high-rise apartment, saying that it keeps him safe, protected from attacks. The pigs wouldn't dare blow up a penthouse. He adds that he and Eldridge Cleaver are in solidarity. They remain close comrades.

Cleaver is patched into the program. Without warning, as if he is back in North Korea, he begins reading from a prepared statement. "I just want to comment on the present situation that exists within the Black Panther Party," Cleaver begins in a steely voice. "The Party has fallen apart at the seams."

Newton is stunned. Trying to compose himself before the live TV cameras, he interrupts: "I hate to disagree here, but you leave me with no other choice."

Cleaver curtly responds: "We will deal with that in a report to the Black Panther Party."

Then he hangs up.

Tim watches as the young Panthers in Algiers shoot the Black Power salute and cheer. Cleaver is kicking ass, taking names, asserting control. Newton, the so-called Supreme Servant, is a fucking fraud.

Tim studies Cleaver. He seems very relaxed, as happy as Tim has ever seen him.

Minutes later the phone rings again. Tim watches as Cleaver lights a Winston and placidly picks up the telephone. The new tape recording system quietly clicks into action:

Newton: Eldridge. You dropped a bombshell this morning.

Cleaver: Yeah.

Newton: Don't you think so?

Cleaver: I hope so.

Newton: It was very embarrassing for me.

Cleaver: It had to be dealt with, man...

Newton: Your whole section is expelled.

Cleaver: Right on, if that's what you want to do, brother. But look here.

Newton: What?

Cleaver: I don't think you should take such action like that.

Newton: I'll take that, brother. You dropped a bombshell... As far as you're concerned, you can go to hell, brother... You're expelled, all communication will be stopped, and that's the end of it.

Cleaver: Hey, Huey—

Newton: What? I'm going to write the Koreans, I'm going to write the Chinese and the Algerians to kick you out of our embassy.

Cleaver: Hey, Huey—

Newton: Or to put you into jail, because you're a maniac, brother. You and Timothy Leary, I think you're full of acid this morning...

Newton: I like a battle, brother. We'll battle it out.

Cleaver: That's not the best way to deal with that.

Newton: That is the way *I* want to deal with it.

Cleaver: Well, I think that you're a madman, too, brother.

Newton: Okay, we'll battle then, two madmen will lock horns.

Cleaver: We'll see, okay?

Newton: I think I have some guns.

Cleaver: I've got some guns, too, brother.

Newton: All right. You put yours to work, and then I'll put mine to work, but I'm not a coward like you, brother... You're a coward because you attacked me this morning... You're a coward and you're a punk, you understand?

Cleaver: Hey, Huey—
Newton: YOU'RE A PUNK!

Cleaver hangs up and more cheers begin echoing in the grand old colonial villa. Newton just walked into Cleaver's trap. The audiotapes and the video can be edited for release in Babylon. Newton can be snitched out and punked, revealed as a madman and deposed.

☀ ☀ ☀

The next morning, at the embassy, Tim tries tapping into his professor of psychology mode, earnestly analyzing the big trouble in the house of revolution. "A tragic, sorrowful spectacle...the bravest, strongest men in Afro-American history attacking each other instead of the mutual enemy."

Now the Panthers are putting together their anti-Newton videos and calling them "The Voodoo Tapes."

Tim listens carefully as Eldridge speaks directly into the camera, denouncing Newton's faction as "the right wing" of the Black Panther Party. Kathleen appears on camera, more vibrant and healthy than Tim has ever seen her. She rips Newton as a revisionist playing patty-cake with the pigs. When she finishes, Kathleen stabs her fist overhead and yells: "Power to the people, death to the fascist pigs!"

Like it's a call-and-response at a tent revival, Eldridge shouts back: "Death to all revisionists!"

During a break in the filming, Tim stands near Cleaver and Field Marshal DC as the Panthers discuss the best way to get the videos to as many people as possible in Babylon. DC puts his arm around Tim's shoulder:

"At least we have a captive audience of one," he says, laughing.

Tim chuckles: "Don't forget that I'm an escape artist."

DC laughs even harder.

IN THE MIDDLE OF THIS SHIT

March 1–6, 1971

An hour after midnight on the first day of March, a U.S. Capitol switchboard operator receives a call from a man speaking in a very low, flat voice: "This building will blow up in thirty minutes...Evacuate the building."

Thirty minutes later, a bomb stashed inside a first-floor restroom, packed with fifteen to twenty pounds of dynamite, explodes, blowing out walls and shattering windows. A column of white smoke rises from the Capitol as police sirens begin to wail.

❁   ❁   ❁

When Tim shows up for his work at the embassy, he's greeted by a jubilant Eldridge Cleaver, who is braying about the bombing in Washington. The only thing Cleaver is pissed about is that no pigs were killed. In Babylon, President Nixon is ordering a massive manhunt and condemning the attack: It is "a shocking act of violence which will outrage all Americans."

Not long after Nixon's order, Yippie leader Stew Albert is driving through the Pennsylvania countryside with his wife. He hears a police siren and glances at the rearview mirror. Several cop cars are closing in, fast. He pulls over. Within seconds, more than a dozen policemen are surrounding the car. Pointing their guns at Stew's head, they order him to step outside.

The cops refuse to say why he's been stopped, but as they methodically search the car, it becomes obvious: They are looking for explosives.

Once Stew and his wife are released from custody, they drive to Washington, DC, and call a press conference on the Capitol steps. There, they address the recent bombing:

"We didn't do it, but we dug it."

✺   ✺   ✺

Tim is back at the embassy, broom in hand, watching in wonder as a giddy Eldridge Cleaver soaks up the breathless reports about the attack at the heart of the pig empire. And then another urgent call is coming in for Cleaver. It's Huey Newton, and the Panthers once again record the exchange. Somewhere else, the FBI is also listening in. Newton's little-boy voice is rising: "I will do all that is possible with the life that is in me to destroy you."

Cleaver hangs up and calls the Panthers to an emergency meeting. He orders around-the-clock surveillance of the Algiers airport, just in case Newton tries to invade with a team of assassins.

Tim notes that Eldridge's normal, nearly somnolent way of speaking has been replaced by crisp, clear orders. Suddenly, Cleaver stands and motions to Tim, telling him to stop sweeping and follow him outside. From the balcony, Tim sees the sun beginning to poke through the clouds. Rainy season is finally ending. Cleaver reaches into his jacket pocket. A few feet away, a young Panther guard clutches his rifle and keeps watch.

Cleaver pulls out a piece of paper and carefully unfolds it. He turns to Tim and says that he's been disappointed by the stupidity of the radical press in the United States. Despite the clarity of his statements, despite their "debate," the underground press is still hassling Cleaver about his treatment of the great Dr. Leary.

He has decided to remedy the situation by publishing an open letter. He has titled the missive "...About the Revolutionary Bust of Tim and Rosemary Leary and In Answer to the Punkassed Sniveling from Motherfuckers Who Know Me Better Than That."

Tim listens as Cleaver recites it out loud:

> I'm speaking to you as a brother, as a revolutionary, as a Total Outlaw, and I have on my hand shit deeper than you know exists. In the middle of this shit I've got Leary—Timothy and Rosemary.
>
> I'm in the shit that you're in, and in an extension of that shit, out here, and I know, even if you don't, that all of this

shit has to be dealt with at the same time, as a whole. And in the world that we live in today, the shit has no geographical center, and it's just as deep here as it is there, perhaps even deeper.

Right now, on a balcony overlooking Algiers and baked by the warm African sun, Tim's ability to be in the moment but hovering above it is emerging. As he considers Cleaver's paranoid rant about deep shit in light of his reputation as a major American author, Tim realizes that his early hunch about Cleaver was right.

The man should have done way more Orange Sunshine.

It would have made his writing soar.

Cleaver continues reading:

Meanwhile, I can't relate to irrelevant behavior and activity, even if it does come in pretty colors—Psychedelic. Pretty colors. Really beautiful. But not LETHAL.

ALL POWER TO US, THE PEOPLE, THROUGH THE INSTRUMENTALITY OF THE DICTATORSHIP OF THE LUMPEN—THAT IS, IF ALL THE PEOPLE GET ARMED!

He glances at Tim, apparently finished. Tim sighs. But there's more. Eldridge has added a postscript:

P.S. If some of you longhaired cats, motherfuckers, would get crew cuts, a "clean shave," put on a suit, white shirt, and a tie, and go down and join the local police force, the Army, GM, AT&T . . . and then begin imaginatively to turn that shit around, blowing it away, delivering crippling blows from the inside, by sabotaging shit, ripping shit off, giving up useful information, setting pigs up to be ambushed and ripped off, such would be much more useful . . .

There's also a second postscript:

P.P.S. Don't worry about Tim and Rosemary. Pappa's seeing after them.

Eldridge refolds his letter and stuffs it back inside his pocket.

Tim mentions, as nonchalantly as possible, that he's expecting his money from America very soon, but he and Rosemary need their passports—their real passports, the ones with their real names on them—in order to claim the money when it is wired over. If they get the money, they can immediately give the Black Panthers their $10,000.

To Tim, Cleaver looks pleased. But then he wants to know why Tim needs both passports.

Tim explains that he and Rosemary have a joint account and may need to provide both passports.

Eldridge thinks it over and decides it is impossible for Tim to go anywhere without his knowing about it. The Algerians will rat Tim out and give him up to the Panthers. Not to mention, Cleaver will have Tim followed around the clock.

Cleaver leads Tim back into the embassy mansion and retrieves the passports from the Panthers' vault.

❋   ❋   ❋

At the apartment, Tim and Rosemary retreat to their bedroom and lock the door, whispering so Malika can't hear them. Tim spells out the options and the dangers. Only one thing is clear: It's been nearly two months since Cleaver had them kidnapped and then publicly denounced them, yet they've seen no signal the Algerians are looking to deport them. And just like before, back when Rosemary first came to see him in prison, they are talking about escape.

❋   ❋   ❋

On March 4, the official Black Panther Party newspaper, run by Huey Newton, hits the streets of Babylon. The front page screams: FREE KATHLEEN CLEAVER AND ALL POLITICAL PRISONERS. A photograph inside shows Kathleen with a black eye. Another shows Cleaver's underage mistress, Malika. The story lists Cleaver's affairs and his violent attacks on his wife. It claims he beat his wife in her hospital bed right after she had given birth. It says Kathleen is "a virtual prisoner" in Algiers. The article has one more bombshell—it says that in Algiers, Cleaver murdered a fellow Panther he suspected had slept with his wife: "He killed—which act he could never seem to be able to commit against any of the People's oppressors— killed this brother...he murdered him and buried his body right in Algiers."

Tim tells Rosemary that things are beyond madness. As they whisper inside their apartment, as they wonder if Cleaver's mistress is listening in, Tim suddenly understands the million-ton gravity behind Cleaver's earlier boast: *We bury people here in Algiers.*

In America there's been a break in the case of the Capitol bombing. The Associated Press has received a five-page typed communiqué from Bernardine Dohrn and the Weather Underground. "We have attacked the Capitol," the letter reads, because "it is a monument to US domination over the planet."

For the next several days, Tim goes to a pay phone where no one can eavesdrop. He's making international collect calls, one after another, desperate to find anyone who can get him the hell out of Algeria. *I'm an indentured servant to a murderer who is caressing his weapons, beating his wife, and shooting people point-blank in the heart.*

He finally gets through to Michael Kennedy in San Francisco. The connection is bad, and Tim can't hear exactly what the attorney is saying. Tim asks about the money—Kennedy's office has long been the conduit for donations to Tim, yet he's received nothing in months. Suddenly the static clears and Kennedy's voice comes through. He says Tim owes more in attorneys' fees than he's getting in donations. He keeps speaking as more pops and hisses erupt, then suddenly the line goes dead.

Tim dials the operator and asks to place another call, then another. He finally reaches one of his *real* friends—one of the blissed-out hippie investor-smugglers inside the Brotherhood of

Eternal Love, still a trusty band of appearing-and-then-disappearing outlaw sprites, magically moving tons of goodies from Oaxaca, Acapulco, Kabul, and the underground Orange Sunshine laboratories hidden away in California. The friend assures him that the Brotherhood is still loyal, and they will find a way to get him some money. But just like when he was in the California Men's Colony, Tim is going to have to find his own way to get past the prison walls.

A VANISHING PINPRICK

March 7–30, 1971

Early on Sunday morning, March 7, Tim and Rosemary are tiptoeing behind the locked door of their bedroom while Queen Malika lolls and sleeps in the living room. Tim carefully unlatches the balcony door that leads to their patio, six floors above rue Lafayette.

In the apartment next door, where a quiet Algerian family lives, their friend Khali—the manager from Le Mediterranee—is stepping out onto the adjoining balcony. The two men nod at each other without speaking. Carefully, Tim picks up a suitcase and leans over the railing, handing it to Khali. More and more items are passed across—Tim's typewriter, rugs, furs, cushions.

Tim ducks inside and walks with Rosemary into the living room, locking the bedroom door behind them. Malika is now awake, stretching and arching her back. Tim tries not to linger on her skimpy nightgown. He tells her they're going out for breakfast and will be back soon. Downstairs, they hail a cab and head to the beach hotel in El Djamila, the little village outside Algiers. A room is waiting for them. All the possessions Tim had handed over the balcony are already inside.

Tim places a call to Cleaver and puts on his most soothing, acquiescent prisoner voice. He tells Cleaver he and Rosemary are going to chill out, lay low at the beach hotel. The Panthers, after all, were the ones who had told him about the place, had once put him up there.

"No!" Cleaver yells.

Tim says: "We have to have a few days of rest. You can dig that."

There is a second of silence and then Cleaver speaks in a flat, menacing tone: "I want you to come up here right now—and bring the passports."

Tim quickly says that the Panthers' money should be arriving at any minute. He still needs the passports for the exact moment when the cash is wired to Algiers.

Cleaver hangs up on him.

Tim and Rosemary collapse on their bed.

❁   ❁   ❁

After the revelations in the Black Panther Party newspaper, U.S. officials are pressing the Algerians to investigate whether their guest Eldridge Cleaver is tied to the missing Black Panther—a murder committed in the heart of Algiers.

At the same time, at the Algerian presidential palace, President Boumédiène is reading a letter sent to him directly by Huey P. Newton explaining that Eldridge Cleaver and the other residents of the embassy are, in fact, no longer members of the Black Panther Party. Newton tells the Algerian president that the embassy should be closed.

❁   ❁   ❁

For Tim and Rosemary, the next few days pass in a sunny glow. Everyone in the village is friendly to them. Khali introduces them to the mayor and police chief and Tim is very gracious and charming, thanking them for their hospitality. Later, he and Rosemary hear from Khali that the cops turned back a carload of Black Panthers that tried to enter El Djamila. It's a bizarre feeling, being protected by the police.

One evening, they meet with a British journalist and her Algerian boyfriend—a man who has been rising in the government. The couple had been invited to Tim and Rosemary's ill-fated dinner party. Cleaver had warned Tim to avoid them, fearing they could be CIA agents. Now the couple is taking Tim and Rosemary out to dinner in El Djamila and explaining that the Algerian government might be willing to protect the Learys, to offer them permanent residency status and free them from Panther control.

Tim's mind is spinning—back in America, his attorney and other militants are apparently siding with Cleaver, but here in Algeria the socialist revolutionary government is favoring him? The Algerian man confides something else: Richard Nixon's government is trying to play hardball with the Algerians in negotiating oil concessions. President Boumédiène may be looking to poke the Americans in the eye, and Leary will be his sharpened stick.

✹   ✹   ✹

Back at the beach hotel, the phone operator patches a call through to Tim. It is Cleaver and he is in screaming Papa Rage mode: He is coming for Leary. He wants Leary back in the embassy. He wants the passports. He wants the money.

A pro-Cleaver Panther has just been gunned down on a New York City street. Cleaver assumes the assassinations have begun. He's expecting an attack on his villa at any moment. And the Algerians are calling nonstop, asking hard questions about a murdered Panther in Algeria, who is going to pay the mounting bills—and why Supreme Servant Huey Newton is telling them to shut the Black Panther embassy down...and kick the Panthers out of the country.

To Tim, Cleaver sounds manic, and whatever comes after paranoid. Dr. Leary's dealt with people at the final mental breaking point, people who can't handle prison, can't handle the heaviness of peyote, mushrooms, and lysergic acid, let alone the heaviness of their minds. Cleaver is losing his shit. It doesn't help that the newest edition of the Black Panther newspaper has a demeaning cartoon in it: The artist who created the Black Panther logo—the same image that adorns the embassy's bronze plaques—shows Cleaver naked except for a peace symbol medallion on his neck, his hands up in complete surrender. His cock is a dot, a vanishing pinprick. The FBI is mailing extra copies of the cartoon directly to the Panther embassy.

✹   ✹   ✹

One afternoon, Tim and Rosemary receive a trusty courier from the Brotherhood of Eternal Love. He has made it through customs and past the Panthers staking out the airport, fixated on intercepting black assassins sent over by Supreme Servant Huey Newton.

In the hotel room, the envoy opens a sack and spills out several hundred dollars and plenty of Orange Sunshine. Outside, birds are cresting over the water. Clouds move in from the coast. All Tim wants to do is find a wondrous place to trip under the blue desert sky.

✸ ✸ ✸

On March 29, Tim answers a call. The man on the line, speaking in French, says he is from the president's office.

"The president of what?" Tim asks.

The man laughs. "The president of Algeria," he says. He asks if Tim would be willing to come in and meet with a few Algerian officials.

A few minutes later, a sleek black government sedan pulls up at Le Mediterranee. Tim and Rosemary look at each other and kiss tenderly before Tim steps into the car and is driven away.

The sedan follows the winding, tree-lined road to El Mouradia, the white presidential palace. In the distance, Tim can see the Bay of Algiers sparkling in the crisp sunlight. They walk past the uniformed members of the Algerian Republican Guard, each man clutching his sharpened dagger. Inside the cool, dark building, Tim is led to a conference room.

Six senior government officials are seated at a table. They rise as he walks in, regarding him with some amusement. Here at last is the American drug fugitive, the man they've been hearing so much about for months and months.

The lead official offers his hand to Tim and introduces himself as Algeria's advisor on foreign affairs. He reports directly to President Boumédiène.

He hands Tim two cards. One has his McNellis picture on it; the other, a photograph of Rosemary. The documents are Algerian residency cards.

"It is a pleasure of the Algerian government to have you join us," the president's assistant tells him. "We want you to know that you are a free person here. This is a free country. You and your wife are our guests here. When we gave you political asylum we took you under the protection of our government."

Tim's head is bobbing with gratitude.

"This is not Texas," the man says as everyone laughs. "You are safe and free to live your life here as you wish."

There is one more thing, though: It would be best if he and Rosemary had no further contact with Eldridge Cleaver and the Black Panthers.

Tim readily agrees.

❋　　❋　　❋

The next morning, Cleaver receives his own summons to appear downtown. No government car is sent for him. He presents himself to the *wali* of Algiers, a hero of the revolution who runs the city on behalf of President Boumédiène. Cleaver is questioned closely about the negative news reports bouncing around the world—and why he believed he had the authority to arrest an internationally recognized figure, a man known for opposing President Richard Nixon. He is grilled about a missing Black Panther.

After several tense hours, Cleaver is dismissed—and ordered to stay away from Dr. Timothy Leary.

REVOLUTION WITHOUT REVELATION

April 1–May 4, 1971

An Algerian official assures Tim that he and Rosemary will be assigned their own house by the government. There are intimations that he may even be given a teaching job at a university. The return of the dry season and the bright sunlight is reviving Rosemary. She's looking stronger and healthier than she has in months. They want to have a baby, but Rosemary needs to have surgery on her fallopian tubes, which were probably damaged by the endometriosis. It's a complicated procedure and she wants to see doctors in Europe.

Tim wants to go to Europe, too, and there is a gambit that might get them there: He shows Rosemary a letter inviting him to Denmark to lecture on "the Psychedelic Revolution" at an international conference. It's been eighteen long months since his last public address. It's a trifecta: There's money; Rosemary can see doctors; and maybe the Danish will deem him an intellectual, a thinker, an artist who needs asylum. Algeria is never going to be the fountainhead for the sonic mind-and-sex revolution. There's no place for Jimi Hendrix's music, no place for Orange Sunshine. If they stay it'll be nothing more than a backwater retirement—a cheap place to live out their final years.

Tim thinks it through: Denmark is a member of NATO and maintains full diplomatic relations with the United States. But the Scandinavians are cool and seem to lean away from Nixon. They've given sanctuary to conscientious objectors, defectors, and soldiers who went AWOL. The women are pretty; the free love movement seems to be moving along nicely. But what's to stop the Danes from turning him over to the CIA?

Tim reads the invitation letter again. It says that Danish television will broadcast his lecture. His eyes linger on the mention of a generous honorarium—he and Rosemary are almost completely broke.

And there is this sentence:

> We have now obtained the informal guarantee from the
> Danish government that you will not be handed over to the
> American authorities during your stay in Denmark.

The first Sunday in May dawns bright and sunny. Tim and Rosemary Leary arrive at Maison Blanche Airport with their suitcases packed. They've checked out of their room at Le Mediterranee, and the trustworthy hotel manager, Khali, has agreed to store their rugs, books, and typewriter in the basement.

As they approach the ticket counter, Tim suddenly spots two Black Panthers on duty, monitoring the exit gate. Cleaver is still ordering surveillance of the airport, still waiting to intercept the assassins coming for him from Babylon.

Nervously, Tim buys their tickets to Copenhagen and tries to melt with Rosemary into the crowd. They wait in the customs line, out of sight of the Panthers. When they inch to the checkpoint, an Algerian officer asks for their passports and studies them hard. They have no exit visas. Summoning his French, Tim explains that the chief of the airport knows all about their departure, that everything has been approved by the government.

Guards appear and Tim and Rosemary are pulled out of line and sent to the immigration office. They are ordered to sit, and Tim watches various airport officials making phone calls, staring at him, speaking rapidly in Arabic. Minutes tick by and the plane to Copenhagen takes off without them.

Early the next morning, Tim heads out for frantic meetings with various Algerian officials. Everyone is unfailingly polite. One suggests that Tim and Rosemary consider a flight to Paris instead of Copenhagen. Another man warns Tim to avoid any flights to Paris, whispering: *Paris is a trap.* France is an Interpol country and the international police have a warrant ready for the arrest of Dr. Timothy Leary.

Finally, on Tuesday, May 4, they are told that they can board the next flight to Copenhagen. There's just one catch: When they leave Algeria, they will not be allowed to return.

Tim is given an exit visa stamped with his real name. He must fly out under his own U.S. passport, not the fake William McNellis identity.

He fishes out his dull brown William McNellis suit, the one the Weathermen bought for him in Seattle, and tries it on again. He studies himself in a mirror and then rushes back to the airport with Rosemary.

Two Black Panthers are on guard again. One is Field Marshal DC, who immediately spots them and begins striding toward them. Tim holds his breath. He has never known exactly what to think of this Panther, a man who can laugh easily one moment and then coldly turn his guns on him the next. Tim senses that DC has always wanted to free his mind, to expand his consciousness, but somehow chose to remain loyal to Cleaver.

He can't understand DC's continued allegiance, and Tim's now come to his own firm conclusion about Cleaver: "Eldridge was the new candidate for the Kim Il-sung club, the elite clique of planetary strongmen, heavyweight champions who have fought their way to power...It's a familiar vocational aspiration of the oppressed... There are probably a hundred thousand men in the world who dream and scheme about the violent steps which lead to the top."

Now DC is standing in front of Tim, checking out the luggage. Tim glances over to the Algerian security officials. Surely they know that the Black Panthers have been ordered to have no further contact with them.

DC is beginning to smile.

You are *an escape artist.*

Now a grin is spreading across Tim's face. DC shakes their hands and wishes them the best of luck.

Tim walks away from the Black Panther, holding Rosemary's

hand. Within minutes they board the plane, flying north and looking down at the blue-and-green Mediterranean.

As they settle into the flight, Tim is wondering if, by now,
Cleaver is staring at the little warning note Tim sent to him:

Revolution without revelation is tyranny.

PART III

HIGH ON A MOUNTAIN

I'LL SHOW YOU EUROPE

May 4, 1971

Tim and Rosemary settle into their seats on Swissair Flight 233 and sip glasses of chilled Champagne as the tang of cologne and perfume from the first-class passengers fills the air. The DC-9 purrs reassuringly as a young blond stewardess bends over in front of Tim, softly attending to another passenger. He has been studying the Swissair brochure tucked into the seat pocket. "You can fix your eyes pleasurably on numerous hostesses whisking past," it reads, "prettily dished up."

Tim's lecture in Copenhagen promises to bring desperately needed money, along with a chance for a new life. But beyond simply escaping from Algeria, he and Rosemary have no real plan. There is no network waiting for them, no detailed, coordinated blueprint for safe haven. The lawyers back in the States, Kennedy and the others, have not set up any kind of shelter, money stream, or infrastructure.

Maybe I can seek out some publishers in Denmark; maybe they'll want to publish my lectures from the conference.

Maybe he and Rosemary can visit Sweden and petition for asylum. There are fans, followers, all over Europe, where music and dope feed a hungry counterculture. At the very least, there will be a hell of a lot more Panama Red, Thai sticks, Acapulco Gold, and LSD than they could score in Eldridge Cleaver's Algeria.

The blond stewardess is rolling a cart up the aisle. She serves them a full meal on white china with cloth napkins: veal steak with Swiss sausage, fresh rolls, and a side salad. For dessert, they receive nicely wrapped Swiss chocolates. Tim asks for two and pockets the second. It might be a while before they can eat again. They're nearly broke and have only a few crumpled American bills along with some leftover Algerian dinars.

As he munches the last of the food, his mind is bouncing again.

Maybe the invitation from Denmark didn't really come from a university? Maybe it's an ambush plotted by Nixon's CIA?

And even if the invitation is authentic, what guarantee is there, really, that Danish cops or American agents won't suddenly appear alongside them at the airport, gripping their arms and steering them into a dimly lit back room—putting them in handcuffs and then sending them back to America in chains?

He wonders if he still looks like an ordinary American tourist— the yokel who won the Rotary club's vacation prize and is looking forward to buying his first cuckoo clock and maybe some Swiss candy for the girls in the secretarial pool. As the plane begins its descent into Geneva, where they'll wait for the connecting flight to Copenhagen, the paranoid vibes are beginning to slither through the cabin:

What's to stop Nixon from sending someone to arrest us in Europe?

Tim looks at the window and wonders what's really down there.

The FBI, CIA, and State Department have known for at least a week that Dr. Timothy Leary has been planning to travel to Copenhagen. The CIA had sent incognito agents to monitor the airport in Algiers, waiting to see if Leary and his wife would make a move. Now that Tim and Rosemary are in the air, an agent in Algiers sends a confidential cable to Washington:

LEARY AND HIS WIFE HAVE BOARDED THE SWISSAIR FLIGHT AND ARE DESTINED FOR COPENHAGEN.

Nixon's State Department quickly secures cooperation from the Danish government. The FBI and Danish police are coordinating their plan to arrest Leary when he arrives.

The plane dips out of the clouds and swoops low over Lake Geneva, touching down at the city's sleek new airport. Tim and Rosemary step off the plane, subdued and trying not to stand out. They take an escalator to a moving sidewalk that carries them into the terminal. They duck into a thickly carpeted airport lounge and retreat to a quiet corner. Their connection to Copenhagen won't leave for several hours.

"Will you buy me a drink while I think?" asks Rosemary.

She nurses a Dubonnet as Tim walks to the airport's telegraph office. He has learned that an old friend named Pierre, the Paris psychologist who harbored them in France when they first fled America, is going to attend the same conference in Copenhagen. Pierre has promised to send a cable to alert "William McNellis" in Geneva if he hears about any trouble in Denmark. At the telegraph office, there is a message waiting, along with a number to call.

Tim steps into a phone booth and listens as Pierre tells him that cops and reporters are crawling all over Copenhagen. Pierre says that even he has been pulled aside and questioned, just to make sure *he* wasn't Timothy Leary.

"Don't get on the plane to Denmark," he warns.

Tim sags as he listens to his friend's backup plan.

There are friends in Geneva who will let you crash at their house for the night. Beyond that, I know someone else who will give you and Rosemary a deeper, secret hideout in Switzerland.

As Tim tries to dissect the warnings, Rosemary is cradling her drink at the airport bar and watching her husband inside the telephone booth. As she looks, a big-bodied man dressed in an exquisite suit strolls in front of her. He's regal-looking and guiding a muscled German shepherd on a very tight leash.

He stops and looks at Tim in the phone booth, watching for a moment. Then he turns toward Rosemary. She can see his leonine features, a thick mane of silver hair swept back from his forehead. He turns and leads his lunging dog away. Rosemary nervously fingers the seven cents in her pocket.

Tim returns, his eyes wide from Pierre's warning.

He tries to sort it out.

We can't go to Denmark . . . but maybe the cosmic forces are aligning to bring us to Switzerland.

In 1943, just across the border from Nazi Germany, a gentle

Swiss chemist named Albert Hofmann accidentally absorbed a
trace amount of a rye fungus he'd synthesized for medical research.
Hofmann, a father of four, had felt a pleasant sense of intoxication
accompanied by an intense, florid play of color. Three days later, he
intentionally dosed himself. He took the smallest amount he could
think of, 250 micrograms. As it turned out, he could've gotten by
with much less. An hour later he was pedaling his bicycle across
the Swiss countryside as terrifying hallucinations gripped his mind.
Hofmann was certain he was going insane. Once he came down
and figured out the correct dosage, he tripped again. This time he
realized that LSD could spark visionary insights "that otherwise
happen only in spontaneous ecstatic states and to a very few blessed
people."

And as Dr. Timothy Leary, esteemed member of the Harvard
University faculty, had begun his earliest explorations into the
curative powers of ancient remedies—the Native Americans' peyote and mushrooms—he learned about the interesting research in
Switzerland and something called lysergic acid. Very quickly, Leary
and his own researchers arranged for shipments of legal LSD—sent
directly from the Swiss laboratory where Dr. Hofmann, the father
of LSD, was working.

✺   ✺   ✺

Tim nervously orders his own drink and turns to Rosemary, telling
her that they've got to forget about the flight to Copenhagen.

It's a setup. We've got to stay on the run.

Their luggage has already been checked through to Denmark.
They literally have nothing. The *only* option is to find those people
in Switzerland, the friends of Pierre, who've agreed to let them hide
out for a while.

Rosemary's head is swimming.

"What if Switzerland won't let us enter?"

Tim snaps back: "I've watched people going through. They just
check the color of your passport."

They shuffle to the "Nothing to Declare" line, act polite, and
Tim is right—no one blinks at them. Almost unbelieving, they step

outside. The sun has broken through the clouds. Rosemary turns and she can see the same aristocrat from the airport coming out behind them. He's leading the German shepherd toward a silver Rolls-Royce.

Tim speaks French to the cabdriver, directing him to the crash pad address his friend furnished. Geneva looks lovely, with flowers peeking out from the old terraces and balconies.

Tim grins at Rosemary.

"I said I'd show you Europe one day."

GOLDFINGER

May 5, 1971

The next morning, Swissair Flight 420 arrives in Copenhagen at 9:15 a.m. sharp. Danish cops and Interpol agents swarm the terminal, accompanied by edgy American agents ready to point out Timothy Leary, the international fugitive wanted by the Nixon White House.

The media has been tipped off about the big bust, and reporters are jockeying for the one photograph that captures the exact moment handcuffs are slapped on Leary's wrists and he is strong-armed away by the CIA and FBI agents. The passengers file off the plane, and as each one enters the airport, he or she is scrutinized. Some are abruptly pulled aside for questioning. Several are frisked. Some are told to turn over their carry-on luggage. The cops and the reporters keep watching and waiting as each new face appears in the Jetway. Finally, the last passenger strolls out. There is no Timothy Leary. In the baggage area, two stuffed suitcases from Algeria stand together, unclaimed.

The reporters race to file international news alerts:

DR. TIMOTHY LEARY, THE LSD PROPHET AND FUGITIVE FROM A CALIFORNIA PRISON WHO WAS SCHEDULED TO SPEAK HERE, HAS DROPPED FROM SIGHT.

❋　　❋　　❋

At FBI headquarters, word arrives that the fugitive Timothy Leary has avoided the ambush and vanished during a Swiss layover. Agents are scrambling to track his whereabouts, even as they are being pulled in a thousand directions: Somebody has just tried to blow up Bank of America branches in Santa Cruz, San Bruno, and

Chico, California. A state office building in Fresno is attacked. The ROTC buildings at Claremont McKenna and Pomona Colleges are assaulted—and the president's office at Claremont McKenna is also set on fire. A Molotov cocktail is thrown into a Los Angeles post office. There is an attempted bombing at the Selective Service branch in Braintree, Massachusetts, and a huge explosion at the Selective Service office in Kansas City.

In the White House, the bruising fighters inside the Nixon Administration, including the bloodhound operative G. Gordon Liddy, are convinced that the longer Leary remains on the loose, the more the freaks and stoners and dynamite heads will feel like they can get away with murder.

More than ever, Leary is making a mockery of Nixon, the FBI, and American values.

❋ ❋ ❋

Tim and Rosemary have spent the night at a safe house with their discreet hosts. Now they are mapping out their next move—still following the mysterious instructions from Pierre, their psychologist friend, to go to a specific address in the city of Lausanne and try to connect with a "powerful" figure.

As their train moves along Lake Geneva and approaches Lausanne, they see the dense cluster of medieval buildings and a towering Gothic cathedral. Across the lake are stunning views of the French Alps. Paloma Picasso, Coco Chanel, and other high-society stalwarts move in and out of the city's elegant homes and apartments. Tim and Rosemary take a cab from the train station to an impressive white marble building with an ornate façade. They find the elevator, press the PENTHOUSE button, exit into a private entryway, and instantly an apartment door swings open for them.

Rosemary gasps.

It's the haughty-looking man who had strutted through the Geneva airport with his German shepherd. He is six feet tall, wearing a bespoke Savile Row jacket, and has the puffy physique of a former prizefighter who has decided instead to conquer fine food. He introduces himself as Michel Hauchard and offers a slight bow as he invites them inside. The guard dog, now untethered, leans forward and sniffs Tim's private parts.

Hauchard leads them into a wide living room with sweeping views of the shimmering blue lake. Two very young, aristocratic-looking women, Gabrielle and Antonia, are draped languorously across a couch. To Tim's practiced eye, they appear to be on muscle relaxants. A servant glides up with drinks and Tim and Rosemary settle into overstuffed white chairs.

The Learys and Michel Hauchard study each other. Hauchard looks, to Tim, like one of those perpetually smooth and ultimately ominous power players from a James Bond movie like *Goldfinger.*

"Pierre tells me you are rich and writing a book that we shall sell to the movies," says Hauchard.

"I'm afraid we're poor and very much on the run," Tim quickly replies.

"That is nothing," says Hauchard. "It is my obligation as a gentleman to protect philosophers. The police are no problem to me. I have a dozen of them on my payroll."

❀   ❀   ❀

Michel Hauchard might have once served in the French Resistance during World War II. Exiled under the suspicion of fraud, he gravitated to Switzerland. He has a handsome Italian speedboat, named *Joanna* after a stunning young woman he had chased around the world—including dropping bundles of white and yellow roses into her swimming pool from an airplane. In the summer, he races the boat in and out of Monaco; in winter, he decamps to the luxurious ski chalets in Gstaad. When he walks into Monte Carlo casinos, the maître d' and the roulette dealers know his name. He is admitted to the back rooms where the heavy rollers spend thousands on a single play, and where his lucky number is 8. One evening, he made it rain with francs, riding a winning streak until members of the casino staff blanketed the roulette table with a shroud, signaling that Hauchard had squeezed out all the money. In London, he stays at the Savoy, orders Russian caviar, and calls for a Rolls-Royce Silver Cloud to ferry him around the city. The rumors are persistent: that he spent time in the infamous Prison de la Santé in Paris, where the writers Jean Genet and Guillaume Apollinaire had been held—and that he has shifted easily into international arms smuggling, maybe selling weapons to the Palestine Liberation Organization. When a Red Cross relief plane was blown out of the sky over Biafra, rescuers found it crammed with guns—and some said Hauchard knew all about it. He is friends with the king of Morocco and has connections in Lebanon who help him free friends from jail.

Hauchard steers Tim and Rosemary to a guest bedroom and tells them they are welcome to stay as long as they like. He invites them to join him later for dinner.

In the bedroom, Rosemary glances at Tim.

"He's a crook," she says.

"We have no choice," he replies. "He's our crook."

❈   ❈   ❈

In the morning, Hauchard asks Tim to accompany him to a meeting with his personal lawyer—an expert in all manner of criminal investigations. As they step out of the apartment building, Tim feels bulletproof alongside Hauchard. A security guard salutes them as they walk to the Rolls-Royce. As the chauffeur speeds them through Lausanne's streets, cops wave them past busy intersections.

At a lakeside café, Tim is introduced to another regal-looking man, Horace Mastronardi, who has worked on some of the highest-profile criminal cases in the country, including representing Hauchard against fraud accusations. A waiter stands at a discreet distance as the lawyer speaks bluntly to Tim.

The Swiss don't really want you here. They would have arrested you at the airport if the FBI and CIA weren't so sure they'd catch you in Denmark.

Nibbling on biscuits and sipping his coffee, Tim listens intently as Mastronardi continues.

You can find a place here, but you'll have to insinuate yourself into Swiss life. Build a network of champions, make your stay in the country seem important, inevitable.

Tim begins to slowly smile. The Swiss have a long history of granting residency to free thinkers, no matter how controversial.

Vladimir Lenin and Jean-Jacques Rousseau were once given refuge here.

A thought is forming: *Switzerland could be a good place to let things cool down, blow over.*

Maybe, in Switzerland, he could become an American genius in exile—just like the great black jazz artists who had to flee to Europe to find freedom and respect. It's part of a long, hip American tradition. Writing, creating, living the expatriate dream. Besides, he's seen the U.S. revolution from the inside, and it looks like the same old squabbling for power and wealth. *What's wrong with being a funky Erasmus in European exile?*

Mastronardi adds one more thing.

You especially have to stay away from drugs.

Tim smiles at the well-dressed men, sips more coffee, and nods—even as he sees Hauchard winking at him.

"You just be silent," Hauchard tells him, "and let me be cunning."

I'LL PAY ALL THE BILLS

May 7–8, 1971

The next day, when Tim and Rosemary emerge from the comfortable bedroom, the clouds are hanging low over Lausanne. Boats are slowly drifting across Lake Geneva, the water barely moving. There are already some visitors arriving and Hauchard is introducing them: various playboys, countesses, and high-lifers. Hauchard's servants are running back and forth from the kitchen with platters of fresh bread, croissants, jam, cheese, and thinly sliced meat.

Tim and Rosemary settle at the dining table, which is covered with a freshly ironed tablecloth, and Hauchard's guests move toward them. Hauchard is smiling, puffing on a Cuban cigar: *Why don't you share a few tales about what you've been up to the last few months?*

Tim looks up from his breakfast plate, grins, and begins talking about his prison escape, hiding in the woods with bomb-throwing revolutionaries, living with the Black Panthers in Algeria. Hauchard's well-dressed guests are murmuring their approval, their excitement. Tim glances at Rosemary for a second. *Is this what the rich and bored do in Europe—they collect people? Am I becoming Hauchard's living, breathing court jester?*

Tim strolls to the window and soaks in that breathtaking view of the lake and the people scooting along the waterside roads on Vespas, their hair blown back and scarves whipping in the wind. When he turns and walks back into the living room, the maids are darting about, making cappuccino and carrying armloads of silk linens. Tim feels energy coursing through his body; he's feeling optimistic, like a young man.

Suddenly, Hauchard is calling him, urging him and Rosemary to get dressed for a trip into the city. He has a look bordering on a smirk.

I've arranged for Rosemary to receive medical treatment at one of Switzerland's best gynecological clinics. I'll pay all the bills.

In Washington and in several U.S. embassies around the world, American intelligence agents are chasing down leads: *Leary landed in Switzerland, but we have no clue where he has disappeared to. Maybe he took a back door to France? South to the Italian Alps? North to Sweden? On to India?*

In the U.S. embassy in Rome, field agents are checking into tips that he is roaming the city, passing himself off as a tourist. An American traveler calls the FBI to say she saw the fugitive boarding a flight from Rome to Zürich. In Philadelphia, an FBI informant calls in to say that Timothy Leary is en route to Chile. In Greece, a spy at Ethiopian Airlines tells the CIA that Leary has taken a flight out of Athens and is on his way to seek refuge in Addis Ababa.

KIDS SAY THE DARNDEST THINGS

May 18, 1971

Richard Nixon's overnight guest at the White House is emerging from the Lincoln Bedroom and joining the president for breakfast. Art Linkletter is a well-known TV and radio personality, famous for teasing children in a segment called "Kids Say the Darndest Things." He is a father of five, but his youngest child, Diane, committed suicide two years ago. She was twenty when she jumped to her death from a sixth-story window.

Linkletter went public with his grief, lashing out in anger at what he assumed had caused his daughter to die: LSD.

"It wasn't suicide, because she wasn't herself. It was murder... she had a tiger in her bloodstream."

An autopsy revealed no drugs in his daughter's system, but Linkletter insisted that she had been tripping on acid when she made her leap. He launched an anti-drug crusade and focused his anger on one man:

"Leary called LSD 'God's greatest gift to man...' And when somebody like Timothy Leary comes out and justifies it, we have got to jump on him with hobnailed boots."

In Washington, Nixon watched the unassailably genial Linkletter target Leary. It was beyond fortuitous. They were after the same man, and Nixon contacted Linkletter—and asked him to join a national narcotics commission. He invited Linkletter to the White House, and to spend the night in the Lincoln Bedroom, before they planned how to take down Dr. Leary and his drugged-out followers.

As he heads to eat with the president, Linkletter is thinking about an article in that morning's *Washington Post*—a story about a Nixon Administration official who said that penalties for marijuana should be "minimal or non-existent...a fine, like for a parking ticket."

Sitting down to eat with Nixon, with the White House waiters leaning over to pour coffee, Linkletter jumps right on it: "Well, I'm not very happy about what I read in the paper today."

Nixon looks up: "What happened?"

Linkletter begins explaining what he just read in the *Post*. Suddenly, he sees the president picking up a phone at the breakfast table. Linkletter listens as Nixon orders that the administration official who was quoted in the story—the one advocating lenient marijuana sentences—be fired immediately.

"I want [him] out of the building and his desk cleaned out, and gone before dusk tonight," Nixon demands.

"Good night, you shouldn't do that," Linkletter interjects.

Nixon glowers at his guest.

"If I have a man in my group that thinks that way, I don't want him in there—he's out."

In the afternoon, Nixon and Linkletter meet again, this time in the Oval Office.

Linkletter begins by saying, "There's a great difference between alcohol and marijuana."

Nixon replies: "What is it?"

Linkletter says: "The worst that you can have when you're in with other alcoholics is more to drink, so you'll throw up more and get sicker and be drunker...But when you are with druggers, you can go from marijuana to, say, heroin. Big difference."

Nixon, quiet for a second, responds: "I see."

Linkletter tells him, "If, if, if you're with a guy who suggests you have three more drinks than you should have, you're just going to get sicker. But if you're with a guy who you're already high and he suggests you try, this instead of this, you can go much further."

Linkletter lets it sink in with Nixon and then continues his explanation: "Another big difference between marijuana and alcohol is that when people smoke marijuana, they smoke it to get high. In every case, when most people drink, they drink to be sociable. You don't see people—"

Nixon, growing more engaged, interrupts him: "That's right, that's right."

Linkletter goes on: "They sit down with a marijuana cigarette to get high—"

Nixon: "A person does not drink to get drunk."

Linkletter: "That's right."

Nixon: "A person drinks to have fun."

After a bit, Nixon muses out loud: "I have seen the countries of Asia and the Middle East, portions of Latin America, and I have seen what drugs have done to those countries. Uh, everybody knows what it's done to the Chinese, the Indians are hopeless anyway, the Burmese. They have different forms of drugs."

Linkletter: "That's right."

Nixon: "Why the hell are those Communists so hard on drugs? Well why they're so hard on drugs is because, uh, they love to booze. I mean, the Russians, they drink pretty good."

Linkletter: "That's right."

Nixon: "But they don't allow any drugs. Like that. And look at the north countries. The Swedes drink too much, the Finns drink too much, the British have always been heavy boozers and all the rest, but uh, and the Irish of course the most, uh, but uh, on the other hand, they survive as strong races."

Linkletter: "That's right."

Nixon: "And your drug societies, uh, are, are, inevitably come apart. They..."

Linkletter tries to finish the thought for Nixon: "They lose motivation...No discipline."

Nixon responds: "Yeah...At least with liquor, I don't lose motivation."

✸　✸　✸

A few hours after Linkletter packs his overnight bag and leaves the White House, Nixon is in his limousine and heading toward the Potomac River and the presidential yacht, the *Sequoia*. He thought about bringing King Timahoe with him, the Irish setter he has named after a town in Ireland. Sailors in dress whites offer crisp salutes as he boards the vessel, followed by his closest aides: Henry Kissinger, Bob Haldeman, and John Ehrlichman. Joining the party is a new advisor, Charles Colson, whom the president had looped into the inner circle after he had heard him say: "I'd walk over my own grandmother to reelect Richard Nixon."

Nixon grips a glass with scotch and soda as the captain steers the *Sequoia* into the deeper waters of the Potomac, a sludgy open sewer too polluted for any fish to survive in. As evening shadows descend, the yacht passes Mount Vernon and George Washington's tomb. Nixon and his aides stand at attention as the *Sequoia*'s bell rings a salute.

Dinner is served inside the mahogany-walled cabin, and Nixon continues drinking. Now he's sipping wine, a 1957 Château Lafite Rothschild. His companions are poured a California chardonnay. Nixon tries to disguise the difference, and the servers have standing orders to hide the labels while pouring wine.

All eyes turn to the president as the boat bobs and sways in the water. He is talking about enemies—the enemies they all have in common. *It's no longer just the anti-war protesters or the radical left.* Now America's opponents include "the madmen on the hill." Democrats in Congress.

"One day we will get them," Nixon tells the others. "We'll get them on the ground where we want them." He looks at Colson. "And we'll stick our heels in, step on them hard and twist—right, Chuck, right?"

Now the president is staring hard at Kissinger: "Get them on the floor and step on them, crush them, show no mercy."

There is a moment of complete silence. No one knows what to say, what to do. Colson decides to respond for everyone:

"You're right, sir. We'll get them."

SQUARE IN THE PUSS

Late May 1971

At Hauchard's penthouse there is another evening party in full swing. The rock music is cranked up, the liquor is flowing, and the drugs are passed out like candy. Tim walks into the crowd, appearing refreshed, radiant, and in control. His face is fuller, far less haggard, than it had been in Algeria. Hauchard is looking on approvingly as young women nearly spill out of their dresses as they move close to Tim, laughing merrily, holding his elbows, squeezing his arms.

Rosemary has retreated to her bedroom. She's had surgery to repair her fallopian tubes and she needs rest.

Without warning, there are screams and growls echoing across the wide living room. People are pushing away from one another and pointing: Hauchard's German shepherd is snarling and lunging at one of the servants. Hauchard's voice is suddenly booming, commanding the animal to stop. The room grows deadly silent as Hauchard orders one of his people to take the dog away and kill it.

The party rolls on.

※　　※　　※

On Wednesday, May 26, in Washington, Nixon is talking to his chief of staff, Bob Haldeman: "I want a goddamn strong statement on marijuana," the president says. "Can I get that out of this son-ofabitching, uh, Domestic Council?"

"Sure," Haldeman replies.

Nixon continues: "I mean one on marijuana that just tears the ass out of them... You know it's a funny thing, every one of the bastards that are out for legalizing marijuana is Jewish. What the Christ is the matter with the Jews, Bob, what is the matter with them? I suppose it's because most of them are psychiatrists, you know, there's so many, all the greatest psychiatrists are Jewish. By God we are going to hit the marijuana thing, and I want to hit it right square in the puss."

On Thursday, May 27, Tim steps into Hauchard's wood-paneled study, which is furnished with Parisian antiques and an enormous desk that looks like it might have once belonged to Napoleon. He settles into a chair behind the big desk and writes a letter to his new Swiss attorney:

> Dear Dr. Mastronardi: Pursuant to our conversations I am glad to furnish you with the following declaration: If I should be granted temporary residence in Switzerland I pledge that:
>   1. I shall at no time possess any illegal drug.
>   2. I shall not engage in any political activities or make any public appearances.
>
> *Sincerely yours, Timothy Leary*

When he's through, Leary finds Hauchard and begins outlining his plan to pay the millionaire and his attorney back, and to provide a living for himself and Rosemary in Switzerland: He has contacts in the States who will fund him, New York publishers and magazines that want him to write books and articles.

Psychology Today *wants me to write a story about "The Psychology of Pleasure." I've also been working on a book about my prison escape. Much of the writing is already done. I'm just waiting for some straight answers from the publishers. Things were messy and unclear in Algeria.*

Tim goes on, explaining that his manuscript is probably being held hostage by his radical lawyers—who only want to work with the bloody revolutionaries. They wanted a political manifesto.

Hauchard slowly presses his fingers together. He nods, thoughtfully, as though he is deciding something.

WAR ON DRUGS

June 1–16, 1971

Hauchard asks Tim to sit with him in the yawning living room. Outside, in Lausanne, the temperatures are cresting in the seventies. The flowers along the waterfront are running riot.

Hauchard explains that a philosopher-raconteur like Dr. Timothy Leary should be in his own lair, a place where he will have fewer distractions, a place where he can begin working in earnest on his book.

Hauchard adds that he has a perfect place in mind, a ski chalet in the exclusive resort town of Villars-sur-Ollon.

Within an hour, Tim and Rosemary are strolling the winding streets with the sweeping views of the Rhône Valley and thirteenth-century châteaus. Lake Geneva is on the horizon and majestic Mont Blanc looms in the distance. Bouquets of blue clouds float just over the village. The Learys stop to eat at an inn with a toasty fire and order plates of local Gruyère cheese.

It's clear that Villars is not as intentionally showy as St. Moritz or Zermatt, the other famous Swiss ski zones. Tim puts his arm around Rosemary and they walk up a hill to the chalet Hauchard has arranged for them to live in. It is called Le Dauphin and it sits alongside a trickling stream. There's a fireplace, two bedrooms, and even a fallout shelter sealed by a vault door. Out front is a blue Volkswagen van, a gift from Hauchard.

❁ ❁ ❁

In mid-June, Hauchard sweeps in for a visit and says he wants to take Tim out to hobnob with royal families checking on their children at the town's exclusive international boarding schools.

Hauchard's chauffeur-driven Rolls-Royce is waiting and Tim steps inside, sinking into the deep leather upholstery. The car glides silently down the hill, through the narrow, winding streets. A few strangers turn and stare for a second.

In the old town center, the chauffeur parks and Tim steps out, feeling the bracing mountain air. He can hear some excited chattering in English and he looks up to see a small group of young Americans traveling through the Alps for the summer. The pack is pointing at him, calling his name and moving toward him. The tourists run over to chat him up, hoping to score an autograph. Within moments, an even bigger crowd surrounds Tim. He's smiling, radiant.

The commotion draws the attention of the local newspaper.

❈   ❈   ❈

When the first news reports emerge that the infamous Dr. Leary is living in a small Swiss resort town, alarms quickly go off inside the Nixon White House. The FBI sends cables: *Leary has surfaced again.* His location is pinned down—and it looks like he is *still* mocking the hell out of the president of the United States.

Nixon knows that crime will be a major issue in the next election, and he's eager to position himself as a law-and-order leader. He's just declared a war on drugs, calling it a "national emergency." He's asked Congress for $155 million to lead the fight against "America's Public Enemy No. 1."

Nixon's old friend, Secretary of State William Rogers, is also a law-and-order man. He and Nixon had originally become friends hunting Communists together during the McCarthy era, chasing them out of the shadows. But now that Nixon is president, Rogers has seen a darkness fall over his old ally. Nixon has always been obsessed with the enemy within, but now he's increasingly vengeful, intent on punishing anyone who might oppose him. The president has even been steadily easing Rogers out of his inner circle. Rogers knows there's one way he can prove to Nixon that he is still just as unforgiving when it comes to law and order: by bringing back Timothy Leary in chains.

Rogers contacts the heads of the Swiss Federal Department of Foreign Affairs and spells it out:

There is a dangerous escaped American criminal on the loose, residing in Villars-sur-Ollon. Can your people hunt Timothy Leary down and hold him in prison until we can ship him back to the United States?

BRING US DR. LEARY

June 17–30, 1971

O n June 17, as Nixon and his secretary of state wait for a reply
from the Swiss, something else is raging inside the Oval Office.
The *New York Times* is publishing "the Pentagon Papers,"
a secret history of the Vietnam War, and with each revelation,
Nixon is growing increasingly obsessed with leaks inside his inner
circles.

He tells his aides that he's certain there is now a clearly coordinated effort to destroy his presidency. Nixon insists that the Democrats are hiding clandestine files, hoping to blackmail him. The
plots, their so-called evidence, must be stashed at the Brookings
Institution, a liberal think tank in Washington, DC.

Inside the Oval Office, Nixon begins yelling:

"Goddamn it, get in and get those files. I want it implemented
on a thievery basis... You're to break into the place—blow the safe
and get it."

❀   ❀   ❀

Tim picks up the phone in the chalet and Hauchard is on the other
end, talking in his rapid Parisian French, ordering Tim to come see
him immediately in Lausanne.

Tim drives the blue VW van the thirty-five miles to the city.
When he arrives at the penthouse, Hauchard steers him right away
to his oak-lined study.

Hauchard gets to the point.

*My high-ranking sources inside the Swiss government are telling me
that now that you have been exposed, Nixon is applying enormous pressure
to get you extradited.*

Hauchard points out that U.S. newspapers are already running stories claiming that the Swiss are about to brand Leary as an "undesirable foreigner" who has to leave the country.

Tim tries to fathom what it all means.

Hauchard goes on:

I can still keep you out of prison, maybe keep you permanently in the country, but it is going to cost a lot of money.

Slowly, Hauchard insists that many people will have to be paid. Expenses will mount. And then there will be unpredictable twists and turns that can be cured only with timely payments to even more people.

We can go belowdecks and bribe Swiss officials and even police officers to look the other way, to come up with imaginary reasons why fate and the Swiss laws are conspiring to allow you to remain untouched.

Hauchard is almost purring.

It won't be easy, but it is doable. Given your notoriety . . . it will just cost far more money than imaginable.

Tim soaks it in.

This is the payback moment. Hauchard runs deals, scams, and underground banking maneuvers. And now the gun-running Mephistopheles is armed with Montblanc fountain pens and paperwork that he is placing in front of Tim.

Hauchard produces a two-page document in French:

1) Mr. Leary cedes exclusively to Mr. Hauchard for the length of twenty (20) years all the rights of authorship for the entire world, without exception or reserve, including the United States, of his book actually entitled "It's About Time."

2) Mr. Leary gives to Mr. Hauchard for the duration of twenty (20) years . . . all the rights . . . for three (3) future books, two (2) in preparation, which Mr. Leary is engaged to remit to Mr. Hauchard before July 1, 1972.

3) Mr. Leary cedes to Mr. Hauchard . . . for the duration of twenty (20) years . . . all other books.

Tim looks through the papers. There are a few more items—ones that seem to give Hauchard the ability to control the *content* of the books—and clauses that outline the financial arrangements: Hauchard will get half the profits from the books and a "deduction...for expenses required for the personal needs of Mr. Leary."

Tim looks at Hauchard questioningly.

There really is no choice. It's like being in prison in California, where his lawyer told him, *Escape is your only choice...joining the revolutionaries is your only salvation.*

It's no different than the fait accompli the Weathermen had shoved in his face at his most vulnerable moment: *Write us a thank-you note that tells the world how grateful you are that we freed you from the clutches of Amerikan fascism.*

It is, in the end, no different than what Cleaver and the Black Panthers had threatened: *Turn over your money or be buried in Algiers.*

Tim reaches for the fountain pen and signs the contract.

❋ ❋ ❋

On June 28, on orders of the Nixon Administration and the United States secretary of state, the American Embassy submits the required formal request to Switzerland's Federal Department of Justice and Police. Citing the 1900 Treaty with Switzerland, the United States asks that the dangerous prison escapee Dr. Timothy Leary be arrested and extradited to face punishment in America.

❋ ❋ ❋

Fat clouds are rolling over Villars and a steady morning rain is splashing outside the cozy chalet. Little streams of water are beginning to slide down the forested hillside. It's June 30, the day Rosemary has been looking forward to ever since her surgery, a moment she's been anticipating, really, ever since she married Tim. She's completed twice-weekly fertility treatments at the clinic, and the doctors, carefully studying her cycle, have told her that today is the perfect day to conceive a child.

The astrological forecasts and tarot cards have been muted, with no clear signs, but she and Tim have resolved to make this a holy day. They are planning to burn incense and light candles, preparing the launching pad for the voyage of a new life into the cosmos.

Still in bed, waiting for Tim to wake up and make love to her, Rosemary hears some voices shouting outside in French. There are loud knocks at the front door.

The alarms are sounding inside her head: *There is, of course, dope in the chalet.*

She panics and then begins flitting around, knocking things over and wildly cramming the LSD and other drugs into a little metal box under the fireplace.

She tightens her robe, opens the door, and there is a burly uniformed cop and two more dressed for undercover work.

"Bring us Dr. Leary," they say.

She runs back up to the bedroom, fighting the fear. Tim dutifully reports to the front door.

"We are here to arrest you," they say.

The men talk to Tim in low tones. They spot some flowers that he and Rosemary have put in a vase: "It is illegal to pick those in Switzerland."

Tim retreats to the bedroom and tells Rosemary: "I'm under arrest. The Americans have filed extradition papers."

The three Swiss cops lead him into a small Volkswagen and roar away. Rosemary watches from the door. Whatever chance she and Tim had to make a baby together has cratered, maybe forever.

SOME KARMIC MISTAKE

July 1971

Tim is being led into Prison du Bois-Mermet in Lausanne, an ominous gray fortress built in 1905 and surrounded by a thick wall fifteen feet high and capped with razor wire. The cells are filled with the ghosts of desperate, doomed souls, including Jewish refugees housed here during World War II until they were expelled to face Nazi-occupied Europe.

Because the Americans have classified him as a dangerous criminal, the Swiss place Tim in solitary confinement. He's locked in a brick-walled cell with a metal toilet, washbasin, desk, and bed. Twelve feet up is a small window with metal bars.

Tim asks: *How long am I going to be inside?*

A guard freezes him with a look.

You're going to be locked up until the extradition papers are processed. Then you'll be shipped to America.

At the chalet in Villars, Rosemary places a desperate call to Mastronardi, the Swiss attorney.

He tells her he has been preparing for these high-level deals being cut between the Nixon White House and the Swiss government—and he has developed a plan: He is going to inform the Swiss justice ministry that Dr. Timothy Leary, a notable opponent to the United States' unpopular war in Vietnam, is seeking political asylum.

Secretary of State Rogers arrives at the White House and delivers Nixon the news firsthand.

Timothy Leary is in solitary confinement in Switzerland.

Now it is simply a matter of processing extradition papers—ones that will prove just how evil Leary is, how many laws he broke in the United States, what a threat he is to millions of people. Once the Swiss get the laundry list of Leary's crimes, they'll rush to expel him. California governor Ronald Reagan has already pledged his complete cooperation. Reagan has ordered his staff to send Leary's criminal files to Switzerland.

Nixon is very pleased.

It really is like putting Al Capone behind bars, like dragging the most dangerous man in America back to justice.

Rosemary is frantically writing a note to Allen Ginsberg, the bearded, goggle-eyed Beat poet. He and Tim share a deep connection, and Ginsberg has always felt indebted to Tim for guiding him to LSD. The two men are from the same generation, much older than many of the hippies, radicals, and freaks worshipping them.

> Allen: Tim in Swiss prison…locked in solitary as "most dangerous etc"…Some karmic mistake, having to repeat last year all over again. Handicapped by language difficulties and vast amount of money needed…What to do?

Inside Prison du Bois-Mermet, Tim is perched on the edge of his metal bed, wrapping himself in his wool blankets. His mind is wandering.

Is Hauchard a CIA agent? Did he set me up?

Tim gazes at the bars on the window, wondering if they can bear the weight of a man who ties some sheets to them. Suddenly, he hears the squeaking wheels of a cart and heavy footsteps in the corridor. Two guards and two trustees unlock the cell door and tote in cardboard boxes overflowing with delicacies: a half dozen cartons of Camembert, Gruyère, and Brie; roasted chicken; plump, fresh shrimp; lobster already extracted from the shell; Dijon mustard; a medley of Swiss chocolates; salamis, liverwurst, tins of Danish meat, apples, desserts, orange juice, crackers; a fresh carton of unfiltered Gitanes cigarettes; three bottles of French wine and a corkscrew. There is a typewriter. Packages of writing paper, carbon sheets, bundles of mailing envelopes.

"Merry Christmas!" shouts Tim.

The guards say: "This is just the beginning."

They tell him that everything is from Hauchard. The guards lock the cell door and retreat down the dank, damp hallway. Tim fires up a Gitanes and slides the corkscrew into one of the bottles of wine. He examines the label as he drains the bottle. He opens a second bottle and falls into a foggy stupor. One of the guards returns and gingerly opens the cell door. He removes the third bottle of wine and tells Tim that his ration is only one bottle per day.

Tim crashes asleep, realizing that Hauchard wants him well fed behind bars.

Maybe he arranged to have me locked up just so I could do nothing— but write something that will make him money.

Every morning for the rest of the week, Tim nibbles at the cheese and the crackers and pours himself another glass of wine. The typewriter remains untouched.

On Saturday, as he paces the cell, the tinny-sounding transistor radio in the prison is crackling with news: Jim Morrison, the lead singer of the Doors, has been found dead in a Paris apartment bathtub. Maybe a drug overdose. The radio reports are sandwiching in some of Morrison's songs. *"The future's uncertain and the end is always near."*

On July 4, back in Babylon, Allen Ginsberg has taken note of the calendar and is composing a "Declaration of Independence for Dr. Timothy Leary":

> Dr. Leary is, for a modern intellectual, a solitary splendid example of a Man Without a Country. Refused entry by most governments, he cannot visit other countries lest he be extradited to face the cruel and unusual punishment of now

more than 20 years jail if forcibly carried back to America's shores…Though arrested for grass, he was sentenced for Philosophy. Jailed for grass, he was long prisoned for Opinion. Denied bail for grass possession, he was detained behind barbed wire for Ideological Heresy.

Ginsberg gets the document signed by thirty-two prominent writers, including Anaïs Nin, Ken Kesey, and Norman Mailer. He sends it to the international literary organization PEN, which Ginsberg hopes can put pressure on the Swiss. Copies are sent to the Swiss Consulate and the U.S. State Department. The "declaration" is forwarded to the *New York Times*, *Newsweek*, *Time*, Agence France-Presse, the Associated Press, United Press International, and *Rolling Stone*. On Bastille Day, July 14, excerpts are printed in European papers.

Hundreds of people begin writing Swiss officials. Some stoned hippies in California demand a boycott of Swiss cheese. A rank-and-file member of the Brotherhood of Teamsters and Auto Truck Drivers in Oakland sends a letter on union letterhead that compares Tim to Jesus.

Mr. Leary was originally persecuted for his research of increased awareness through the use of substances foreign to the human body…Jesus, before becoming the Christ said, "…Cast not your pearls before swine, lest they trample them and turn to attack you."

In Copenhagen, where Tim was once expected to show up after he had fled Algeria, university students are mobilizing their own letter-writing campaign. They contrast Tim's intellectual explorations with the warmongering of the uptight American leaders.

"When is he likely to be delivered to Ronald Reagan?" one student asks anxiously.

Other people are stuffing cash into envelopes. Two soldiers from the Third Battalion, First Basic Combat Training Brigade each put in five dollars and send it to Rosemary, in care of Michael Kennedy's law office in San Francisco.

Kennedy still officially represents Tim in the United States, and he decides to dispatch his partner, Joseph Rhine, to Switzerland to see Leary. Rhine had visited Leary in the California prison the day before his escape. He was the one who copied down Tim's pro-revolutionary statement, and who gave him the details on where to rendezvous with the Weatherman getaway car. *God knows what Leary is telling people.*

❇ ❇ ❇

Tim is informed that he's finally being allowed to have a visitor, someone he can see, if only for a few minutes. He shuffles into the waiting room and is astonished to see Rhine. His U.S. lawyers have been impossible to reach for months, but one of them is here inside this gloomy Swiss prison.

As they sit, Rhine tells Tim he has given Rosemary the cash that people around the world have been sending for his defense. Then he adds something else.

Your home in Berkeley is in default. The house had been paid off, but Tim's children were left in charge. They'd collected rental monies but never made any of the property tax payments.

Fortunately, the lawyers have a solution.

Sign a power-of-attorney giving us the right to sell the home and to use the money to settle the bills you owe us—and we'll write you a big check for the difference.

Rhine produces a flurry of legal papers. Tim looks down at them.

Rhine can see Tim hesitating. He gently points out that no one knows when it will be safe for Tim to return to the United States—or if he'll ever live in that house again. And right now he could use the money from the sale.

Tim reaches for the papers, and for the second time since he has been in Switzerland, he signs away something he owns.

❇ ❇ ❇

In Zürich, several prominent Swiss artists and intellectuals are assembling a petition, arguing that Dr. Leary is an extraordinary philosopher who has helped the world better understand the writings of notable Swiss thinkers like Hermann Hesse, the visionary Swiss author of *Steppenwolf* and *Siddhartha*, and Carl Jung, the psychoanalyst, whom Leary had spent years studying.

In New York, the playwright Arthur Miller and the PEN American Center are also sending a letter to the head of the Swiss Federal Department of Justice and Police.

> No good purpose will be served by returning this writer/scientist to an American prison. He...qualifies as an intellectual refugee and we ask the Swiss government to grant him asylum as it has hundreds of other writers, artists and political figures who have sought refuge in Switzerland after having been forced to flee from other countries.

And at his bucolic home in the woods outside of Basel, Dr. Albert Hofmann, who took the life-changing ride on his bicycle while on a new drug called LSD, is reading a letter sent to him by one of Leary's most faithful supporters, a hippie archivist named Michael Horowitz. He is begging Hofmann to help Leary.

The aging chemist responds with his own letter:

> I've followed with deep concern the arrest of Dr. Leary in our country. Although I do not agree with all ideas of Dr. Leary, I am convinced that it was a pronounced injustice to sentence him with 20 years of prison for a minor offence.

In the upper echelons of Swiss government, there is a moment of reassessment. President Nixon seems intent on bombing Vietnam back into the Stone Age, and at the same time, his government is portraying Timothy Leary as a massively dangerous prison escapee with an extraordinarily dark criminal background in narcotics... but now high-ranking Swiss ministers are concluding that, in fact, Leary really *does* have an international intellectual reputation.

He's not Charlie Manson with a Harvard pedigree.

And now, into the summer, Swiss officials are deciding they

will not bend instantaneously to Nixon's White House. The Swiss will move at their own chosen speed, and Leary will be given time to pursue his request for asylum.

※　　※　　※

Tim receives a visit from Swiss officials who tell him that he might even be eligible for release on bail—but it won't be cheap: 75,000 francs—about $20,000 U.S. dollars—the highest bail ever set in Switzerland for an extradition case.

He'll need to raise a lot of money, and fast. Not just for the bail, but for the spiraling attorney's fees. He begins typing a letter to Hugh Hefner at the Playboy Mansion.

> Dear Hugh: This letter is written from a solitary confinement cell in which I have been practicing enforced meditation for one week. As you know, the U.S. is trying to extradite me back to prison.
>
> If returned to the U.S., I will spend the rest of my life in prison.

Tim studies what he has written. He pecks at the keys:

> Can you arrange to send $25,000 for my bail fund? A loan. I ask you as a colleague and friend...it is a good investment, Hugh.

※　　※　　※

After three weeks in prison, the guards tell Tim that his wife is finally being allowed to visit. The two will have only fifteen minutes together. In the small visiting center, Tim tries to explain what he's been doing inside his cell all alone—spending ten to twelve hours a day analyzing the numerical consistencies among the *I Ching*, the tarot, and the periodic table of elements. He looks haggard, like he had in his final days inside the California prison. Suddenly, he brightens and says that one of the guards brought in something special for him.

"A thick package, already opened. Removing the brown paper wrapping and cardboard cover I discovered an oval painting of a landscape."

Tim describes it for Rosemary in rapturous tones.

There is a Swiss lake, sturdy trees, and a blue sky. When I flipped the canvas over I saw that it was signed by Hermann Hesse.

❋   ❋   ❋

At the White House, Nixon fully expected Leary to be handed over immediately and flown back to the United States. But it's been nearly a month now and there's still no word on any extradition arrangements.

Secretary of State Rogers is informed that Leary's Swiss lawyer, Mastronardi, is "using every legal dodge available."

Worse, the Swiss are raising difficult-to-answer questions about Leary's long prison sentence in California for possessing a tiny bit of marijuana. Rogers studies reports saying that if Leary had been busted in Switzerland for the same amount of pot, he would never have set foot in jail—he would have only had to pay a small fine. The Americans are demanding the return of a man whose "crime" amounts to an unpaid traffic ticket in Switzerland.

When Rogers relays the news to the White House, Nixon is infuriated at the stonewalling. All week he has been planning to boost his approval ratings through his war on drugs.

He had even convened a strategy session inside the Cabinet Room—and his aides had urged him to single out Leary, to make him public enemy number one. Nixon and his aides had started chanting like football players getting psyched for the big game:

"*Leary, Leary, Leary . . . Timothy Leary, Timothy Leary!*"

A boisterous Nixon finally yelled out: "*We've got room in the prisons for him!*"

And now, his disappointing secretary of state has failed to crack the backs of the Swiss, failed to bring Leary back to the United States.

Nixon decides to play hardball: He summons his imperious attorney general, John Mitchell, and informs him that he is going on a secret mission to Switzerland to get Leary.

Maybe sending the highest-ranking U.S. law enforcement officer, the man who oversees the FBI, will scare the Swiss into forking over Leary.

The pipe-smoking, oval-faced Mitchell is Nixon's closest confidant. His apartment in the Watergate complex has a direct line to Nixon's desk inside the Oval Office. The president leans on him heavily, and will be counting on Mitchell to run his reelection campaign next year.

If anyone can get Leary, it will be the attorney general of the United States.

✺   ✺   ✺

In days, Mitchell is quietly making the rounds in Bern. His trip has been kept secret and so far reporters seem unaware he is even out of the country. Through the State Department and the White House, Mitchell sets up a series of meetings with high-ranking Swiss officials. At each meeting, after the formal handshakes and the toasts are made, Mitchell impresses on his hosts the idea that President Richard Nixon believes Timothy Leary is the most dangerous man in America.

Satisfied, Mitchell flies back to Washington two days later and the media still has no idea he ever left. On July 29, he reports to the Oval Office. Nixon and some key advisors are waiting.

A White House staffer is snapping pictures, and after the photographer finally leaves, Nixon utters one word at his attorney general: "Leary?"

Before Mitchell can speak, Nixon asks if there is any movement at all: "Get off the deck a little?"

Mitchell knows Nixon is brimming with anger about the way the heartland sees him as weak on drugs. And how Leary would be a prize catch. Mitchell hems and haws, bringing up "the pushback from Switzerland." That's not what Nixon wants to hear. Mitchell quickly adds that the visit to Bern was a success:

"We've got it pretty well set..."

THE POPE OF DOPE

August 1971

Tim is told he has another visitor and he is led from his cell. It's Mastronardi, the Swiss lawyer. He soberly tells Tim that Nixon's attorney general has been in the country, twisting arms and making threats. Mitchell has told the Swiss that if they release Leary on bail, he'll flee the country and remain a danger to children everywhere. Now some ministers are suggesting that Tim should remain behind bars until the extradition issue is resolved.

Tim blanches. No sunlight is reaching his cell, and he feels himself shrinking, growing older and weaker.

Not to worry, Mastronardi whispers. He quietly explains to Tim that he has a master plan to hasten Tim's release on bail—the same method he used to get Hauchard out of prison in France.

The next day, Tim walks to the exercise yard and mills around for a few minutes. Suddenly, he begins spiraling, collapsing to the ground and clutching his chest. He is writhing and gulping for air. The guards summon a prison doctor, who hurriedly examines him. The doctor hears Tim's weak voice mumbling in French:

I've had crushing chest pains for several days.

The guards transport Tim to the prison hospital. Nurses race to hook him to an electrocardiogram machine. The results are inconclusive, but eight other doctors, each sent by Mastronardi, begin arriving to also diagnose his condition. They all agree that Dr. Leary is in grave danger. Rosemary is telling reporters that her husband "has been feeling very sick."

Swiss officials decide that the profoundly ill prisoner can be freed, but that he will still have to pay the 75,000 francs for bail.

✸   ✸   ✸

Back at the chalet in Villars, there are allies moving in to help, especially Brian Barritt, a wild-eyed, scraggly-bearded mainstay inside the acid scene in Europe. A former British army infantryman who segued from being a 1950s beatnik artist into a full-blown LSD evangelist, Barritt is a seeker, a pusher, and on the fastest lanes on the hippie highways crisscrossing Europe and Asia—those paths that the restless freaks are following as they move to German communes, and then to hash dens in the souks of Morocco, and then to the Kathmandu Valley. He had sought Tim out in Algeria and the two sealed their bond with acid trips in the Sahara, convinced that they could communicate telepathically.

Rosemary is explaining to Barritt how Tim still needs money to get bailed out when there is a phone call and another familiar-sounding voice saying: "Renting a Hertz, see you soon."

An hour later, there is a knock at the door and two Brotherhood of Eternal Love freaks from California are on the steps, both traveling on forged passports. They are toting a briefcase crammed full of cash. Most of the money is on its way to help fund a hippie commune in South America, but they want to assist with Tim's bail and expenses.

Then one of the smugglers pours out some aromatic Panama Red hidden inside a cassette player. The other smuggler slips off his leather boots and pours out a mound of Afghani Gold Seal hash. One of them flicks his tongue for a second on what looks like a baby's pacifier dipped in the Brotherhood's Orange Sunshine.

As the drugs take hold, Rosemary has a moment of clarity: *The cops! They're probably watching the chalet at this very moment, through binoculars, telescopes, periscopes, hidden cameras, electronic listening devices.*

She asks Barritt to run and hide the money somewhere, and to not even tell her where, just in case the cops suddenly connect a million microdots. Just in case they arrest the drug dealers and then come back to take Rosemary away.

Barritt nods quickly.

Yes, of course, I understand. It's a sacred obligation.

He finds some stray plastic and seals fat wads of hundred-dollar bills inside, some $20,000 in all. He creeps into the darkness outside the chalet. He hopes he looks like a nature lover out for a late-evening stroll.

The Swiss woods are so incredibly beautiful at night, alive and pulsing with energy.

He threads his way through some trees toward a stream. It sparkles in the speckled dabs of moonlight floating through the trees. He spies a tumbled pine that has fallen across the water. Working furiously in the dark, he stoops nearby and digs a small hole. He stuffs thousands of dollars into the damp soil and throws dirt on top. He tamps down all signs of the hole, lopes along the creek for several yards, and then circles back to the chalet.

In the morning, the Brotherhood dealers are gone and the sunlight is streaming through the windows. Rosemary picks up the telephone and calls Mastronardi with the good news:

I have cash for Tim's bail.

He tells her that he will file the necessary paperwork and that she should bring him the money in two days.

The night before she goes to meet the lawyer, she asks Barritt to recover the money. He's tripping again, and when he steps outside, his mind fractures. Millions of tiny faces are studying him from between the blades of grass. The air is thick with magic. He remembers the trickling mountain stream, the capsized pine tree. He shuffles off in what he hopes is the right direction. He comes across a stream.

Yes, this must be the same one.

He looks for the fallen tree, only... *Which one?*

The entire creek is lined with crisscrossing patchworks of fallen timber. Barritt pauses and looks back in the direction of the chalet. He surveys the dark trees.

This is as good a place as any to start.

He kneels and begins digging frantically in the dirt.

The next morning the Swiss lawyer counts the cash. Oddly, some of it is dirty and a bit damp, but that's not a problem. Swiss banks know how to clean money.

At 4 p.m. on August 6, Tim walks out the front gates of Prison du Bois-Mermet as Rosemary, dressed in angelic white, rushes to greet him. He hugs her and looks at the cluster of reporters shouting questions. He is beaming. His eyes are bright, and he has grown a graying mustache that makes him seem, well, European. He suddenly appears to be the picture of perfect health.

"Rosemary and I came to Switzerland for many reasons," he announces. "We hope to live here under the great symbolic aura of Hermann Hesse and Carl Jung. We're time travelers and hope to stay because of a tradition of freedom."

Rosemary adds: "Perhaps we'll raise some children."

The Swiss newspapers run huge front-page headlines. In the beginning, the Swiss weren't quite sure how to translate Leary's American moniker, "the High Priest of LSD."

By now they've settled on "le Pape de la Drogue": *the Pope of Dope.*

Secretary of State Rogers demands answers from the United States Embassy in Bern. The chastened American ambassador reports back:

> SWISS HAVE BEEN UNCOMFORTABLE IN THIS CASE SINCE THEY HAD APPARENTLY NOT ANTICIPATED LOCAL AND INTERNATIONAL PRESS INTEREST WHICH LEARY'S ARREST OCCASIONED. MOST PROBABLY SWISS HOPE THAT LEARY'S RELEASE FOR MEDICAL REASONS WILL PLACE THEM IN GOOD LIGHT.

Rogers is livid and fires off a confidential cable:

> USG EXECUTIVE [PRESIDENT NIXON] UNIFORMLY OPPOSES RELEASE ON BAIL OF PERSONS WHOSE EXTRADITION HAS BEEN REQUESTED BY FOREIGN GOVERNMENT.

Tim is put under house arrest as part of his bail agreement. He also surrenders his fraudulent William McNellis passport, turning it over to Swiss authorities. He's ordered to stay close to the chalet.

Police expect him to report in three times a week. He can see his lawyers, but only if he tells the police where and when.

The day after he settles back into the chalet, Tim walks down the steep hill and into the town center. No one seems to notice him. He is bundled up against the wind as he sits at a café, orders a coffee, and lights a cigarette. He has agreed to meet a reporter from a Lausanne newspaper.

"If I go back to the United States, I'm a finished man," he tells the reporter as he blows a cloud of smoke into the air.

PHANTASMAGORIA

September 1–8, 1971

Tim steps outside the front door of his ski chalet. Like Martin Luther, he affixes a declaration to the door:

To: All visitors
Subject: Law and Order

 This house is maintained in a manner conforming to the laws of the Swiss Confederation. There is no illegal substance present.
 In visiting us, please abide by the law.
     Welcome and God bless you, Timothy Leary

Finished with his work, he steps back and admires the message. This should keep away some of the goons, the drooling freaks, the stoned imbeciles who keep seeking him out, wanting to get high with him, offering him dope, offering their girlfriends or themselves, hoping he will lay some knowledge on them like he's the twinkling mystic swami machine that you can put quarters into on the carnival midway.

At the least, the short and tight message should placate the cops keeping an eye on him.

   ✺   ✺   ✺

On September 3, he dresses carefully in some nondescript clothes. He is never supposed to leave Villars, but Hauchard has arranged something very special for him. Tim pulls away in his blue Volkswagen, checking the rearview mirrors. He guides the van down the hill and out of the village, gunning the engine for Lausanne.

At a coffee stand at the bustling train station, Tim greets Dr. Albert Hofmann. The mild-mannered, sixty-five-year-old retired chemist and the fifty-year-old fugitive size each other up. Hofmann is wearing a dark suit and exudes a quiet, dignified intelligence. Tim is in his muted turtleneck, feeling springy and alive with nervous energy.

They climb into the Volkswagen and Tim drives them alongside Lake Geneva. Tim is laughing and trying to draw Hofmann out as they travel. They arrive at a country restaurant and sit under a gazebo. They order fresh perch and a bottle of white wine. Hofmann remembers how Leary ordered LSD from Switzerland in the early 1960s, when the drug was still legal. The amount Leary had requested, 100 grams, was huge—enough for one million doses—and Leary had never secured the proper paperwork. Ever since, Hofmann had been wary.

Now he is telling Leary: "LSD is too powerful for young people, including teenagers . . . you should not tell everybody, even the children, 'Take LSD! Take LSD!'"

Tim looks at the one man who found the key.

How can I tell him that dosing the young is the only hope to bring about real cosmic consciousness?

Tim concedes that he was wrong to publicize LSD's benefits so much: *But I had no real control, not as much as people give me credit for, especially over young people.*

Hofmann is quiet as Tim adds: *Things are different in the United States. Maybe it was a mistake to promote LSD. But it was inevitable that somebody would have spread the word.*

They finish the bottle of wine, climb back into the VW van, and begin the short trip back to Lausanne. They park the car and walk side by side to Hauchard's penthouse, where they have been invited to have drinks. When they step off the private elevator, Rosemary is there. So is Brian Barritt, the caffeinated hippie scenester.

They linger for a few hours, talking, debating; and then, as twilight descends, Hofmann and Tim stroll along Lake Geneva. They stop at a café for dinner. As they finish eating, they are joined by Tim's Swiss attorney, the elegant Mastronardi.

The lawyer tells them: *Your meeting must remain secret. Leary's asylum request will be shot down if Swiss officials learn he is consulting with the father of LSD.*

After they say their good-byes, Tim slips back into Villars and secretly returns to his chalet. Hofmann goes to his home in that small village outside Basel. Before he goes to bed, he thinks about his meeting with Tim. Hofmann reaches for a pen. He writes in his diary:

He is imbued with a faith in the miraculous effects of psychedelics and extreme optimism leads him to underestimate or even overlook undesirable facts and dangers.

❈   ❈   ❈

Emboldened by how easy it is to slip past the cops and see the very man who discovered LSD, Tim takes Rosemary to Zürich to hang out at Café Odeon, where Albert Einstein, James Joyce, Benito Mussolini, and Leon Trotsky had spent time.

He wanders to the C. G. Jung Institute, housed in a two-story residence on the shores of Lake Zürich. He still sees himself in Jung—someone who had traveled a long way to study the *I Ching*, *The Tibetan Book of the Dead*, Eastern religions, and mysteries. Tim had once helped write a tribute to Jung and his thoughts:

"The phantasmagoria of a lunatic . . . the end of all conscious, rational, morally responsible conduct of life."

AT LEAST HE'S OUR HITLER

September 1971

In the Oval Office, Richard Nixon is bristling and his aides are tiptoeing around him. He has created an "Enemies List," which includes journalists, Democratic congressmen, and celebrities. The original list of twenty is quickly expanded to include more than two hundred names. Nixon gathers his aides and lays out a plot to use the full force of the United States government to harass each of his antagonists, to fuck them really hard: *IRS audits, FBI investigations, smears, litigation, and criminal charges.* All of them will come tumbling down: Senator Ted Kennedy; singer Barbra Streisand; Joe Namath, the charismatic quarterback for the Super Bowl champion New York Jets; eighty-three-year-old painter Georgia O'Keeffe; actor Paul Newman. The list goes on and on.

Nixon is still fuming over the leak that led to the publication of the Pentagon Papers. He has also established a secret White House investigative team, called the Plumbers, to stop all unauthorized leaks—and to harass the president's political enemies. One of the chief Plumbers is the most fervently obsessed of Leary's pursuers: ex-FBI agent G. Gordon Liddy, who had carried out the earliest drug raids against Leary at the Millbrook mansion in New York.

Liddy is still a manically dedicated man, consumed by a need to continually prove his toughness. As a boy, he conquered his fear of lightning by climbing into a tree during a violent thunderstorm and lashing himself to a high branch. He overcame his phobia of rats by cooking and eating one. When his father banned him from owning a gun, he made his own out of spare parts. He deliberately got a job butchering chickens—in order to learn to kill without emotion. Now, at age forty, Liddy's favorite party trick is to hold a cigarette lighter under his hand, letting the flame get closer until his flesh starts to sizzle and burn and his intense eyes take on an unholy gleam. Liddy's busts of Timothy Leary had brought him to the attention of the Nixon White House, where he was originally hired as an anti-drug warrior. At presidential dinners, Liddy relishes telling the stories of his personal confrontations with the High Priest of LSD:

During one bust, Leary complained to Liddy: "This raid is the product of ignorance and fear."

"This raid," Liddy replied, "is the product of a search warrant issued by the State of New York."

Leary jabbered back to Liddy about how one day society would be grateful for his work: "The time will come when there will be a statue of me."

Liddy responded: "I'm afraid the closest you'll come is a burning effigy in the village square."

Now that Liddy is deep inside the Nixon Administration's domestic affairs task force, he is viewed as an enormously potent counterintelligence specialist despite his reputation as a loose cannon. He's fascinated by Nazi pageantry and has gotten in trouble for making unauthorized pro-gun speeches. At staff meetings he volunteers to assassinate the president's enemies, boasting that he can kill a man instantly by jamming a sharpened No. 2 pencil into his neck.

One Nixon aide cracks to the others, "Liddy's a Hitler, but at least he's our Hitler."

Liddy and the other White House Plumbers are working out of the basement offices in the Old Executive Office Building. They've set up wiretaps on reporters and several White House staffers. Nixon's staff orders Liddy to smear Daniel Ellsberg, the man who leaked the Pentagon Papers to the press. One idea is to dose Ellsberg with LSD in advance of a widely publicized speech. That plan falls through, but Liddy and his handpicked operatives are given another assignment: They are told to burglarize the office of Ellsberg's psychiatrist, looking for damning information.

Over the Labor Day weekend, Liddy flies to Beverly Hills with an elite team of operatives, veterans of the botched Bay of Pigs invasion. The men are told only that they are targeting a "traitor" to the United States. They dress in fake wigs, beards, and glasses and speak through voice-altering devices. They understand that if the police apprehend them, they are to claim they are addicts looking for drugs. Liddy directs the men to enter through a window and he keeps watch while they rifle through the office.

The results prove to be negligible, but the ease of the burglary is deemed a huge success—and now the Nixon White House knows it has a cunning team of covert operatives trained to break into enemy offices.

THEY SAY IT'S YOUR BIRTHDAY

October 1971

Tim and Rosemary are arguing as they slip out of Villars and drive to Geneva to pick up Michael and Eleanora Kennedy at the airport. Rosemary had bonded deeply with the Kennedys back in California while Tim was in prison.

Tim argues that Kennedy is the one who sent them into the quicksand of Algeria. He's the one who probably helped squash Tim's manuscript, since it didn't crackle with his radically chic politics. Kennedy has to be skimming donations people are sending to Tim in care of the law office. And now Kennedy is selling Tim's only asset, his home in Berkeley.

"I knew they were going to rip us off," Tim tells Rosemary.

"You're paranoid," Rosemary replies. "He put his life on the line for you. He risked his whole reputation. Let him have the house."

He stabs back: "Yeah, yeah, you're right. I'm just a bad-tempered person who's not grateful to his friends."

The Kennedys are all smiles, bearing perfumes for Rosemary and bottles of booze for Tim. They head to dinner and the visitors are bursting with uptight news from Babylon.

Things have gotten weird and intense in San Francisco since Tim's escape. Everyone is being followed by the FBI. Phones are clearly tapped.

Tim listens as Kennedy says they might move out of the country and become exiles, too, maybe living in London until things cool off.

Rosemary nods and coos sympathetically as Kennedy talks, but Tim is bitter about so many things. *Why did you send me to Algeria? Why did you let me stay there for seven months as Cleaver's prisoner? Why didn't you come get me?*

Kennedy says everyone admired Tim's tightrope act in Algeria, how he'd navigated a crazed situation and found a way to liberate himself.

Tim is angry. "Eldridge Cleaver is nothing more than a petty tyrant," he says. He's trying to "seize control of the militant revolution."

Cleaver's trip is "the politics of despair."

✸   ✸   ✸

After seeing the Kennedys off at the airport, Rosemary and Tim consult their horoscopes for the month ahead.

Rosemary has still been unable to conceive a child with Tim. Her eyes widen in recognition as she reads her forecast: "If your partner seems to be intent on indulging his or her streak of egotism at your expense this month, do not waste time in self-pity."

Tim's outlook is equally worrisome: "Those close to you are getting tired of your promises, promises...the last embers of an emotional involvement are cooling fast."

More visitors arrive, led by Dennis Martino, the short, curly-haired hustler who had managed to smuggle twenty thousand hits of LSD to Tim in Algeria. With a wispy goatee and a leather motorcycle jacket, he is as jangly as ever. He has brought his heavily pregnant girlfriend, a teenager with a hollow face and big liquid eyes. Martino has ties to the Brotherhood of Eternal Love and his brother is married to Tim's daughter. Martino still thinks Leary is a holy man, but he makes others nervous. Tim is tolerant and has anointed him "the sorcerer's apprentice." Martino is also a wanted fugitive: After being convicted on drug charges, he skipped out, traveling with a false passport supplied by the Brotherhood.

They have another visitor with them, someone Rosemary asked Martino to bring along. He is a tall, handsome, strong-looking man with flowing black hair, one of the original cofounders of Tim's League for Spiritual Discovery—the early attempt to treat LSD as a sacrament. John Schewel has been close to Tim and Rosemary for years, and then he became even closer to Rosemary while Tim was in jail in San Luis Obispo.

Younger than Rosemary and about half Tim's age, he also has ties to the Brotherhood—and a seemingly steady supply of money. Rosemary leaned on him in the weeks and months before the breakout. He ferried her around, ran errands, and eventually slept with her.

The visitors have a stash of treasure: a trunk full of furs, coats, clothes, beadwork, jewelry, shawls. Batches of Rosemary's favorite makeup from Kiehl's. More hashish, more LSD, and the intense, fast-acting psychedelic DMT. A bundle of money—$5,500.

The three visitors crash on a waterbed plopped onto the floor. The "No Drugs" sign that Tim put on the front door is still out there.

❀ ❀ ❀

Tim's fifty-first birthday is coming in a week. Whenever the day nears, he finds it hard to forget the fact that his first wife committed suicide on his birthday sixteen years ago.

A few days before the party, he tells Rosemary he wants to see a doctor about his hearing. Now that they have some extra money he can have a minor ear operation that might boost his flagging ability to understand what people are saying. Martino drives him to the clinic, and later to the hospital. While they're gone, Rosemary and John Schewel retreat to the bedroom and make love. Last summer their time together had been a diversion. Now it's beginning to feel like something deeper.

When Tim returns from the hospital, he strips down and slumps onto a couch. He is naked except for a fur-lined leather coat. Rosemary and John come into the room. Tim watches Rosemary as she begins crying:

"You never looked better," she says.

She adds: "I won't be here for your birthday."

Tim gazes at her and then at her lover. "It's happened before."

She replies: "You're sending me off, you know. It's your decision."

Tim replies: "I'm doing nothing."

She looks back and says: "Exactly."

❀ ❀ ❀

As soon as she leaves with her lover, Tim can feel the loneliness wrapping around his head.

For two straight days he drops acid and feels the sonic whip from the DMT as he goes stumbling through the chalet, chanting, pumping up the stereo, and trying to hold it together while the hallucinations come in roaring waves. Two days before his birthday, Rosemary is in contact to tell him she and her lover are moving into a nearby farmhouse. As he absorbs the news, Tim is slumped on his bed—with Dennis Martino and his pregnant girlfriend, all of them surrounded by clumsily separated portions of acid, hash, DMT, and dollar bills.

Pushing himself off the bed, Tim gets dressed and goes for a morning walk down the steep hill and into the village.

Anything to get away.

As he gets closer to his favorite café, there is a stoner up ahead, a hippie he has gotten to know in town, walking with an oddly behaving teenage girl. She's younger than Tim's daughter, and when Tim stops to talk with them, she is clearly, quickly flirting:

I'm high, right now, on mescaline . . . I really want to go see what's happening in Amsterdam . . . but now that we've met, I'd really like to go home with you and cook you a meal.

Tim invites her back to the chalet and she wobbles into the kitchen, trying to make something at the stove, but she's so high she is setting the pans on fire and shouting and flapping her arms. She and Tim fall into the drug-stuffed bedroom and collapse on the waterbed.

There's no time for Tantric sex.

No time for the hundreds of orgasms Tim says a woman can have on psychedelics.

A VICTORY FOR LOVE

November–December 1971

everal days later, Rosemary is pushing open the door to the chalet, ready to talk about the marriage, to see if they can figure out a way to make it work again.

As she walks in, shaking off the rain and cold, she sees the teenage mescaline chick in the front room. Rosemary's jaw drops.

She's wearing my clothes.

The girl offers a sweet smile and gently pats her tummy the way some women do when they are pregnant. She has already moved into the bedroom and is using Rosemary's makeup, her kohl eyeliner, and the good perfumes Rosemary brought back from North Africa.

Rosemary looks for the rest of her clothes.

They're all gone.

Tim has already given most of them away—except for what the mescaline chick would like to keep.

Tim walks into the room, but before he can say anything, Rosemary turns and storms out.

In the morning, Tim makes the slog to the post office to collect the mail—pausing to laugh at the anti-drug sign still posted on his door.

At the postal station, there is a large manila envelope from the United States, sent from 105 Bank Street in Greenwich Village. It is from John and Yoko. They have been closely following Tim's asylum request. Lennon can sympathize. The Nixon White House has been trying to deport him to England and the FBI is spying on him relentlessly, hoping to bust him for "undesirable alien" activity. Lennon has been faithfully supporting Tim ever since his prison escape. Today's letter from the former Beatle arrives with a check for $5,000.

There is also correspondence from the law firm of Kennedy & Rhine in San Francisco.

Your house in Berkeley has sold.

There is a check inside. His share, after deductions for legal fees, amounts to just $4,000.

❉   ❉   ❉

Winter mountain winds are rocking the roof of the chalet, and sheets of snow come slapping down, falling past the windows and hitting the cobblestone streets. From the window Tim watches the ski lifts carrying the jet-setters and celebrities up the mountain. In the distance, he can hear the shooshing sound of skiers racing down the hills, their shadows chasing them on the moonlit sparkle of snow—all under the brooding glare of a series of craggy peaks known as "the home of the devil."

Tim steps back from the window. In the room, there is a bottle of speed and an autographed photo that William S. Burroughs had just dropped off during a short visit. Tim paces the chalet, ignoring the phone calls from Hauchard and thinking of people he can hit up for loans, for help. The Stones have been taking breaks in Villars after being locked in a heroin-and-blues swirl in southern France, recording their sluggishly brilliant *Exile on Main St.* Stones guitarist Keith Richards likes Tim's charming little Swiss village so much that he is talking about moving there.

Sitting by the fire, staring outside, Tim wonders why the fuck Richards is not calling him back. He had gotten his phone number in Villars and Tim has been calling him every day, nonstop.

❉   ❉   ❉

Four days after Christmas, a message is delivered to President Nixon at the White House:

THE SOVEREIGN NATION OF SWITZERLAND HAS OFFICIALLY REFUSED TO TURN OVER DR. TIMOTHY LEARY.

The Swiss stiffly point out that in their country, Leary's marijuana offense would never have resulted in the same severe punishment imposed on him in Ronald Reagan's California:

THE CONDITIONS OF THE 1900 EXTRADITION TREATY BETWEEN
THE UNITED STATES AND SWITZERLAND HAVE NOT BEEN MET.

Despite the visit from Attorney General John Mitchell and the Nixon Administration's bullying, every Swiss law professor and judge who was consulted about Timothy Leary is in agreement.

The decision is unanimous.

Photocopies of the Swiss newspaper articles announcing the decision are being distributed through the State Department, the White House, and the U.S. embassy. There are big photos of fugitive Timothy Leary in front of a mob of reporters in a quaint Swiss village. He's gleaming, wearing a white wool sweater.

"The Swiss people have all been very good to me," he is saying. "I want to thank the government of Switzerland for protection of human rights...This was a victory for love."

I OWN TIMOTHY LEARY

January 1972

Knowing it is what Richard Nixon wants, G. Gordon Liddy is busy harassing one of Nixon's chief enemies, the muckraking columnist Jack Anderson. The journalist's phones have been tapped and he is being secretly followed. Liddy is now assigned to "CREEP"—the Committee to Re-Elect the President—and along with his partner, E. Howard Hunt, he has suggested another way to target Anderson: dosing the straitlaced, nondrinking columnist's steering wheel with LSD. At the very least, Anderson will go temporarily insane and make a fool of himself. Maybe he will lose control of his car and crash.

Before Liddy can carry out the plan, Nixon's White House counselor tells him to hold off. There's a bigger project in the works: Attorney General John Mitchell has ordered Liddy to come up with a plan to punish and destroy the Democrats.

On January 27, Liddy reports to the attorney general's office in the Department of Justice. He proudly unveils "Operation Gemstone" and asks for a million dollars to charter a yacht during the upcoming Democratic National Convention in Miami. Nixon's enemies will be lured aboard and put in compromising positions with "the finest call girls in the country...not dumb broads but girls who can be trained and photographed." Liddy says there should be an additional plot to kidnap radicals around the country, drug them until they're senseless, and then stash them in Mexico.

The attorney general, puffing on his pipe, frowns and says: "Gordon, that's not quite what I had in mind."

But Mitchell brightens when he hears about one other option: bugging the Watergate offices of Nixon's Democratic enemies.

❋   ❋   ❋

Tim puts on his winter coat and walks back to the post office, his breath forming billowy puffs in the frigid air. Stomping his boots to shake off the snow, he sorts through the mail and sees a postcard with a sketch of a beautiful, tree-laden stretch of the Swiss countryside. It is from Albert Hofmann, who has been following the news that Leary will be staying in Switzerland. He would very much like to see Tim again.

But not everyone in Switzerland is pleased that Tim is allowed to be free, and Nixon's government is not giving up the fight. Secretary of State Rogers is demanding that the Swiss confiscate Leary's U.S. passport. Attorney General Mitchell is using his law enforcement contacts to apply pressure at the local level.

Complaints are being lodged against Tim; angry letters are being sent to local officials in Villars-sur-Ollon. The police are expressing concern about the hedonists and day-trippers rolling into town to see Leary. After he picks up his mail, Tim steps inside the local municipal offices for his weekly check-in with the police. As always, he is prepared to lie through his teeth and swear that there are no drugs being consumed at the chalet—and that he has not traveled anywhere away from the village.

Tim is stunned as the local officials make an announcement: *You're being ordered to leave Villars in the next few days.*

❋   ❋   ❋

State Department officials are closely monitoring the moves and they alert the press: SWISS CANTON SAYS LEARY MUST LEAVE reports the *New York Times*. The *Washington Post* headline reads: LEARY EXPELLED.

The papers indicate the end is near for Leary: "Expulsion from one canton usually means expulsion from Switzerland."

In Bern, the United States Embassy sends a brisk forecast back to Washington.

FEDERAL ALIEN POLICE MAINTAIN IT ONLY A MATTER OF TIME BEFORE LEARY MUST LEAVE SWITZERLAND.

Tim is still doing his uneasy dance with Michel Hauchard, charming the guests at Hauchard's penthouse parties, talking up the book he is supposedly working on. Now Hauchard is telling him to quietly skip out of Villars and aim for ultra-chic Gstaad, where Hauchard owns a chalet and will let him stay. If Leary plays it carefully, no one will know that he's slipped from town. Hauchard has fixers and handlers, people on the payroll, in Gstaad. They'll keep Leary hidden.

Tim throws his cashmere sweaters and extra winter socks into a bag. He counts out the cash left over from John Lennon. He sifts through the remaining drugs—the hash, DMT, and acid—that Barritt and Martino and the mescaline chick haven't devoured. Peeking out the window, making sure the cops aren't following him, he sprints to the Volkswagen van, tosses his duffel inside, and quickly winds his way down the hill to the highway.

❋   ❋   ❋

The U.S. embassy's secure telegraph machine is running nonstop with demands from the White House and State Department: *What's Leary's status? When is he being booted out of Villars? Where is he going?*

Field agents are glumly filing replies: Leary has slipped out of Villars. None of the usual sources have any idea where he's gone, but everyone worries that he may have fled the country.

The embassy sends an urgent message back to Washington:

We heard a rumor that Leary had left Switzerland and departed for Scandinavia.

❋   ❋   ❋

Speeding the twisting highway to Gstaad, Tim keeps checking the side mirrors. Dark Mercedes-Benzes zoom alongside him, the draft making the Volkswagen sway. He's half expecting a roadblock, or for one of the cars to cut him off. FBI agents coming out of the dark, guns drawn.

Tim hunkers into the driver's seat, trying to look like an old-timer on a holiday in the Alps, a weathered man chasing one ski slope after another.

It's just like escaping into Northern California, then Oregon, then Washington, pretending to be a rocking-chair angler instead of a wanted fugitive.

He finds the chalet, just as Hauchard had promised, and drops his bag on the bed and tries to decompress. Within moments, there is a knock at the door. It is one of Hauchard's employees, delivering food and wine. The man also brings in an electric typewriter and plugs it in. He carefully arranges a stack of blank paper next to it and bows toward Tim.

By now, Tim knows that Hauchard has been telling people:

"I own Timothy Leary."

THE WORLD CHANGED FOREVER

February 1972

Tim contacts Michael Horowitz, the faithful, learned hippie archivist who has been trying to preserve his papers, letters, and writings back in California. Horowitz had visited Tim in prison in the California Men's Colony, hoping to share some acid with his hero—but the tab he was planning to give to Tim had fallen from his fingernail to the visiting room floor.

Tim tells him to fly as soon as possible to Switzerland, to bring money, and to be ready to document another summit meeting between the two most important figures in the history of LSD.

On February 24, Tim and Horowitz drive the A6 motorway two and a half hours north to Basel. When they arrive at the winter Fasnacht carnival, some revelers are hoisting a psychedelic LSD float and parading through the streets.

It is a brisk afternoon and Dr. Albert Hofmann appears dressed in a dark suit. Leary is in a bomber jacket and white sneakers. They greet each other like old friends and then Hofmann steers his Toyota down the same road where he had once pedaled his bicycle after ingesting that first deliberate dose of pure LSD.

Hofmann is again scolding Tim: *LSD should be used only by older, mature people with stable personalities.*

Leary insists it is far too late to put the genie back in the bottle.

Things grow quiet in the car as they follow the winding path to Hofmann's old house, the place where he crawled to bed in an LSD panic, convinced he was going insane. It is a comfortable, sprawling home high on a hill. Seeing it brings a flood of memories back to Hofmann, all centered on that fateful day he did LSD in 1943:

"My wife and children were away. It was just me, and I barely managed to crawl to bed."

Tim listens and says, "It was the first bad trip. There was no precedent. You must have felt that you poisoned yourself."

Hofmann answers, "Yes, but in the end it was good. In the morning, it was fantastic."

Tim nods. "For me, the world changed forever."

The men drive on.

"I would have remained a boring professional psychologist the rest of my life, making money and accomplishing nothing," offers Tim.

"Instead of the most dangerous man in the world," Michael Horowitz chimes in from the backseat.

ALWAYS ERR IN EXCESS

March–May 1972

Tim picks up the phone and feels the dread wash over him as he hears Hauchard's ominous whisper: "It's getting too hot. You'll have to move again."

Tim repacks his bags and races to a small thirteenth-century hamlet outside of Zürich. Legend has it that William Tell had been here, and there are extraordinary views to the Alps and the shimmering Lake Zug. Tim pushes open the door to a two-story chalet that is only fifteen feet from the water. The place is decorated like a ship. He steps onto the balcony and watches the fog lifting and the fish rising for the mayflies.

Hauchard calls and asks if he can see the manuscript for Tim's book.

Tim says that he's nearly finished, but that he needs assistance to wrap things up. He asks Hauchard to buy an airline ticket for the hippie showman Brian Barritt, the acid freak who'd buried and then nearly lost $20,000 of Tim's money. Barritt is now living in London, but Tim is certain he'll come help.

Hauchard agrees, but pointedly adds that it's getting harder and harder to protect him in Switzerland. Hauchard says he's found publishers who are interested in the book and he's certain they'll pay big money.

Finish the book and you'll be able to convince the Swiss to keep you out of prison and in the country forever.

Finish the book and we'll both make money.

A few days later, Tim opens the door and Barritt is standing on the steps, dressed in a bright orange suit. Tim knows Barritt is a risk, a temptation; he is into heroin, a drug Tim has always resisted.

Tim offers him Afghani hash and some lines of coke and then they go for a giggling walk. They decide to pick up spray paint so they can work on some kind of trippy art project. Barritt picks up six cans, but Tim bellows at him that it's not enough:

"Always err in excess!" he shouts.

✺　　✺　　✺

In Washington, Nixon's handpicked National Commission on Marihuana and Drug Abuse calls a press conference to announce its startling recommendations. The august group is led by a Republican governor. Its members include a Republican senator and a Republican congressman as well as prominent academics and law enforcement officials. They've spent a year researching pot, and some of the members have even toked up themselves.

Now, the chairman is announcing that Nixon's war on drugs should make a separate peace with marijuana. *"We feel that . . . citizens should not be criminalized or jailed merely for private possession or use."*

Nixon is furious. He's been double-crossed by people he should have been able to trust. *Where will it end? If marijuana is decriminalized, what does that mean for the hunt for Timothy Leary?*

Nixon, his face taut and his eyes flashing with anger, goes before White House reporters and assails his own commission: "I oppose the legalization of marijuana and that includes its sale, its possession, and its use."

Secretary of State Rogers sends a cable to the American operatives in Bern, demanding that they keep leaning on the Swiss to banish Leary, no matter what the hell happens with pot laws in the United States.

As Rogers sends his directive, American agents have finally tracked Tim down to his lakeside chalet—and quickly, the Nixon White House decides on a new strategy, based on their success in getting Leary kicked out of Villars. Maybe they can pressure local authorities, urging every single Swiss canton, one by one, to ban Leary if he tries to settle in. It will be a coordinated campaign, working directly with individual police jurisdictions. Leary is a prison escapee wanted for dozens of crimes—a malevolent, debauched criminal who will terrorize each quiet, tidy Swiss village. Town by town, Leary will be squeezed out of the country.

The plan is ramped up and executed. One after another, Swiss cantons are issuing edicts to keep Leary from becoming a resident. Tim is ordered to leave his lakeside chalet, and he's quickly running out of options.

On Wednesday, May 3, the U.S. ambassador sends a triumphant message that Secretary of State Rogers can pass on to the White House:

FEDERAL ALIEN POLICE NOW PLAN [TO] INFORM LEARY DIRECTLY
THIS WEEK THAT HE HAS ONE MONTH TO DEPART SWITZERLAND.

✹   ✹   ✹

Some of Tim's tripped-out aristocratic friends, relatives of Hermann Hesse, offer him a place in Lugano, a refuge near the Italian border. He packs again and barrels down the highway connections, winding his way to a fifteenth-century mountaintop castle once owned by a cardinal. The fortress has thick stone walls with views of rolling vineyards.

Barritt is with him and they retreat inside, trying to work on Tim's opus. Tim says he wants to call it *Confessions of a Hope Fiend*, a nod to the deviant English sorcerer-explorer Aleister Crowley's written "confessions" about dabbling in drugs. Tim feels a connection to Crowley and it seems only right to offer a tribute.

Crowley scandalized Victorian society with his lurid adventures in the dark arts. He was denounced as "the wickedest man in the world," and the Beatles put him on the cover of *Sgt. Pepper's Lonely Hearts Club Band*. Led Zeppelin's Jimmy Page decided to buy Crowley's freaky Loch Ness estate, the scene of ritualistic debaucheries and various attempts to reach the lords of the underworld. Decades ago, Crowley had been to Algeria for kinky séances and mescaline-hash desert dances in the same dunes where Tim and Rosemary had taken acid.

By Tim's count, this will be the seventeenth version of the manuscript he began in Algeria. The book has changed, dramatically, each time. The stories are bending, growing, shrinking over and over again. The reinvention is by design. His writing philosophy is inside his new favorite phrase:

"You can be anyone this time around."

※ ※ ※

Tim's retreat in Lugano is quickly overrun by visitors: old friends, Swiss hippies, underground journalists and filmmakers, American jazzmen and German rock musicians. Many visitors arrive bearing pot, hash, acid, coke, peyote, and DMT. Someone bakes one hundred hash cookies. Thin French socialites are showing up, lolling around half-naked. Incense is burning as strangers pad through the kitchen, looking for Leary, offering him drinks with melting tabs of acid. There is talk about telepathic wave sculptures, astral travel, things that are infinitely luxuriant to the touch, egos dissolving, and the thin, steely constraints of the world being melted in a perpetual orgasm.

Dennis Martino, the twitchy drug runner with the connections to the Brotherhood of Eternal Love, is also back from a trip to Afghanistan. When Tim asks him about Rosemary, Martino says she is now living in Afghanistan with her lover, John Schewel. There was a big bust in Kabul led by some macho drug agent, and things got very tense, with undercover narcs circling around. The Brotherhood moved to Kandahar, where they have more freedom to operate. Rosemary is there with Schewel, and wearing a burka to avoid drawing too much attention—the garment is perfect for hiding drugs.

Martino has brought something special from Afghanistan: a bottle of pure hash oil, one of the higher-end products that the Brotherhood offers to its most favored customers. Tim dips a toothpick into the bottle, licks the tip, and melts into a blissful high for the rest of the day.

※ ※ ※

Inside the Swiss government, resentment is building over the Nixon Administration's heavy-handed meddling in the Leary case. Horace Mastronardi informs Tim that he will not be expelled, that he will be allowed to stay indefinitely.

The Americans are beyond frustrated. They nearly had Leary in their grasp, and now the Swiss are claiming that he poses no danger. Surely there must be some way to convince the Swiss, to convince the rest of the world, that Dr. Timothy Leary is no ordinary criminal; that he really is, in fact, one of the most dangerous men alive.

✹ ✹ ✹

Back in the United States, the presidential campaign is reaching full boil and Nixon's extralegal dirty-tricks team is in high gear. G. Gordon Liddy and his operatives are using the playbook from the FBI's COINTELPRO operation: wiretaps, surveillance, forged letters, planted stories, informants, double agents, professional provocateurs, and smears. Nixon's team has successfully sabotaged the moderate Democratic frontrunner, Edmund Muskie. Now the likely nominee appears to be George McGovern, a pacifist senator from South Dakota. CREEP is salivating at the prospect of running against the unabashed leftist. They will portray McGovern as the candidate of "Acid, Amnesty, and Abortion."

On May 15, another Nixon opponent, segregationist Alabama governor George Wallace, is shot while campaigning in Maryland. As the wounded Wallace fights for his life in the hospital, Nixon meets with his senior aides in the Oval Office. Wallace's exit from the race clearly benefits Nixon, and the president is worried that the would-be assassin might have ties to the Republican Party.

Nixon tells his men: "Put it on the left right away...It must get out fast before they pin this on the right wing...Just say he was a supporter of McGovern and Kennedy. Now just put that out. Just say you have it on 'unmistakable evidence.'"

Nixon knows that the FBI will be searching the suspect's apartment. He asks: "Wouldn't it be great if they found left-wing propaganda in that apartment?" He adds, pointedly, "Too bad we couldn't get somebody there to plant it."

An aide immediately phones G. Gordon Liddy's partner at CREEP, ex–CIA agent E. Howard Hunt, and tells him to break into the suspect's apartment and bait it with Democratic materials.

Meanwhile, Liddy is busy with his own assignments. He's been casing George McGovern's campaign headquarters inside the Watergate complex, hoping to bug it. But the lock is too difficult for his Cuban burglars. Another target inside the Watergate proves to be easier to penetrate: the office of Democratic National Committee chairman Lawrence O'Brien. Near midnight on Sunday, May 28, Liddy's men slip inside the Democratic leader's office, photograph the documents on his desk, and plant the bugs.

Everything goes smoothly; no one suspects a thing. Liddy is elated.

HE JUST ISN'T WELL SCREWED ON

June 1972

The Weather Underground's revolution is sputtering. They managed to pull off only one big operation all year—detonating a bomb inside a Pentagon restroom. The brutal series of nonstop attacks seems to have ended. They had trumpeted their war on the Capitol and the Pentagon in extravagantly worded communiqués. But the fire never spread. The revolution was not happening. All they've managed to do is blow up a bunch of government commodes. FBI agents are laughing at them, calling them "the terrible toilet bombers." There is even a mocking ditty: "Weatherman, Weatherman, what do you do? Blow up a toilet every year or two."

And in Algeria, Eldridge Cleaver is watching his revolutionary hopes go up in smoke: A new Panther recruit hijacked a Western Airlines flight and scored a $500,000 ransom. In Algiers, Cleaver prepared an effusive welcome. Yet when the plane landed there, the Algerian government interceded and returned the money to the Americans. Then more Panther devotees from Detroit hijacked a Delta plane and grabbed a $1 million ransom. The Algerians confiscated that money, too. Cleaver, Papa Rage, sent out ominous statements criticizing the president of Algeria. Soldiers quickly surrounded the Black Panther embassy and ordered everyone to come out with their hands up.

❁　　❁　　❁

Tim presents Michel Hauchard with a hefty, carefully typed manuscript and Hauchard immediately travels to Geneva. He meets various publishers for business dinners at a luxury hotel. He is also hosting film director Roman Polanski, whose eight-months-pregnant wife, Sharon Tate, had been murdered by the Manson family.

From Geneva, Hauchard calls Tim:

We're going to make a lot of money.

❊ ❊ ❊

At the old castle in Lugano, Tim is gently lowering the record player needle onto the new Stones album, *Exile on Main St.* Heroin seems to be inside many of the tracks, and Barritt, who sees no real boundaries between drugs, has been nudging Tim to experiment.

Tim tells him he has always avoided heroin.

I've seen too many worn-out junkies with that droopy nod, too many beat-up writers, poets, and bebop musicians who loved their needles and spoons. It is living, liquid death. The warm embrace that disconnects you from the world, from other people.

Suddenly, to Barritt's surprise, Tim agrees to try some smack.

"Okay," says Barritt, "but I'd hate to be known as the person who got Timothy Leary hooked."

Tim sits very quietly as the drug slips into his veins. He nods, relaxes, starts to giggle. And then he falls into a deep, deep sleep. Barritt watches his hero. "All his ambition drained away, all his dreams became fulfilled and all he had to do was lie back and dig it."

❊ ❊ ❊

When Tim wakes up, he studies the soiled mattresses covered with saris and Indian blankets. There's the sticky smell of bodily fluids and pot. Ravi Shankar is blaring from the stereo and the raving Barritt is pogoing from room to room, completely naked except for a cape. A few zombie hippies are lurching out of the bedroom and shaking medicine-man rattles. There is a wanderer from California, someone called Walking Horse the Train-Meeter.

Dennis Martino is there, too, and talking to himself, muttering that the drugs aren't enough: "I'm coming *down*," he says. "Let's *do* something. Let's go back to the other room and smoke some more dope—or *something*."

In the attic, a group of bearded men are launching into a new acid trip while two androgynous German teenagers have sex on the floor. The two lovers are completely ripped, chortling with joy each time the short-haired girl farts during the intercourse. Tim decides that he has to leave. That he'll camp outside, under the stars.

When he wakes up, there is a reporter asking for an interview.

Tim looks at the stranger and says: *I'll give you an interview, but my answers will be channeled telepathically through Brian Barritt.*

When the convoluted interview session is done, another reporter arrives—a visiting *Penthouse* writer. Someone slips hash into his meal and as the drugs wrap around his brain, the reporter is getting flustered and then angry.

Tim chuckles at him:

"If you go into Che Guevara's camps, you gotta expect you might get shot at or get dysentery."

In Washington, G. Gordon Liddy is summoned to CREEP chief John Mitchell's office. Apparently there's been a problem with the earlier bugging of the Democratic headquarters. One of the listening devices isn't working correctly. Mitchell orders Liddy to return to the Watergate and fix the problem.

At 2 a.m. on Saturday, June 17, Liddy's men are spotted by a security guard. The cops are summoned, and the burglars sent by the Nixon White House to the Watergate are arrested. Liddy, monitoring the operation from a hotel room across the street, packs up quickly and leaves. He understands what is coming next. He goes home and tells his wife: "Some people got caught. I'll probably be going to jail."

A few days later, Nixon is asked about the Watergate burglary at a news conference.

"This kind of activity...has no place whatever in our electoral process or in our governmental process," Nixon says, before lying: "The White House has had no involvement whatever in this particular incident."

The next day, inside the Oval Office, the president is seething about who fucked up the operation.

"Who was the asshole?" Nixon asks. "Is it Liddy? Is that the fellow? He must be a little nuts."

"He is," Nixon's aide H. R. Haldeman responds.

"I mean he just isn't well screwed on, is he?" Nixon asks. "Isn't that the problem?"

HE HAS DESTROYED MORE LIVES

July–October 1972

Michel Hauchard summons Tim to Geneva for a final business meeting with visiting publishers from America. Everyone is gathered inside a hotel banquet room that Hauchard has reserved. Waiters arrive with huge platters of meat, fish, and vegetables. Bottles of vintage wine are opened and poured. Tim grins and answers questions. Then, as the meal ends, Hauchard announces to the group that the book is going to the highest bidder.

Tim steps out and one of Hauchard's aides closes the door behind him. When the publishers finally file out, Hauchard walks up to Tim and tells him, with a smug smile, that he's sold the book for a quarter of a million dollars—one of the largest publishing advances in history.

✸　　✸　　✸

Federal narcotics agents from Nixon's drug agencies are holding high-wattage emergency strategy sessions with special officers from Reagan's California Bureau of Narcotic Enforcement. Together, they have formed a secret task force to track the Brotherhood of Eternal Love, that loose-knit collective of hippie dealers that views Dr. Timothy Leary as a patron saint.

The agents are swapping stories: Brotherhood men and women celebrate successful drug deals with ritualistic orgies where the men lie in a circle and women take turns riding them. Fleets of Volkswagen vans are still arriving at the Port of Los Angeles stuffed with tons of hash. Chemists are holed up in Southern California and around the country, churning out millions of hits of acid. As investigators put the pieces together, they are beginning to maintain that the Brotherhood is one of the most sophisticated, far-reaching criminal enterprises on the planet.

Some skeptical agents are drowned out as they argue that, really, the Brotherhood is not as organized as Nixon and Reagan might think.

The hippies are just too high all the time, too disorganized.

A reminder sweeps the sessions: *Nixon's prime directive is to get Leary.*

A strategy takes shape:

What if Leary is painted as more than simply a spiritual leader for this group? What if the notorious fugitive is cast as the diabolical criminal mastermind of the largest drug conspiracy in the history of the world?

The agents sketch out pyramids of power: There are Brotherhood members in Southern California, deep in the jungles of Hawaii, and along the coast of Oregon. At the top of the pyramid, at the head of the Hippie Mafia, is Timothy Leary. He's the Godfather, Carlo Gambino, and Lucky Luciano all rolled up into one.

Now, there's a headline.

It is, after all, what President Nixon wants.

❂   ❂   ❂

In the early-morning hours of Saturday, August 5, a strike team of two hundred federal and state narcotics agents storm several homes in California, Oregon, and Hawaii. They arrest or indict dozens of members of the Brotherhood of Eternal Love. They find 1.5 million hits of acid, thirty gallons of hashish inside a makeshift canning factory, passport forging equipment, 5,000 pounds of hash, two kilos of cocaine, and $20,000 in cash.

A massive press conference is staged to announce the news. The bust has been carefully timed to make the front pages of Sunday papers all across the country. Dr. Timothy Leary, currently enjoying refuge in Switzerland, is identified as the criminal leader, the mastermind behind the Brotherhood of Eternal Love. Twenty-nine felony charges are filed against Leary and others, representing hundreds of years in prison. The opening sentence of the front-page *New York Times* story delivers the "drug kingpin" news that Nixon had been wanting: "Fifty-seven persons connected with Timothy Leary's sex and drug sect, the Brotherhood of Eternal Love, were arrested or indicted."

The bail for the fugitive Godfather is set at an astonishing $5 million—the highest ever levied in the history of law enforcement in the United States. And the task force's spokesman, Orange County prosecutor Cecil B. Hicks, is blasting Timothy Leary as the head of the biggest drug cartel in the world:

"Leary is personally responsible for destroying more lives than any other human being. The number of his victims destroyed by drugs and LSD literally runs into the hundreds of thousands."

❋　　❋　　❋

Hauchard receives a check from the publisher and completes his accounting. He informs Tim that, after deducting everything Leary owes him, his share will come out to $40,000.

It is, by far, the single biggest payday Tim has ever seen—but Hauchard is keeping nearly all the money. Hauchard looks triumphant.

"Timothy...how do you think I make my money?"

When Tim receives his share, he sends $5,000 each to his son and daughter back in California. He spends another $10,000 on a new yellow Porsche with a sunroof and a kick-ass quadrophonic stereo.

❋　　❋　　❋

A few days later, Tim is jolted by a call from Mastronardi, the Swiss attorney: In the wake of the news from the United States, the Swiss want to wash their hands of him. They want him gone.

Mastronardi says he's done everything he can, but the forces aligned against him have grown too strong with these new criminal indictments. The Swiss will give Tim a bit of time to find a new home, but he is expected to leave the country as soon as possible.

Tim hangs up the phone and crams some clothes and toiletries in his new Porsche. He roars away, farther south to Carona, a few miles from the Italian border. He hides for a few days and then moves to a farmhouse outside of Bern. Unsure whether he's being followed, he moves again, this time to a lakeside chalet in Immensee.

As he ducks in and out of the villages, news drifts in: Many people are convinced that Nixon's five-million-dollar bond is actually a five-million-dollar reward. Mercenaries, international bounty hunters, are looking for him, ready to strike it rich by kidnapping Dr. Timothy Leary and turning him over to the Americans.

THE GODDESS LAKSHMI

November–early December 1972

Racing across Switzerland, Tim keeps hearing the new Moody Blues album, *Seventh Sojourn*, blasting out of the four speakers in the Porsche.

The record's seventh song is "When You're a Free Man," the band's latest tribute to Timothy Leary:

> *You left your country for peace of mind*
> *and something tells me you're doing alright.*

Tim stops to place a call to Mastronardi, and he listens as the attorney says he pulled one last string:

I convinced the Swiss to let you stay until the end of December.

Hanging up the phone, Tim presses his hands into his leather coat, trying to stay warm. He can see his breath in the frigid air. For the last several days it has been gloomy and bitterly cold.

I have less than two months before being launched into the great unknown.

He's been meditating, thinking about what's in the soul of Switzerland:

"Switzerland is so green and beautiful because it rains, rains, rains in the damp, gloomy Alps. The Swiss are good people, but soggy and bored."

❄   ❄   ❄

In New York, a few days after Nixon's landslide reelection over George McGovern, a willowy socialite named Joanna Harcourt-Smith agrees to meet Michel Hauchard at the St. Regis–Sheraton Hotel bar for drinks.

Joanna is twenty-six and honey-blond, a fixture in the posh

stratosphere of European high society. Born in St. Moritz, she is descended from royalty on her mother's side and British admiralty on her father's. Her family includes several notable citizens, from wealthy publishing magnates to the scientist Stanislaw Ulam, who helped invent the hydrogen bomb. She speaks several languages and is friends with the Rolling Stones, movie stars, and wealthy industrialists. She wears a necklace of looped-together wedding and engagement rings, scalps from her previous conquests. Eight years ago, Hauchard had made her his teenage mistress, dressing her in baby-doll outfits. Their short-lived affair was often stormy. Since then, the former lovers have retained a wary distance, except when they want something from each other. Now Hauchard wants to show something to her—something that might win her back.

He kisses Joanna on both cheeks and strikes a match for her Gauloise. They settle in their seats, conversing in French. He orders a bottle of Cristal Champagne and offers a toast. He puffs on a cigar and reclines in his chair, admiring her. She's wearing a black-and-white dress borrowed from a friend, the designer Diane von Furstenberg.

After some small talk, Hauchard says he has been assisting the Pope of Dope, the fugitive Dr. Timothy Leary.

I've helped keep him out of prison and I've brokered an extraordinary publishing advance for his new book.

Reaching into his suit pocket, he pulls out a check and slides it across the table. It's another payment from Bantam Books, made out to him for $86,000.

"Look what I am doing now with your generation's hero." Hauchard chuckles. "The guy is worth a lot of money and I own every bit of him."

Joanna is stunned.

She's never met the infamous Timothy Leary, but he's one of the three men she's always wanted to sleep with, along with John F. Kennedy and Jimi Hendrix.

Hauchard keeps talking and blowing his cigar smoke, and Joanna says to herself: *Timothy Leary needs to escape.*

She decides that she is going to free him—from Hauchard, and maybe from Richard Nixon.

❂   ❂   ❂

A week later she flies into Switzerland, accompanied by her latest lover, a smooth Danish playboy nicknamed "Tommy the Tumbling Dice," who helps keep the Rolling Stones supplied with drugs—sometimes smuggling coke by taping half kilos to his children's bellies. With the children in tow, Joanna and Tommy head to Hauchard's penthouse apartment. She gives Hauchard's Moroccan butler some hash and while the servant and Tommy light up the pipe, Joanna quietly retreats into Hauchard's study and rifles through his address book. She finds five numbers for Timothy Leary and copies each one down carefully.

The next day, she begins calling the numbers repeatedly, until someone sounding like Leary answers. She explains in her French-accented English that she knows Michel Hauchard, she has seen him in New York, and she also knows that she and Tim need to meet.

He is wary: "What kind of drugs are you on?"

Joanna laughs: "Every one I can find, but especially psychedelics."

He says they really should meet the next day.

❂   ❂   ❂

The following evening, Joanna and Tommy and the kids arrive at Tim's chalet on Lake Zug. It is dark and cold outside. A fresh snowfall has blanketed the mountains overlooking the lake. Inside, crackling logs pop and hiss in the stone fireplace. Several of Tim's hangers-on are there, including the wiry, fast-talking Dennis Martino and the wild-eyed psychedelic explorer Brian Barritt. Martino is eager to impress Joanna and Tommy. "I'm a triple Gemini," he says by way of introduction.

The small talk continues, everyone trying to get comfortable with one another. Tommy the Tumbling Dice looks forlorn, defeated. He can see that his time with Joanna is ending. He goes off to check on the kids. While he is away, Tim asks if anyone has any LSD. Martino volunteers to fetch some from upstairs. As he clambers away, Joanna reaches into her bag and pulls out two hits of Clearlight, each a tiny chunk of hard gelatin. Tim is impressed. Clearlight is the good stuff, the most powerful acid on the market.

Joanna and Tim stand in front of the roaring fireplace and stare into each other's eyes. They sip some white wine and Joanna lifts one of the hits of LSD and places it on her tongue. Then she chases it with wine.

She pinches the other tab between her thumb and forefinger, the way priests offer the Holy Communion wafer. She holds the LSD aloft in one hand and raises her wineglass with the other:

"Who loves me will come with me."

Tim steps forward and licks her fingers, letting the acid hit his tongue. He lifts his glass to toast her: "To you, beautiful woman. Just tell me what you want."

She says: "Everything."

❊   ❊   ❊

Joanna and Tim quickly fall in together. He drives her all over Switzerland in the gleaming yellow Porsche as they continue to drop acid, talking the whole time, discussing his theories of the seven levels of consciousness and the way DNA works, tucking in stories of Freud and Lenin in Switzerland, talking about how he is going to star in an upcoming movie based on Hermann Hesse's *Steppenwolf.* They have dinner with the directors of Sandoz, the laboratory where Hofmann invented LSD, and Joanna sits on the lap of one of the uptight Sandoz executives, laughing uproariously at how his face is reddening.

One day, Tim tells her he will be her guide, and that she has passed all the tests: "You are looking for a way out of the decadent aristocratic game, the limbo of Jet Set desperados. Your intelligence has always told you there is something more. I'll show you the way."

She's not sure what to think—he still hasn't made love to her, but he seems to be intently bonding with her mind. Each morning they take a fresh dose of LSD and set out, Joanna climbing into the Porsche, wearing oversize sunglasses despite the weak November light. She marvels at how he can be twice her age and launching into these daily acid trips—and yet always reemerging so refreshed and renewed.

They go skiing and enjoy long, languorous meals over bottles of

Champagne. They talk, over and over again, about an escape plan for him, for the two of them. They talk about conning Hauchard, using his money to buy a big sailboat, maybe a yacht. They can make the boat their own country, and they can be free, high, and happy.

Tim wonders about Sri Lanka:

"We can live on the beach with sand between our toes and flowers in our hair. Let's never talk to anyone but each other."

❀　❀　❀

In early December, he tells her he wants to drive to Gstaad to stay in the Palace Hotel, a grand, castle-like outpost on a bluff overlooking the village. She understands what he's saying:

This will be our first night alone with each other.

Tripping on acid, they race along the twisting, unforgiving mountain roads as the stereo blasts David Bowie's "Ziggy Stardust" and the Eagles' "Take It Easy." They take a third-floor suite with thick, comforting wood beams and a corner fireplace. Outside the windows are stunning views of the snowy mountains.

On the table is an iced bottle of Veuve Clicquot Champagne, a discreet note tucked next to it: "Welcome, Mr. and Mrs. Leary."

Joanna soaks in a bath while Pink Floyd plays on her portable stereo. They're beginning to come down from this morning's acid trip and Tim insists that it's time for more of the sacrament. For a second, Joanna pauses. She's beginning to feel exhausted from the intensity of tripping every single day since she has met him. He's smiling as he offers the tabs and she reaches to put one on her tongue.

The drapes are spread apart and moonlight glistens in the window. The LSD hits them full force. Tim pulls his brown Samsonite briefcase closer and unclasps the lock. He carefully removes several items: tarot cards, a jade Buddha statuette, amulets, wooden Tibetan prayer beads, a woven liturgical mat, and an old issue of *Life* magazine. Finally, he extracts a magical golden Tantric ring, intricately engraved with depictions of people fucking. He lights several candles and begins assembling an altar from the objects.

He opens the *Life* to an illustrated article about the human brain. Joanna has slipped on a purple silk robe.

He points to the magazine:

"These are pictures of the inside of the human brain. Look at them carefully so you will know that when I make love to you, I am caressing you in the innermost way, touching you everywhere, in every precious river and valley of your brain."

The waves of acid are washing over Joanna, lifting her away.

Tim continues:

"You are the goddess Lakshmi who brings wealth and abundance, consort of Vishnu who dreams the world. I promise you that I dreamed and created you just as you are now before me, covered with jewels, in this room, in the light of this moon. I am Vishnu the World Dreamer. Our lovemaking will be the union of god and goddesses making us free in all the worlds."

He slips the Tibetan prayer beads over her head, slides the gold Tantric ring on her finger, and takes her to bed.

GARDEN PARTY

December 1972

December is like a sticky blur of fucking, fine food, velvety clothes, and harem dreams arranged, day after day, by the high-society mainstays who welcome Joanna and her lover Timothy Leary in Gstaad and then St. Moritz, all of them traveling in the perfumed wake of counts and countesses and manservants and courtesans called "assistants."

Tim still has money to burn from his book deal and there are cashmere sweaters, rose-colored pillows in five-star hotels, more bottles of Veuve Clicquot, hot bubble baths in marble tubs, fresh croissants and apple strudel at luxurious chalets where the maître d' knows Joanna's name and guides them to a table with a view.

Outside, they can see how the snow has coated the Alps, and the skiers look like beautiful children's toys gliding over tiny diamonds of cocaine, with the flakes shooting up from the slopes and glittering in the falling light like angelic confetti.

☀ ☀ ☀

Inside the White House, Nixon is still exulting at his reelection, one of the largest landslides in U.S. history. He is buoyed by news that his aides and the FBI have coordinated one more thunderclap to destroy Leary, to make him persona non grata in every country in the world.

An announcement is being drafted to declare that Timothy Leary and his disciples in the Brotherhood of Eternal Love have evaded federal income taxes on their drug profits—and they will face dozens more felony charges while owing the U.S. government at least $75 million in back taxes.

❄ ❄ ❄

Nixon is swaggering, flexing his political and military muscle. He orders a massive Christmas-season bombing of Hanoi to force North Vietnam back to the negotiating table:

"I will do things that are goddamn rash as hell," he tells his staff. "I don't give a goddamn what happens. I don't care."

Within days, hundreds of massive B-52s are swarming the country, dropping tens of thousands of bombs on the capital city. It is the most punishing air attack since World War II.

Henry Kissinger chirps to the president, "It's going to break every window in Hanoi!"

Night after night the planes sweep in, aiming for military targets but sometimes hitting hospitals or neighborhoods. As the waves of bombers appear and the air-raid sirens scream, the Vietnamese children run for the shelters, shouting the only English word they know:

"Nixon, Nixon."

❄ ❄ ❄

It's Christmas Eve in the Alps and Tim is driving with Joanna to St. Moritz, passing through ancient villages where he can see the curls of smoke swirling up from the wooden roofs of the centuries-old homes.

They are on their way to Chalet von Opel, the home owned by one of Joanna's best friends, an heir to the Opel automobile dynasty. Tim and Joanna are swept inside the mansion, where people are already gathering around the roaring hearths, handing one another beautifully wrapped presents. Servants are circulating with platters of food and drink. Lines of cocaine are being tapped out on tables.

The famous pop artist Andy Warhol arrives with his own entourage of handsome young men dressed in identical tuxedos, along with several feral-looking women outfitted in red and gold dresses designed by Coco Chanel. Tim and Joanna marvel at the sight, still tripping from their daily hit of LSD and buzzing on cocaine.

Tim and Warhol sit next to each other on a couch. After a moment of uncomfortable silence, Tim tries his best to charm Warhol.

He says with a smile: "There are only three real geniuses in America. You, me and the third one changes all the time."

Warhol remains mute. He intently studies the scene, all the pretty young people mingling, talking, flirting. Tim watches Warhol watching and sees that he is appraising Joanna.

Pointing at her, Tim says to Warhol: "This is the most beautiful woman in the world and I love her."

Warhol throws Joanna a cutting look. He raises his arm and snaps his fingers. One of his aides instantly reaches into a bag and pulls out a copy of Ricky Nelson's hit single "Garden Party"—the hard-eyed autobiographical song about how all the famous people wanted him to amuse them, to put on a show and do party tricks.

The record is rushed to the turntable. When the song comes on, Warhol suddenly stands up and grabs Joanna's hand. The pale artist leads her, spinning and dancing, across the room.

Tim watches for a long moment and then begins clapping to the beat.

✸　　✸　　✸

It's the day after Christmas and Tim wakes up with Joanna resting lightly next to him. The clock is ticking. He has to be out of Switzerland in five days. Tim and Joanna glumly retreat to the chalet on Lake Zug, trying to see if there is any magic, some move they can make, anyone they can call—*Mick Jagger? John Lennon?*

Dennis Martino is waiting for them, and he is more jangly than ever. Joanna, like Rosemary before her, finds something creepy about him. Warning lights begin flashing when Martino makes his cartoon strut into the room. She looks away when he begins yakking about yoga or astrology or bragging about the time he caused a woman to have a spontaneous abortion by playing his Moog synthesizer at full blast. It feels like Martino is always watching her, checking to make sure she's taking all her drugs, that she's staying high. Maybe he's hoping to catch her at a vulnerable moment, ready to pounce so he can experience his own "cosmic orgasm" with her.

And right now he's hopping up and down like a flying monkey in *The Wizard of Oz*, yipping that he has come up with a way to stay alive: There are some filmmakers he's heard about in Austria, just across the border, who are making an official anti-heroin documentary for the government. Maybe Tim can appear in the Austrian movie...and rail against drugs. It just might work—Austria has no extradition treaty with the United States, and denouncing drugs might get the Austrians to let him stay.

On December 29, Tim straps his skis to the top of the Porsche and loads the car with Joanna's luggage. Still tripping from that morning's acid, the couple flies along the icy mountain roads and frozen rivers, aiming east toward Austria. At the checkpoint, they are waved through without being stopped—in the Porsche, they look like two more rich skiers.

HE HAS TAKEN LEAVE
OF HIS SENSES

January 1–11, 1973

Tim has booked the luxury suite at the Hotel Bristol, a baroque palace near the opera house in Vienna. They contacted the filmmakers Martino told them about, but it turned out they were making a *pro*-drug movie. *Not the best way to win asylum in Austria.*

Martino shows up and instantly reaffixes himself to their orbit, sleeping on the couch. Joanna is losing it. Every morning there's been acid for breakfast, often followed by hashish for lunch, a dinner spiked with cocaine and Champagne, and then more hashish and some valium or Quaaludes to mellow things out late at night. When she stands and looks in the mirror, her face is drawn and haggard, her tangled hair hanging in greasy clumps. When Tim hands her a hit of acid, she often simply palms the tab, flicking it away when he's not looking.

Tim is talking on the phone to his twenty-five-year-old daughter, Susan. She's been on a wandering odyssey to India, using the $5,000 her father gave her after his book deal with Hauchard. She was traveling with her husband, Dennis Martino's twin brother.

Now she's telling her father: *He's been doing too many drugs and is hearing too many voices.*

Susan adds that now she is spooked and wants to see her father before flying back to the United States. She's traveling alone through Europe with her one-year-old child. She adds something else:

I'm eight months pregnant.

Tim tries to soothe her. His daughter and his son, Jack, grew up in a house filled with peyote, mescaline, and LSD. They'd been turned on to acid at a younger age than most people, and then they had drifted, and he had allowed them to keep going. In prison, in exile, Tim had heard the stories about his disheveled son and emotionally unhinged daughter wandering in and out of pads, courtrooms, and counseling sessions.

They are minor celebrities, thanks to me.

Star-trippers and hangers-on hound them, as if by hanging around Dr. Timothy Leary's children they'll get close to something he has given them.

Tim tells Susan: *We'll meet you in Vienna.*

❃   ❃   ❃

On Christmas Day, Nixon paused the brutal bombing attacks on North Vietnam and his aides gingerly suggested it was time for a truce. Instead, the president ordered the biggest raid yet: More than one hundred B-52s were sent to demolish Hanoi. Some 40,000 tons of bombs were dropped on the capital city, the equivalent of two Hiroshima-sized atomic blasts.

As the bombs fell, folksinger Joan Baez was in Hanoi on a peace mission, talking with government officials and visiting American POWs. She spent much of her time crouched inside a shelter, playing her guitar and singing for terrified Vietnamese children as the explosions thundered overhead.

Fifteen B-52s were shot down, along with eleven other planes. Dozens of U.S. pilots and crew were killed. On the ground, the Vietnamese say more than 2,000 civilians died, including many after Hanoi's major hospital was destroyed.

Now steadfast American allies in Europe are expressing concern. Sweden's prime minister is assailing Nixon's bombing as an outrage on par with Hitler's extermination of the Jews. In Australia, the new prime minister sends Nixon a private letter criticizing him. In England, the *Guardian* writes: "Mr. Nixon wants to go down in history as one of the most bloodthirsty of American presidents."

And on Capitol Hill, senators and congressmen return from

their Christmas recess and gather in the hallways. Several are worrying about the carnage and wonder if a constitutional crisis is looming. A Republican senator from Ohio, William Saxbe, tells people he is afraid that President Nixon has "taken leave of his senses."

Tim and Joanna drive to the Wien Hauptbahnhof, the main train station in Vienna, and watch as Susan, massively pregnant and belly swaying, comes off the train and walks toward them. She is gripping her one-year-old's hand.

Tim hugs his daughter and his grandchild. He remembers how, as a child and even as a teenager, Susan loved to nuzzle up to him. He tries to read her face, wondering if she's jealous of Joanna, his new lover who is her own age.

Susan reaches into her rucksack and rummages until she extracts a small bottle filled with clear liquid. She holds it out to Joanna.

"It's holy water from the Ganges," she says as she pushes it into Joanna's hands. "Drink this. It will make all of your dreams come true."

Joanna unscrews the cap and gulps it down as Susan smiles and Tim nods approvingly.

Vienna is dark and cold, even damper and drearier than Switzerland. Tim's daughter has returned to the United States and he and Joanna have been at the Hotel Bristol for nearly two weeks now, ordering room service and running up bills. Tim finally confesses to Joanna that the money he has been blowing through, the money from his book, is almost all gone. The bill at the hotel is running into the thousands of dollars, and there is no way to pay.

Tim says: *We can sell the Porsche.*

The next morning, Tim and Joanna and Martino swallow LSD for breakfast and see that their drug stash is running perilously low. Martino says he knows where he can score. He takes the Porsche and several hours go by before he finally returns. Bolting into the hotel room, he is bruised and trembling.

I lost control of the Porsche on an icy road and smashed into a wall. The car is destroyed.

Tim blinks in disbelief. There's no insurance. Joanna begins heaving, hyperventilating.

The Porsche was going to pay their bills. It was going to get them some money, some cash, that could get them moving secretly to Sri Lanka—so far away, so hidden.

Joanna begins screaming at Martino, exhausting herself and collapsing into tears before flopping on the bed and trying to sleep.

In the morning, Joanna drags herself out of bed and stumbles weakly into the bathroom, feeling more wasted than ever. She turns on the light and studies the mirror: Her entire face has turned the color of a mottled tangerine. She begins screaming. Her eyes have become orange, too. She closes them and keeps screaming. A flood of fear swamps her: *Too much LSD. Too much LSD. Too much LSD.*

Tim calls for a taxi, trying to calm her down as they hurriedly dress: *There's no such thing as someone turning orange from taking too much LSD.*

He wants to take her to a hospital, but a case of LSD poisoning can't be handled by ordinary doctors. She insists that they go straight to the prestigious Medical University of Vienna, where Sigmund Freud once taught.

Tim replies: "I love your attitude. Let's go to the top. Sure thing."

The taxi races along the gray streets, past the Parliament building, and screeches to a stop in front of the venerable university with its ancient marble walls and red roof. Stumbling inside, Joanna demands to see the dean of the medical school. He is lecturing to a class. She hurries along the corridors, flies up the stairs, and finds the amphitheater. Flinging the doors wide open, she sees the doctor onstage, standing next to a corpse on a marble slab. Hundreds of students are in the surrounding seats.

"Look at me!" she begins shouting in German as the lesson suddenly stops.

"Look at me!" she shouts again, moving toward the stage. "I'm more important than a dead person, but I might be dead soon, too. I am sick and I want you to tell me what's wrong."

She steps up on the stage and tosses off her mink coat and unbuttons her green silk blouse, slipping it off her shoulders. She is nude to the waist, orange under the bright lights. The students quickly rise to their feet, cheering and whistling.

The doctor holds up his hands gravely, slowing the applause. He turns to look Joanna over. "Observe, class," he finally announces. "A classic case of jaundice due to hepatitis."

The holy water from the polluted Ganges, the treasured vial that Tim's daughter had offered her to drink, is poisoning her.

❀ ❀ ❀

The Austrian doctor insists that Joanna go to the hospital, but instead she and Tim return to the Bristol. Martino is waiting for them, smoking hashish and looking like the caterpillar from *Alice's Adventures in Wonderland.* They sit in a close circle and try to make sense:

Joanna could die. We're nearly out of drugs. Just a few hundred dollars left. No car. Nowhere to go.

Martino begins babbling again, this time about other connections:

The Brotherhood of Eternal Love has been traveling in and out of Afghanistan for years. It is the holy wellspring and people have been cultivating hashish there since the time of Jesus.

Martino tells Tim that the Afghanis are welcoming and laid-back. Hash is sold in the old city markets for ten cents a joint. There are even government-run hashish stores with helpful signs posted in English.

Martino talks about how sunny the weather is, how cheap the prices are: *Hotel rooms are fifty cents and you can stuff yourself on lamb kebabs, pomegranates, and fresh yogurt for a quarter. The grapes are plump and sumptuous, some of the best in the world. People feast on steak for sixty cents.*

Martino tells them that the Brotherhood's key drug connection inside the country, the powerful Hayatullah Tokhi, would welcome them. *He owes you the world. If you go there, he'll have money. He'll be glad to protect you.*

Tim is weighing the idea.

Martino adds a thought. *Afghanistan has no extradition treaty with the United States. Nixon can never get you there.*

Tim is smiling. He has his own Afghan connection: The king of Afghanistan has an acid-eating nephew, Hari, who once sought Leary out in Switzerland—Hari had been one of the wanderers on the international LSD highway who managed to make the pilgrimage to Tim's chalet. *Surely the king of Afghanistan will be cool with Dr. Leary arriving in his country.*

Tim announces his decision: "We'll go to Afghanistan. We'll score money. Joanna will get well."

He turns to Joanna: "We will find it all in Kabul. I'll lay you down on satin cushions, make love to you, and feed you light and exquisite foods. We'll have all the Afghani hash we want, and the king will visit us and treat you like a royal princess."

Joanna is convinced: "I'll be dead in twelve hours if I don't get out of this dismal city. Let's head for the sun."

They begin making phone calls. They throw their dollars and francs on the bed, emptying their pockets, seeing if they have enough cash to get three economy-class tickets for a morning flight with a stopover in Beirut. Maybe Joanna can hustle up extra money from her jet-set friends there.

As the escape plan takes shape, there is a jarring realization: *What about the huge hotel bill?*

They run around the suite, grabbing Joanna's designer clothing, the mink coat, her camera, skis, boots, and a pair of binoculars. They build a pile in the room and then, on top, they throw her bracelets and earrings.

Joanna scrawls a note to the hotel manager:

We have to go. Here's my stuff.

PART IV

HAPPYLAND

PEACE WITH HONOR

January 12, 1973

Tim rubs his hands together, trying to stay warm as the morning dawns cloudy and freezing cold. Joanna's face is still glowing like a tab of Orange Sunshine. The hepatitis is not just tinting her skin, it's also seriously draining her energy. Tim bundles her into a taxi and Dennis Martino slides in next to them.

It will be good to get to somewhere warm. First a layover in Beirut, where hopefully Joanna can hit up her rich friends for some money. Then, a few weeks in Kabul hanging out with the royal family and scooping up mounds of hash from the Brotherhood of Eternal Love's excellent suppliers.

Once they get things tight with their royal connections, they can decamp Kabul and go to the next level, a nice long hideout in tropical Sri Lanka. Joanna has really well-placed friends there, heirs to a German fortune, who promise to put them up for as long as they want.

It will be so far beyond the reach of Nixon.

They're traveling light, a few clothes tossed into carry-ons. At the airport, Tim totes Joanna's bag. They stop to let her rest, and it is all she can do to lift a cigarette to her lips. He tries to lighten the mood: *It's your birthday tomorrow, you'll be on the beach in Beirut, digging your toes into the warm sand.*

Even through her haze, she can see that he's actually quite nervous. He no longer has a fake passport and is traveling under his own name.

The Austrians could easily decide to detain him and turn him over to the Americans—and they'll have the perfect opportunity when he tries to get through customs.

Joanna sinks into her chair and Tim skims the morning papers, looking, as always, for news from America.

He sees a small item reporting that Eldridge Cleaver has fled Algeria after finally falling out of favor with the revolutionary government.

Tim pauses for a moment, allowing the schadenfreude to wash over him. He is not a bitter person by nature. But the more he studies the article, the more he hopes Cleaver will end up having to crawl on his knees and beg for asylum in fucking North Korea, with nothing but that shitty ginseng wine to get high on.

✾   ✾   ✾

The Watergate trial is grinding into its first week. G. Gordon Liddy's criminal partner, ex–CIA agent E. Howard Hunt, is pleading guilty on all counts. Despite harsh questioning from the skeptical judge, Hunt swears that no higher figures were involved.

Inside the White House, Nixon is pleased that Hunt is taking the rap. The CIA man will keep quiet and go to jail—knowing that Nixon will get him released after the furor dies down. As Nixon studies the reports coming to the Oval Office, he remains confident that Liddy, the highest-ranking defendant, will also stay silent and take his punishment.

"Liddy is pretty tough," Nixon mutters to his aide, Charles Colson.

"Yeah, he is, he is," Colson responds. "Apparently one of these guys who's a masochist. He, uh, he enjoys punishing himself. That's okay, as long as he remains stable."

Nixon is feeling cocky. His presidential inauguration is in a few days. After his Christmas bombing, the Vietnamese look like they might be buckling. Nixon has a secret cable on his desk from National Security Advisor Henry Kissinger, saying they are on the cusp of a final peace agreement. At the White House, Nixon is talking to his inner circle about getting the hell out of Vietnam, washing his hands of it.

"Peace with honor," he calls it.

✾   ✾   ✾

In Vienna, Tim is still reading the *International Herald Tribune* and puffing on a Chesterfield. As he flips through the pages, he can see how much America is changing in his absence: The draft has been canceled and campus protests are dying off. The voting age is being lowered to eighteen. The Supreme Court is ready to issue a new ruling on abortion in the case of *Roe v. Wade*.

One item in particular catches his eye: Possessing a small amount of marijuana—the crime that got him sentenced to a decade or more in prison—is now reclassified as a misdemeanor.

He stubs out his smoke and stands. He and Martino grip Joanna's arms, supporting her as they walk slowly to the Austrian customs office. Tim hands over his passport and stands very still as the agent examines it.

Suddenly, the customs agent looks up:

Herr Doktor Timothy Leary?

The official seems very pleased, as though he can't believe his good fortune.

Tim nods, his throat tight. The airport around him is buzzing with activity and noise.

Maybe this is it? Maybe the CIA has been following me all over Vienna, stalking me, and they've waited until this moment to pull the trigger.

Now the customs agent is pushing a piece of paper and a pen at him.

Herr Doktor, would you do me the honor of signing your autograph?

Tim writes out his name, finishing with a sweeping flourish as he turns to smile in relief at Joanna.

On board the Austrian Airlines jet, Tim relaxes, lighting a fresh cigarette. He hasn't flown since escaping from Cleaver and Algeria nearly two years ago. The plane climbs above the clouds into the open sky, and he can feel Europe flaking away. He grins at Joanna and pats her hand.

Getting high always seems easy.

At midafternoon, they are making their final approach to Beirut. The city is lovely from the air, nestled between the mountains and the sparkling cerulean sea. They breeze through customs, step outside, and are greeted by the soothingly warm Mediterranean sunshine.

The last time Tim was here, it had turned into a cartoon farce, a madcap attempt to "prove" his revolutionary credentials by trying to stage a serious summit meeting with the Palestine Liberation Organization. He wound up being chased by reporters, offered an old lady's daughter, and trapped inside a tiny bathroom with a shit-stained floor.

It wasn't the steely collaboration that Weatherman and the Panthers wanted—it was Dr. Timothy Leary, Groucho Marx on acid, hiding and peeping and running up and down hotel hallways, making a mockery of the revolution.

Joanna had lived in Beirut as a sixteen-year-old girl, a decade ago, in a palatial apartment while her mother carried on an affair with Lebanon's president. Now they are checking into a low-rent hotel far from the city center.

As Tim opens the door to their dumpy room, Joanna nearly crumples.

"Sleazy," she says.

Sighing, she sits on the bed and picks up the telephone, speaking in French, trying to sound bubbly instead of gravely ill. Tim's eyes are darting and he is jabbering about Joanna recuperating on the beach, finding her strength, but he knows the real priority: They need to hustle some money, desperately.

He listens quietly as Joanna calls one person after another and tries to find some cash.

PURPLE HAZE

January 13, 1973

Today is Joanna's twenty-seventh birthday, and she and Tim are in a taxi bouncing its way through Beirut's chaotic maze of one-way streets. They've been seeing people Joanna knows from the old insouciant, jet-set days, including the rich, obese son of the former president of Lebanon. Everybody sounds sympathetic, but no one is offering any getaway money.

Tim peers out the taxi window at the crumbling, graffiti-covered buildings.

This must be what the Panthers and Weathermen think about when they get their rocks off.

Soldiers are patrolling the streets. The eight-story U.S. embassy is blackened and heavily damaged. Right before Christmas, it had been slammed by rockets. At intersections, desperate children swarm the cab, yapping at Tim, begging for money.

The driver escapes the scene and heads to Télé-Orient, one of Lebanon's two television stations. Joanna had been a minor TV star in Lebanon a decade ago, a bubbly blond teen frolicking in local productions. Inside the Télé-Orient office, Joanna quickly recognizes an old friend—the same program director who'd first hired her. She'd fucked him as a teenager; she'd had sex with many of the older men at the station. He is happy to see her, and he beams when she introduces her new companion, Dr. Timothy Leary. He quickly asks if his famous guest would be willing to do a television interview.

Tim smiles broadly. His ego, the thing he could never kill despite all the LSD, is carrying him to the surface. In moments, he is seated in front of a camera, proclaiming his love for the people of Beirut. He also recounts his successful escape from President Richard Nixon's regime.

After the interview, they return to the cheap hotel and confer with Martino, who has taken an adjoining room. There is only one more hope for funds. Calls are made, and then Tim and Joanna walk outside. They stand in front of the hotel, drinking in the noise from the city as a white Cadillac rolls out of the darkness. A well-dressed young Lebanese man steps out and introduces himself as Hassan, a friend of friends. He adds that he is very proud to meet the legendary Dr. Leary in person. He has some news to share, some things he might help with. Also, there is a gift in the car.

Tim leads Joanna inside the Cadillac, feeling the rich leather seats, and Hassan produces a joint stuffed with hashish, already lit. As the car screeches into the Lebanese night, it fills with swirls of thick smoke and laughter. Hassan races down deserted streets until he pulls up to a brand-new luxury high-rise on the coast. When they step out of the Cadillac, Joanna crumples to the ground. Maybe it's the dope, maybe it's the hepatitis.

Tim tries holding her up and bends down to whisper to her.

Should we go to the hospital? Back to the hotel?

She says to keep going. Tim scoops her up in his arms and carries her to the elevator. On the fourteenth floor, Tim wanders barefoot across the deep plush carpeting. On the balcony, Hassan points out the Mediterranean.

Tim sees nothing but inky blackness. They never did make it to the beach.

❀   ❀   ❀

Back inside, Hassan produces a hash pipe and then offers Tim and Joanna green tablets of what he says is quite good LSD. Joanna is flailing, drowsy, barely awake. She turns slowly, questioningly, toward Tim.

He nuzzles her ear and holds up a tab of acid. "Take this. It's your birthday and whatever happens, this will make you feel better."

Everyone swallows the acid and sits on the floor in a circle. Tim decides that this is a good time to hit Hassan up for money. Hassan shakes his head in sympathy. His parents, unfortunately, control his finances. He offers Tim a consolation gift: more green LSD. Whatever is in the tabs is nudging its way into Tim's brain. Things are getting spacey, shifting. Tim announces they are leaving, they need to take Joanna back to the shitty hotel.

Tripping with a stranger in a penthouse in Lebanon is not the right setting.

Hassan doesn't offer them a return ride in his Cadillac; he slips deeper into his stoned haze, and Tim calls a taxi. As Tim steps inside, the acid begins to rush over him in brisk, bracing waterfalls. He looks at Joanna and she seems filled with light and life, rising rapidly from the dead, her hepatitis forgotten. Tim feels her fingers running through his silvery hair, darting fish touching his skull. She's looking at him with sudden seriousness. They are flying again tomorrow morning, and he is a wanted fugitive.

He hears her voice: "You should really dye your hair black, so that they don't recognize you."

Now they are stopping at a late-night pharmacy, and he watches her, electric with the acid, running into the store and emerging moments later with a bottle of black hair dye. Tim is laughing as he opens the taxi door for her. He kisses her as she slides inside. She is going to disguise him before they fly out of Beirut.

At the hotel, he strips, soaks in a tub, closes his eyes, and tilts back, feeling her rub the coloring into his scalp. He murmurs with pleasure. She settles her orange body into the water with him. They begin kissing, and then they stumble out onto the bathroom floor, giggling as they finally crawl to the bed. The white sheets are smearing with black hair dye as they make love.

Later, as they're smoking and talking, they suddenly remember the hair dye.

You were supposed to wash it out after twenty minutes.

They're on LSD time now and have no idea how many hours have passed. Tim jumps out of bed and goes to the bathroom to rinse his hair. Water pours over his head and into the tub. In the mirror, he can see that his silver hair has gone beyond black. It has turned a bright purple, glowing like a courtesan's cape.

Joanna steps next to him and they gaze at their reflections.

She has an Orange Sunshine body; he has a Purple Haze head.

SUPER BOWL

January 14, 1973

It is Super Bowl Sunday and the undefeated Miami Dolphins are cracking heads with the Washington Redskins at the Los Angeles Memorial Coliseum. Timothy Leary looks like he's starring in the halftime show, doing his loping stride through the Beirut airport with his flaming purple hair, purple satin pants, a purple jacket, and a shimmering silver lamé shirt. He keeps one arm wrapped around Joanna as she leans against him. Dennis Martino shuffles alongside, carrying Joanna's bag.

Who knows what's out there and waiting for us, exactly, in Afghanistan?

All they can go on is what the Brotherhood of Eternal Love smugglers have always told Tim: The Afghanis welcome Americans and the hashish, the *tshars*, is the best on the planet. A *tsharsi*, a smoker, is considered a man of deep knowledge. Afghanistan has that ancient, mystical vibe on the hippie highway, the one that runs from Kathmandu to Kabul. Tripped-out seekers are following Marco Polo's old silk road, coming overland from Europe, traveling by bus, in VW vans, or just hitchhiking.

They walk across the tarmac toward the jet labeled Ariana, the national airline of Afghanistan. The outside of the Boeing 727 is a heady blue, the same color as the billowing fields of opium poppies in Afghanistan. Tim grins as a stunning stewardess, dressed in baggy gold harem pants and a white tunic, guides them to their seats. They are flying nine hundred miles east to Tehran, then another thousand miles to Kabul.

As the plane takes off, Tim and the others lift their fingers to their mouths and swallow green tabs of LSD.

What better way to fly into Kabul?

☀ ☀ ☀

The TV interview Tim did in Beirut is being broadcast and CIA agents in the city are astounded as they stare at the screen.

It's Timothy Leary.

In the murky waters of spy-versus-spy, the CIA has countless confidants, informers, grifters, and fixers on its growing dole. Agents stationed overseas spend good portions of the day not actually spying on anyone but finding, seducing, cajoling people into doing the spying for them—inside hotels, inside government offices, at the train stations and airport counters. The lists are long, getting longer, and the web of information gathering extends deep into the private sector—and Ariana Afghan Airlines, a subsidiary of Pan Am, is no exception:

Acting on urgent CIA requests, a Pan Am employee is thoroughly reviewing the passenger manifests for all the company's outbound flights from Beirut.

There is one name that jumps out from among the hundreds of passengers:

Timothy Leary. Morning flight to Kabul.

☀ ☀ ☀

In Kabul, the sky is clear and blue and the surrounding mountains are laced with a brilliant white snow. James Senner, the thirty-year-old duty officer for the U.S. embassy, is making his way to the sprawling two-story American compound. Senner had joined the army right out of high school in Wisconsin, went to college, gotten married, had kids. And now he is living his version of the American Dream—stationed overseas in an exotic country, spending his days monitoring trouble on behalf of the United States.

Today, he is dimly aware that Super Bowl VII is being played, but there's no chance of actually watching the game. The only TV sets in Kabul are used for decoration. Senner is supposed to be monitoring politics, the anti-American threats, but he's been spending a lot of time shipping hippies, dead or alive, back to America.

The streets of Kabul are pockmarked with long-haired pilgrims who stay too long—chasing the dragon, snorting heroin, smoking it, shooting up. And now there are all these barefoot, strung-out hippies hopelessly addicted to the cheap, constant heroin. Some of the once-serene crash pads in Kabul have turned into shooting galleries with that medicinal, cottony smell and the opened tins of food with flies swirling on top. Hollow-eyed people from Kansas or Texas shuffle into the embassy asking for money or a doctor or just a plane ticket home.

Settling behind his desk, Senner is catching up on paperwork when an urgent call comes in from American agents stationed in Beirut:

Timothy Leary is on today's Ariana flight to Kabul.

Tim is deep into his green acid trip, 25,000 feet high, and making new friends with some American hippies on the flight, taking the jet-age shortcut to nirvana. Tim is cackling and joking, sometimes shouting unnaturally to make himself heard as they soar over the rugged Central Asian landscape. The other passengers try not to notice the weirdly gibbering man with the flaming purple hair, or the wicked turbulence, as they descend into Tehran. The plane is only on the ground for a few minutes. New passengers come aboard, some of them devout Muslims carrying small prayer mats.

Tim has no idea that a fugitive arrest warrant has been sent from Washington to every American outpost around the world—along with official notice that the passport he is holding has been revoked by the United States government.

In Kabul, U.S. ambassador Robert Neumann is in his comfortable office, surrounded by shelves of books, studying the Leary updates from the Nixon White House. Neumann is a somber man with thick black glasses and an unusually large head shaped like an upside-down pear. He was raised in Austria and survived a Nazi concentration camp. He's an old-line veteran of the global diplomatic handshake circuit and a close friend of Henry Kissinger's—and he speaks in the same thick German accent.

Relations with Afghanistan are very delicate—the country leans toward the Soviet Union, but thanks to infusions of American cash it is now showing some signs of becoming more sympathetic to Nixon. Ambassador Neumann has been faithfully carrying out the president's orders to forge closer ties.

Now, with the news that Timothy Leary is headed there, Neumann is weighing whether the drug king's arrival is going to upset all the hard work he has done:

Is Nixon really willing to cause an international scene—and gamble with America's tenuous hold in Afghanistan—by grabbing Timothy Leary in Kabul?

Neumann sends messages to the White House, State Department, and CIA. The reply is swift: This is the best chance to corner Leary since he escaped prison twenty-eight months ago.

Who cares if there's no extradition treaty with Afghanistan?

The details can always be worked out later.

For now, just get him.

✺　　✺　　✺

Duty Officer Senner, brown-eyed and sporting a brown mustache, arrives at the Kabul airport. He is dressed in a suit and tie and carrying two bottles of scotch. One is for the airport director. The other is for the airport security chief. Senner, always dedicated to the mission, has cultivated good relations with both men.

Ariana Flight 710 begins descending from above the snow-covered peaks of the Hindu Kush. A mud-colored ribbon of flat land appears below and the plane dives toward it, maintaining speed to offset the gale-force crosswinds. At the last moment, the jet levels out and spasms onto the runway.

The plane careens to a stop and Afghani airport workers push a rolling staircase toward it. Tim emerges from the door and stops to take in the view. The late-afternoon sun is lighting Kabul with a warm glow. He breathes the clean, dry air and smiles. This will be a grand retreat for the next few weeks, the perfect place for Joanna to recover.

Tim is still grinning as he walks Joanna down the narrow stairway. Dennis Martino is bucking up and down behind them, carrying the bags. Tim is talking about how they can stay at the Inter-Continental, the finest hotel in the city. He'll notify the king's nephew that they've arrived. The sorcerer's apprentice, Martino, can contact the hash-smuggling underground. They can count on an unlimited line of credit at the Inter-Continental.

On the tarmac, Tim's new hippie friends from the plane are crowding around. He's already gathering an entourage. Everyone chatters excitedly as they parade toward the terminal. Tim looks over the group:

"Here we are in Happyland," he says with a laugh.

�֎   �֎   ✖

Inside the terminal, Senner has presented the nice bottle of scotch to the Afghani security chief, Captain Samad Azhar. Together, they have no trouble recognizing Timothy Leary tripping his way into the terminal. He's the one with the glowing purple hair.

Incoming passengers are lining up to present their passports at the immigration station. Tim sees dark-faced, mustachioed Afghani soldiers standing at attention, keeping a close watch. Azhar is behind the counter in his olive-green uniform. Today the captain is personally inspecting the passports. Behind him, at a discreet distance, is Duty Officer Senner in his suit and tie.

Tim presents his passport, and Azhar examines it briefly. Then he passes it over his shoulder to his American friend. Senner steps forward and snatches the passport. He pulls out a sheet of paper and begins reciting to Tim:

Your passport has been revoked by the State Department. Your passport is now being confiscated.

Azhar motions to the Afghani soldiers and they move to take Tim into custody.

"What's the charge?" Tim manages to say, the green acid punting inside his brain as soldiers press around him.

Captain Azhar shrugs. "Not having a passport."

Things are coming into focus, the Great Fear is trying to take hold, and Tim is pacing the airport holding cell. Joanna looks like a weeping pumpkin as the soldiers tear apart her bag, searching for drugs. Everyone's papers are seized and Martino is shaking—he's been traveling with a forged passport created by the Brotherhood of Eternal Love. Tim is babbling incoherently in English:

There must be a misunderstanding. We've been invited to your country as guests of His Royal Highness and the royal family.

The Afghans don't respond and dig deeper in the bags. When they are done, they herd the prisoners to an open jeep. Soldiers climb in around them. Some cling to the rollover bars. Tim's having flashbacks—to Algeria and being kidnapped by the Black Panthers. They stop at a rambling adobe building and Tim and the others are ordered inside. In the flickering light, Tim makes out several Afghans sitting on the dirt floor, holding chickens. A sheep is wandering around, nibbling at the dust. Against the far wall, near a small wood-burning heater, a tall, bearded man in a red turban occupies a chair.

Tim is told to sit. The man is a judge, and this is the courtroom. The judge speaks gravely in Farsi—and when he does, voices seem to pop out of the dark in response. Tim watches the turban bob up and down, like a red ball hopping on a roulette wheel.

Suddenly, there is silence. Tim assumes it is his time to speak. Whatever is left of the green LSD is not helping as he pushes himself to his feet:

Sir . . . we are invited guests of His Royal Highness, not common criminals.

Tim is threshing his hands up and down. The villagers stare at him as he dramatically stabs his finger in the air.

"You must recognize the mistake being made here," he pleads. "We are being detained illegally."

The judge is flicking his eyes impassively and studying Tim's purple hair.

Tim approaches the judge: "We have done nothing wrong. We

demand that our passports be returned to us so that we can check into the Hotel Inter-Continental."

The turbaned vizier continues to study Tim silently. The only sound is the clucking of chickens.

Finally, the Afghani elder speaks in perfect English: "I know that you have escaped from prison in your own country."

The farmers are gaping at Joanna's flaming orange skin and looking back at Tim's purple jacket and hair. Tim makes one final appeal in his best Atticus Finch voice: *Just give us our passports back and we'll return to Beirut. That's all we ask.*

The judge waves his hand dismissively: "You will go to the Plaza Hotel and remain under house arrest until we decide what to do with you."

Tim moves another step forward to keep pleading, but the man shouts sharply in Farsi. The soldiers quickly prod Tim with rifles. Guns punching their ribs, he and Martino are shoved back outside. Joanna stumbles out after them.

She is very weak now. She's had nothing to eat all day and can barely stand. She spies a street vendor with a cart piled high with tangerines, lit by a gas lamp. They are the most beautiful things she's ever seen. She takes an involuntary step toward the fruit. A soldier stops her and orders her into the jeep with the others. Joanna lifts her hand, pointing silently at the fruit and trying to mouth some words.

The man nods in understanding. He breaks rank and trots over to the kiosk. A moment later, he returns with a bag of tangerines. Back in the jeep, surrounded by soldiers, Joanna peels the fruit and eats one after another as they drive.

Tim is yakking:

House arrest won't be so bad, we'll at least be staying in a hotel until the king rescues us.

The Plaza Hotel is leaning as if it is about to collapse. The letter *Z* is missing from the main sign: PLA A HOTEL. There are no cars in the parking lot; no lights shining behind the tiny windows.

Joanna whispers: "Timothy . . . they're taking us to prison."

Inside, a single bulb sways in the reception area. The paint is peeling from the walls and broken furniture is stacked up in a dark corner. The soldiers separate Tim and Joanna. She resists, thrashing and screaming. The men pause and turn to look at their captain.

Joanna locks her orange gaze on him and summons some words: "I am very ill. Look at my eyes. If you separate us, I assure you that I will die and you will have to take responsibility for a terrible scandal. I am the daughter of powerful people in Europe, a British national."

The captain doesn't seem convinced. Joanna summons her haughtiest look. "My godfather is the chairman of the biggest newspaper in England," she is screaming. "You will be in so much trouble that you can't even begin to dream of it."

Suddenly she flops to the floor.

The captain looks down at her for a moment. Then he speaks in heavily German-accented English: "I can see that you are a real troublemaker."

Martino is taken away to one room, and Tim and Joanna are led to another. There is no window and no bathroom, just a single cot, topped with a thin, soiled blanket. Their feet crunch over piles of rat turds. A small oil heater tries to keep away the cold. Four guards are outside the locked door. They offer Tim and Joanna flatbread and tea, but they refuse. *It could be poisoned.*

Tim paces the room while Joanna lies on the cot. She wonders if they will be taken out in the morning and shot.

Tim reassures her: "Don't worry. They're making a deal with Nixon. They're going to trade me for as many helicopters and tanks as they can get. They won't hurt us. We're too precious to them."

Only one thing can make Joanna feel safe. She reaches for Tim. They remove their clothes and crawl under the blankets, holding each other.

❋　　❋　　❋

At the U.S. embassy, emergency cables are flying back and forth with Washington. President Nixon knows that Leary is in custody. The only problem is, so does everyone else. Nixon's men study the urgent, ominous message from the U.S. operatives in Kabul:

LEARY ARRIVAL KNOWN TO AFGHAN PRESS, AND LARGE HIPPIE
COMMUNITY POSES A POTENTIAL PROBLEM.

✸   ✸   ✸

The prime minister of Afghanistan, Mohammad Musa Shafiq, is now in direct conversation with Nixon's White House. He suggests he might be willing to privately cooperate and turn Leary over to the Americans. In return, he would like a windfall—maybe millions of dollars in aid from the United States. The prime minister insists that all publicity be avoided. He doesn't want to be condemned in his own country for partnering with the reviled Richard Nixon, a man now considered a war criminal by much of the world after the Christmas bombing of Hanoi.

The best plan, the Americans and Afghans agree, is to immediately deport Leary to a neighboring country where he can be legally extradited. The Nixon White House is on the case and Secretary of State Rogers is making discreet inquiries, calling foreign ministers around the world, trying to find just the right nation that will take Leary in—and then ship him back. But Nixon's emissaries are finding zero help. No one wants to be seen supporting Nixon. Secretary of State Rogers quickly wires the U.S. embassy in Kabul:

EXTRADITION APPEARS UNLIKELY FROM IRAN OR TURKEY
AND AT BEST QUESTIONABLE FROM MANY OTHER STATES.

✸   ✸   ✸

The U.S. ambassador knows the deal with the Afghani government could fall through at any moment. And what about the royal family? Leary is claiming he is tight with the king's nephew. The ambassador fires one more urgent cable back to Washington:

MOST ANXIOUS EXPEL LEARY ASAP.

AGENT BURKE

January 15, 1973

In Kabul, agents inside the U.S. embassy make arrangements for Dennis Martino to be freed from the dank Plaza Hotel. When they pick him up, they address him as "Mr. Viertel"—the name he had used on his fake passport. They apologize profusely for his detention and assure him that his passport will soon be returned. They drive him to the luxurious Inter-Continental, the one with the nice swimming pool. The strangers sent from the embassy tell him to order anything he wants from room service.

❋　　❋　　❋

At the crumbling hotel where he and Joanna are still being held prisoner, Tim is interrogated by Afghani secret police speaking in German-inflected English. The accents are a holdover from World War II, when Afghanistan favored the Nazis over the British. Many Afghani security forces are German-trained and retain old habits. In some remote provinces of the country, village elders still give the Heil Hitler salute to visitors.

They badger him: *Professor, why are you so important to the Americans, to President Richard Nixon?*

Tim is trying to make sense of the German accents and why his questioners are suddenly calling him "Professor." For the first time in weeks, he is not tripping.

Yesterday's desperate pleading with the old turbaned Afghani judge didn't work. Today he decides to lecture, as though the Afghans are particularly dense undergraduates: "I'm a political refugee. I have been persecuted for my ideas in the United States... I was hoping that the King of Afghanistan was an honorable man, brave enough to accept Joanna and me as his guests for a while.

"Unfortunately, I see I may have been wrong about that."

The secret police eye each other. The king of Afghanistan has been away from the capital. There are rumors flying that he may be losing the throne, that there might be a coup.

In the afternoon, Tim and Joanna brace themselves in the dark room as they hear the door being unlocked. Martino is shown inside, and he arrives with bags of food from the Inter-Continental—huge club sandwiches overflowing with chicken and bacon. He's carrying bags of tangerines and several packs of cigarettes.

Tim wants to think good things, that the Americans have no clue about Martino's true identity—that they really believe he is "Mr. Viertel." He doesn't look like the typical furry freak. He has short hair and a nonstop ability to bullshit. *Maybe they think he's an aggrieved international businessman, someone who can make trouble in high places? Maybe they're nice to him because they don't want him to make waves?* It sounds ludicrous, seems implausible, but what other possibility is there? Martino is a drug smuggler, and if they knew his *real* game, then they'd bust him just as quickly as anyone. *Why the fuck else would the CIA let Martino go?*

Martino is talking, as always, like a hopscotching meth addict trying to con someone out of spare change: "Kabul is crawling with English and American press trying to find out what happened to you." He says he's trying to reach the king's nephew. And he's trying to reach the fabled Tokhi brothers, who run the hashish underground in Kabul. He's trying this, trying that. No luck, no one calling back.

Martino suddenly pulls out a fat, freshly rolled joint.

"I managed to score some hash from a vendor at the market," he says. "This will take care of you."

A sweet, unusually pleasant smoke fills the room. Tim huffs the joint and the high hits him right away. Joanna's voice emerges from the cloud, asking why this hash has such a floral scent.

"Opium," offers Martino. "Afghani hash often has opium in it."

On his way out, he promises he will return soon.

❋   ❋   ❋

Inside the U.S. embassy, all the Timothy Leary cables, documents, and criminal reports are spilled out across desks. Various spies and operatives are pitching ideas on how the hell to pry Leary off the Afghani map. Word from the Nixon White House, from the State Department, is clear: *He can't be allowed to get political asylum somewhere out there on Planet Earth.*

There is only one thing to do: call in one of the most well-known members of Nixon's Bureau of Narcotics and Dangerous Drugs. Ivy League educated, a former Marine and an ex–CIA agent, the thirty-four-year-old Terrence Burke is tall and tanned and sports a trim beard. He's one of the new breed of undercover intelligence operatives sent abroad to work in shadowy realms reaching from Tel Aviv to New Delhi. He is an improvisational player, a roamer, someone who drifts in and out of places scooping up intelligence on the global poppy-heroin-hash trade.

In Kabul, Burke has been focusing on disrupting the Brotherhood of Eternal Love. He's orchestrated major busts and once even managed to get the Tokhi brothers arrested. Of course, they were freed within three hours and all charges were dropped by nervous Afghans. But, still, it was clear that the hard-charging Burke had some balls.

The Nixon White House has been very impressed, so much so that Attorney General John Mitchell once recruited Burke to join a "Special Unit" to work for Richard Nixon's reelection, headed by G. Gordon Liddy. Burke was tempted—it would have been like being saddled up with like-minded soul brothers—but he turned down the offer because he was enjoying the freewheeling atmosphere in Afghanistan too much.

Burke, like the handful of other American agents lurking in the corners of Kabul, has no arrest powers inside Afghanistan. In the mornings, he gets his aboveground intelligence from the embassy. And then he works the alleys and streets, hearing from his underground network of informants, guides, and fixers.

Now Burke is hatching a plot to get Leary back to America—and prison.

It won't conform to diplomatic protocol, but it damn sure will be effective.

THE KING'S NEPHEW

January 16, 1973

The king of Afghanistan's acid-loving nephew Hari has just arrived in Kabul and is demanding to see Timothy Leary.

At midmorning the long-haired Hari, dressed in a mod-style Beatles suit and boots, is at the Plaza Hotel and is steered to the room where Tim and Joanna are being held. He rushes to embrace them: "I'm so sorry about these police. My father and I were on holiday with the King, so I just heard about you today. Don't worry. You'll be out of here in a few hours. I've arranged for some good food from the palace."

Three servants bustle into the dank room, each lofting baskets of fresh food. There is a mound of hashish and more opium. Some cassettes by the Rolling Stones.

Hari proudly announces: "I have read all your books, Dr. Leary. I have also taken a lot of LSD and followed your guidance about how to have a trip that is spiritually directed."

He adds that he has a plan: "I have brought a tape recorder so we can have a good talk which I can take to my uncle. He will hear your words and recognize what kind of man you are, then maybe he will give orders to set you free."

Staring at the hash, the opium, Tim lets the tape spin round and round, and begins talking.

✸　　✸　　✸

In the prestigious Hotel Inter-Continental, Martino, booked under his fake passport name of Richard Viertel, is smoking hash, ordering fresh grapes from room service, and enjoying the hot showers and fresh towels. He lounges on the plush bed, occasionally wondering how Tim and Joanna are getting along at the prison.

There's a sharp knock at the door. Terrence Burke, with the U.S. Bureau of Narcotics and Dangerous Drugs, invites himself in.

He takes a seat and asks: *Enjoying your visit to Kabul...Mr. Martino?*

Martino begins quaking as he listens to Burke: *You are in very big trouble. Passport fraud is a major felony, on top of already jumping parole. You might be spending the rest of your life in prison.*

Burke is now stone-faced and grim. He tells Martino that the situation is even worse. The Afghans are outraged that he slipped into their country under false pretenses, and they are talking about throwing him into Dehmazang Prison. Martino begins squirming. In the hash-smuggling underworld, that prison has taken on dark, mythic proportions as a medieval dungeon where chained prisoners are eaten alive by rats.

Burke shifts in his chair and a gun pops out of his belt and thumps to the floor. Casually, he reaches over to pick it up.

"You can take your chances here," Burke tells Martino. "You have no money and you owe a lot of money at the hotel."

He glances around at the empty room service trays.

"Or," Burke adds, "you can help us."

Martino is shivering. *What can I help with?*

Burke makes it easy: *Tell us about your friends in the Brotherhood of Eternal Love. We'll take care of everything so that you'll never have to see the inside of an Afghani jail.*

And we'll do our best to keep you out of an American prison.

❀   ❀   ❀

Back at the gloomy Plaza Hotel, Tim and Joanna are pleasantly stoned. *Hari left plenty of food, the Stones tapes, and he really is the nephew of the king...a member of the royal family. We have an LSD freak and a friend placed high inside the royal family of Afghanistan...*

The king will free us.

LEARY HIGH AGAIN

Morning, January 17, 1973

A winter storm is moving over Kabul, blanketing the city in a foot of snow. Tim and Joanna, groggy and listless, wake up in each other's arms. It's been days since they've showered. *Hari has to be coming at any minute.* They smoke more hashish and nibble on the food. Suddenly, several soldiers storm into the room, surrounding the bed. "Get up!" the captain commands in a thick German accent. "You are coming with us to the airport. Now."

Tim and Joanna freeze. Ingesting the incredibly pure and potent hashish, delivered so close to the source, is like having your body gently dunked in cotton candy, a sweet cocoon. Tim smiles. *We're going to see the king of Afghanistan.*

Tim wraps his arms around Joanna as she murmurs dreamily. "You see, it works," he tells her. "I told you that perfect love conquers all."

Joanna's legs are wobbly as she tries to walk. She's lost so much weight that her Levi's barely stay above her hips. She slips on her lambskin coat. There's no mirror, but she runs her fingers through her hair. It smells like opium. She fondles the long string of Tibetan prayer beads around her neck, a gift from Tim—who has the look of a seedy aristocrat, unshaven, in wrinkled clothing, yet still undeniably elegant. He wraps a white scarf around his neck, winks at her, and slips on his purple coat, giving her a kiss.

Outside, the winter storm has passed and the sunlight is blinding against the fresh snow. They make their way through the slush toward a waiting jeep. The soldiers are at full attention, gripping their rifles. Tim asks about getting their passports back, but no one answers. *They probably don't understand the question.* As they climb into the jeep, he asks about Dennis Martino. The captain tells him that Martino will be leaving on a later flight.

At the airport, the jeep bypasses the terminal and drives directly onto the tarmac, freshly cleared of snow. Tim's eyes widen as he looks back at the building.

"This is not a good sign," he says.

The vehicle slides to a stop next to a waiting jet. The soldiers jump out and, with exaggerated courtesy, point toward the boarding ramp. Something is horribly wrong.

Tim balks: "I will not enter this plane until my passport is returned and I am told where this plane is going."

The captain points up the stairs. "This plane is going to Beirut and your passports will be given to you as soon as you board."

Tim looks around. For what, he's not sure. A royal motorcade to whisk them to the king's palace? Invading tanks driven by the mysterious Tokhi brothers who supply all the hash for the Brotherhood? A band of barefoot hippies with hollowed-out heroin eyes hoping to liberate him? But there are only armed Afghani soldiers, demanding that he leave their country.

He puts his arm around Joanna and walks up the ramp. He ducks inside the plane and immediately comes face-to-face with a tall, muscular American with a thin beard. He has intense, dangerous-looking brown eyes. He is grinning:

"Burke's the name and dope's the game. I'm here to bring you back to the United States, Dr. Leary."

Tim cocks his head.

"BNDD, stick 'em up," Burke says almost jovially, looking over Tim's purple hair.

Tim mutters: "Bureau of Narcotics and Dangerous Drugs."

Burke pulls something out of his pocket. It is Tim's faded passport, the one with his real name on it. With great fanfare, the drug agent opens it up and flips the pages so that Tim can see that every one is stamped CANCELED.

Tim sags. Burke pockets the passport. He hands Tim a new ID card: AFS Form 225-A. Tim's name and vital information have already been typed in. The top of the card reads:

DIRECT RETURN TO THE UNITED STATES ONLY.

Tim inspects the card. Burke has listed Leary's occupation as *Philosopher*.

Tim is scrambling, trying to find a way out. His mind is flipping into overdrive; he's here on a tarmac with a cocky federal drug agent carrying a .357 Magnum. *This is kidnapping, right?*

Tim begins shouting: "There is no extradition treaty between Afghanistan and the United States. This arrest is illegal."

"You're wrong there, professor," Burke bluffs. "This is an American plane, you're standing on American soil."

He points to the armed soldiers standing outside. *You can stay here*, he says, *but you're not going to like the Afghani prison cells.*

With a grand gesture, he motions Tim and Joanna into the passenger cabin. The two seats at the front have been reserved for them. Burke and another armed agent sit directly behind them.

They are bound for Paris via Ariana, the Pan Am subsidiary. From there, they'll fly Pan Am, first class, directly to Los Angeles. Burke will guard them on both flights. He has insisted that someone back in Washington pay for first-class seats: *I don't want a bunch of hippie backpackers jumping me in economy trying to rescue Leary.*

Ariana Flight 705 finally takes off at 3:35 p.m., more than eight hours behind schedule. Once the plane is confirmed in the air with Timothy Leary aboard, the U.S. ambassador sends a three-word urgent message, via secret cable, that the secretary of state can share with President Richard Nixon:

LEARY HIGH AGAIN.

A QUIET HIJACKING

Evening, January 17, 1973

Tim and Joanna light one cigarette after another, staring dully into space as a smoke cloud forms overhead inside Flight 705. An Ariana stewardess, her harem pants rustling softly, gently places a tray in Joanna's lap. It's a plate of steamed vegetables and rice. "Just what you need for your hepatitis," the stewardess coos.

As she picks at her food, Tim whispers that they should try to bolt away at one of the layovers before they get to Paris and the dreaded flight back to California. The drug agents wouldn't dare shoot at them in an international airport.

The plane touches down in Tehran, but it is only a quick refueling stop. No chance to even leave the plane. They take off again and more food arrives. Tim doesn't feel like eating. He holds Joanna's hand and they lean against each other. It is dark outside now. In a few hours, the plane begins to descend again, this time into Istanbul, the twinkling lights from the city almost seeming inviting.

Tim glances at Joanna. Turkey hates American freaks and stoners. They beat you and throw away the key if they catch you. Running away and disappearing inside Turkey is a long shot for a purple-haired ex-Harvard drug professor and his jaundiced socialite lover.

The plane stops on the tarmac far from the terminal. Flashing police lights are bouncing off the jet. Tim looks out the windows as armored vehicles speed up. Turkish soldiers and policemen are bounding up the steps and into the plane. There is also someone else boarding the plane, another American drug agent who confers with Burke while the Turkish soldiers inspect the other passengers. Then the security forces leave, locking the cabin door behind them. The pilot comes on the intercom, announcing that no one will be allowed to disembark in Turkey. Muttered protests swell in the cabin. The Istanbul-bound passengers have now become prisoners aboard Flight 705.

The next stop is Paris. Joanna turns to Tim:

"Listen, this is great," she whispers. "We'll have to change planes and I can get us out of this mess. When we get there, I will run for a French immigration official and tell him who you are and that you have been illegally kidnapped by American authorities. The French love intellectuals and will protect you from the Americans."

Tim twists across his seat and kisses her. He can see it now. The French are intelligent, sophisticated people. They certainly hate Richard Nixon. They can identify with his love of intellectual freedom. If he can distract the agents long enough, Joanna can get away to make some calls, reach her powerful friends, make a quick case for asylum being granted to the international intellectual philosopher Timothy Leary.

Joanna is going on and on, almost frantic: "Perhaps they will have to put you in jail, but I'll get the best lawyer in Paris—I already know who to call—and we'll fight your extradition to the United States."

They squeeze each other's hands and slump back in their seats.

A short time later, Burke stands and stretches. He struts past them and walks to the flight deck. Tim and Joanna look at each other. No other passenger has the freedom to go into the pilot's cabin. A few minutes later, Burke returns and settles back into his seat. Tim can feel Burke's knees pressing hard against his back.

An hour later, they are nearly dozing when the pilot's voice abruptly announces that due to unforeseen circumstances Flight 705 won't be landing in Paris after all. The flight is diverting to Frankfurt. Now it will land after midnight.

Tim lets the news hit him. The drug agents must have heard him and Joanna talking and strolled into the cockpit and told the pilot to fly to Frankfurt instead. Not only are they being kidnapped, but this entire flight is turning into a quiet hijacking carried out by the U.S. government.

Tim's eyes dart to the side and he sees Joanna pulling out her diary and quickly tearing off little strips of paper, trying not to be heard. On each piece, she writes a message in French and then in English: *"Dr. Timothy Leary is being illegally kidnapped by American agents. Please report this action immediately to the German police."*

She turns to Burke, behind them, and says she has to use the restroom. He gives her permission and Joanna walks unsteadily through the cabin, dropping the folded pieces of paper in the laps of several very confused passengers.

❄   ❄   ❄

In Frankfurt, more U.S. drug agents are waiting on the ground. Tim and Joanna exit the plane groggily. Tim insists Joanna be allowed to see a doctor. Burke talks to a German customs official and Joanna is taken to the airport clinic. A doctor gives her a vitamin shot and says she needs more rest.

Waiting for her to return, Tim watches the late-shift workers shutting the airport terminal down for the night. Burke tells him that he's made new travel arrangements. They'll be flying to London tomorrow: "First class," he adds with a grin. From there they'll fly directly to California.

Burke marches Tim and Joanna to the Pan Am Clipper Club lounge, which the airline has agreed to turn into a makeshift overnight prison. German security officers unlock the doors and Tim and Joanna are told to sleep on sofas. Tim looks up and sees Burke and two other armed American drug agents watching them, sitting with their backs against the exit.

MAKE THEM STOP

January 18, 1973

Nixon is in Key Biscayne, dressed in a dark suit and walking along the beach near his Florida White House compound. In two days he will be inaugurated for a second term. Today the White House is trumpeting its brand-new peace agreement with North Vietnam. The long, costly war will at last be coming to an end, and the country has Richard Nixon to thank. He's already planning reprisals against the naysayers who criticized his bombing of Hanoi.

The president is hopeful that the big news about Vietnam and Timothy Leary will knock the Watergate trial off the front pages. Five of the Watergate defendants have pleaded guilty—and have kept quiet, just as Nixon wanted. Large sums of cash are being raised to reward them, and they're being privately assured that they'll be released soon. But whispers are emerging about some of Nixon's burglars getting restless. Nixon knows that Liddy will never talk, but maybe someone else will crack—and if that happens, it could blow the entire conspiracy wide open.

❀ ❀ ❀

At the Clipper Club lounge in Frankfurt, Tim and Joanna wake to find themselves surrounded by more U.S. agents. Joanna seems revived, maybe because of the vitamin injections. She tells Burke that she needs to use the pay phone outside the lounge to call her parents in London. He agrees. She asks for money to make the call. Burke reaches into the government-provided roll of cash he's traveling with. The smallest bill he has is a fifty. He hands it to her.

She calls her godfather, Sir Max Aitken, chairman of the *Daily Express* newspapers in London. She tells him that she and Timothy Leary have been kidnapped by the American government and will be arriving in London in just a few hours. She hangs up the phone and returns to the lounge. She keeps Burke's change.

Tim and Joanna are escorted to a Pan Am 747 for the flight to England. Tim is amazed; he's never even seen one of the new jumbo jets. The plane seems nearly as long as a football field and the tail wing is at least six stories high. Inside, the cabin has a kaleidoscope-patterned orange carpet, bright orange seats, and off-white walls with pale orange Rorschach-style splotches. The still-orange Joanna blends right in.

A dozen Pan Am stewardesses are aboard, each carefully screened to ensure proper physique. The women are outfitted in blue mini-skirts, blue jackets with gold buttons, white gloves, and blue bowlers. One of the stewardesses gently leads Tim and Joanna to the front of the plane, closely followed by the drug agents. The first-class cabin is like a dream designed by Hugh Hefner and Elvis, with luxurious red carpet, soft mood lighting, and a wood-lined ceiling. A spiral staircase leads to an upper-deck lounge. Other than the two federal agents, Tim and Joanna are the only passengers in first class.

Glancing in the direction of the upstairs lounge, Tim begins to form a plan. The flight to London is brief, so he'll have to work quickly.

After takeoff, another stewardess brings the ubiquitous glass of Champagne. Tim turns to Burke. He casually asks if he and Joanna can go take a peek at the second floor of the plane and its upstairs lounge. Burke looks at the other BNDD agent. They shrug. *Why not?* The cockpit door is locked and there's no danger an acid freak like Leary will storm the flight deck and seize control of the plane. Besides, Burke would like to take a quick nap before landing in London. He watches Leary and his ingénue head for the little stair-case to the airplane's lounge.

Upstairs, they are alone. Tim marvels at the candy-colored couches and the trim-looking bar in the corner. The rounded ceiling curves down to the wide windows. It's like a Tunnel of Love. There is a thick-pile burgundy carpet, and Tim slips off his shoes and lets his feet burrow into the plush fibers. He begins to unbutton his purple pants and his glimmering silver shirt. Joanna is already ahead of him. They're naked on the jumbo jet to London, mulberry hair nuzzling against peachy skin, reaching for each other and very high in the sky.

Burke is just drifting into the first few moments of sleep. A stewardess is shaking him awake, trying to suppress a laugh.

You have to make them stop, she says.

"Stop what?" Burke asks.

"Go see for yourself," the stewardess says, nodding to the upper deck.

Burke darts up the staircase. *Who knows what the Acid King is up to?* There could be drooling freaks falling out of the overhead compartments, cross-eyed children of Charlie Manson chanting to Lucifer Leary. At the top of the staircase, Burke just stops. Leary's bony old-man ass is rising and falling like a wrinkled seesaw, his weird head of hair rocking like a plum in the ocean. Grunts, groans, and tangled legs. The smell of sex in the air.

Burke clears his throat: "Timothy...The pilot states that he will not allow this conduct on his aircraft. You have to stop. You are going to jail tonight so I'll give you five minutes to do so."

Tim is trying to concentrate. He groans and keeps fucking... *Five more minutes.*

✹   ✹   ✹

When they land in London, Tim and Joanna are fresh-faced and astounded: Her telephone call from Frankfurt worked. There's a huge crush at the terminal—journalists, immigration officials, police, and even more U.S. agents. Reporters begin shouting and photographers are shoving one another. It's beginning to feel a tiny bit familiar to Tim, that controlled chaos, the way things spiral out of hand in just the right proportion. Tim begins to grin his toothy, lopsided slice of a smile. In the twenty-eight months he's been on the lam, this is what he's missed. It's nice to be out in the open again, if only for a few moments.

He pulls Joanna close and they walk in a tight embrace, both of them beaming for the cameras.

"I want to go to Algeria!" he yells. "I want to go to Switzerland! I want to go to Austria!"

British immigration officials surround him. Tim draws himself to his full height, trying to adopt a touch of regality, some sort of gravitas, even if he had just been fucking a woman half his age on an airplane a few minutes ago—even if his hair is the color of the mauve gown Queen Victoria wore to the Royal International Exhibition of 1862. The Fleet Street reporters are pressing in, straining to hear every word. Tim proclaims grandly: "I am here in Britain to demand political, intellectual, and spiritual asylum." He bows slightly toward the chief immigration officer. "Joanna and I believe the British have a great tradition of fair play. I am being returned to the U.S. from a country that has no extradition with the United States. My capture is an illegal act."

The British official announces that he will forward the request for asylum to Her Majesty's Home Office.

Reporters rush for the telephones. Terrence Burke sighs. *The Nixon Administration is under the distinct impression that the Brits will fully cooperate with Leary's return. What the fuck is going on?*

There's nothing to do but wait. It's two hours before the Pan Am flight to Los Angeles is scheduled to depart. Tim banters with the press and sees Burke and the BNDD agents smoking nervously. "It would be funny if you were to lose us after all this trouble, wouldn't it?" says Joanna as she joins Burke and they watch Tim in action.

He doesn't respond and she narrows her eyes at him. "I hope you get screwed for this," she says with a sneer.

The British immigration officer finally returns. He's bearing a signed piece of paper, which he reads aloud to Tim and the assembled media: "The secretary of state has given directions for you not to be given entry to the United Kingdom on the ground that your exclusion is conducive to the public good...I have given directions for your removal on Flight 121 to Los Angeles on Pan American Airways."

With a touch of ceremony, he hands Tim the document. The police begin pushing Tim and Joanna to the departure gate and the British official approaches Burke: "We had no intention of granting him asylum," he says, "but we had to go through the motions." Burke appraises the man coolly.

Tim is marched toward the plane, but before he leaves, he turns and throws out some final words to the press:

"A lot of people in high places in the States will be quaking in their shoes when I am on the way home."

A FREE MAN

Evening, January 18, 1973

Pan Am Flight 121 flies a polar route, taking just eleven hours to reach Los Angeles. Tim and Joanna are escorted to first class along with the U.S. drug agents. A stewardess brings them one last complimentary glass of sparkling wine. Burke tells her to let them keep the entire bottle.

Joanna looks around and sees that a famous friend is also in first class: Gunter Sachs, the suave German playboy who was once married to the bombshell actress Brigitte Bardot. He is traveling with his own entourage of jet-setters, clearly viewing the long flight as a chance to party. Sachs looks at Joanna and lifts his glass. Soon everyone, including the U.S. drug agents, is joining in toasts, tossing back drinks, asking for refills.

The party rolls to the upper-deck lounge. Burke joins them, trying to keep an eye on Tim. *No more fucking on airplanes.* More drinks are poured and someone cranks up a portable tape player. Tim is peering at his tarot cards, his purple head bowed down, trying to divine what is in store for the Joker, the Magician. Attracted by the laughs and the tunes, most of first class is bumping around the lounge. Two stewardesses join the party. It's like being on tour with Mick and Keith.

Tim smiles as he looks around the room. He caresses Joanna as they fall back on the airplane's upper-deck couch. He can tell she is high, buzzing from the Champagne, and she is laughing over and over again. He loves her laugh. He reaches for her and kisses her. She lies down on the couch and rests her head on Tim's lap. He strokes her shoulders and runs his hands along the side of her body as she murmurs softly. The other passengers, seemingly oblivious, are giggling and shouting as the music rocks on.

Tim's caresses go lower and lower. He grabs the button on her blue jeans. She sighs as he pulls down the zipper and slides his hand inside. He is rubbing, faster and faster, and now she is moaning louder and louder. A few of the partiers on the plane hear the love groans rising up over the whining engines, the music, and the giddy laughter. All eyes turn to Tim, smiling back at them with Joanna lying across his lap. A stewardess springs up. She knows exactly what to do. She walks to the couch and carefully drapes a blue Pan Am blanket over Joanna's midsection.

The music is cranked up and Tim slides his hand back down.

❋   ❋   ❋

Hours later, dinner is being served in first class. The meal is presented on fine china, one course at a time, by tipsy stewardesses. The filet mignon is charred on the outside, juicy with blood inside. Tim savors each bite and licks his fingers. Prison food isn't anything like this.

The cabin grows quiet after the meal. Joanna falls asleep while Tim is smoking a cigarette and sipping another drink. Burke tells him that they're over the polar ice cap now. Tim looks out the window. To his left, he can see the sun. He walks to the right side of the plane. Out that window, there's a full moon. He shivers. It's as if he's poised between two worlds. As the plane keeps moving, the moon disappears behind the horizon. Now they are turning directly into the blinding sun.

Tim is lost in thought when Joanna finally awakes. Below them, he points out the California coastline. He seems completely sober, despite all he's been drinking, despite the hundreds of hits of LSD that must still be wandering among his synapses. He asks Burke to make sure that Joanna will see a doctor after they land. He pulls Gunter Sachs aside and makes the German playboy promise, man to man, that Joanna will be cared for in Los Angeles.

Settling back into his seat, Tim tries to explain to her what is going to happen next. He can tell she's still drunk. He pulls a small, worn address book out of his bag and shows it to her.

"Here is the entire counterculture," he says. "Use it well and get me out."

She nods, blinking back tears.

"All of my contacts are in here," he adds. "A lot of people will be waiting to see you. Many of them do not understand what I've been saying and have strong opinions about me."

She pushes her body into him as he goes through the book, page by page, marking names for her to call. He tells her to call Allen Ginsberg right away. "They're all good friends of mine and they'll all help you." He gives her the book.

Next, he writes out a note:

> This is to introduce Joanna Harcourt-Smith. She is my voice, my love, my life. She is designated to act in my behalf. Please assist her in any way you can to help me get free.

He pauses for a moment and glances out the window again. There's nothing but clouds below now.

He signs the paper:

Timothy Leary, Amerika, 1973.

❋   ❋   ❋

It is pouring in Los Angeles when they arrive. The raindrops beat furiously against their windows as the jet taxis to the terminal. Tim grabs copies of *Time* and *Newsweek* and quickly stuffs them in the pockets of his purple coat. He looks at Joanna. "It's going to take a long time for me to be processed and I want to have plenty to read."

The plane comes to a stop and the cabin doors remain locked. All passengers are ordered to remain in their seats. Security is exceptionally tight at the airport. The entire area has been carefully swept for bombs. Police are stationed everywhere. Sharpshooters line the roof of the terminal, peering into the gray rain.

A phalanx of Los Angeles–based federal drug agents approaches the plane. The men crowd aboard and order Tim to stand. He gathers Joanna into his arms for one last kiss.

"I love you and always will," he says.

His hands are cuffed behind him and he's led down a stair ramp to the ground. The original plan called for a helicopter to take him directly to the Parker Center jail for booking. But the rain has grounded the helicopter. Instead, a gray VW van with white curtains has been brought onto the tarmac. It is parked near the plane.

Tim is hustled toward the van, closely flanked by the various federal agents. Reporters, photographers, and cameramen are massed behind police barricades. They shout as Leary comes into view. He grins when he sees them and shouts back. He smiles as happily as he can: *I am still a free man.*

He's shoved into the van, which is surrounded by nearly a dozen police cars. The motorcade roars from the airport. Within minutes, it becomes ensnared in a colossal Los Angeles traffic jam filled with honking horns and cursing drivers.

Tim had flown into America at five hundred miles per hour. Now he is crawling, inch by miserable inch, back to prison.

EPILOGUE

im is placed in solitary confinement while Joanna holds a press conference in Los Angeles, saying that she wants to meet with President Nixon: "I plan to tell him exactly how Timothy taught me to be happy and find perfect love."

He is put in a dimly lit cell that has only a bed and a toilet. When he asks for something to write with, he's handed a pencil stub and paper. He begins scratching out a renunciation of his earlier endorsement of the Weather Underground:

"I regret those rhetorical excesses," he writes. "In my anger at my imprisonment...I endorsed their tactics. I was simply stupid and I admit it."

He has no money for an attorney and he wouldn't trust Michael Kennedy to represent him anyway. A Los Angeles–area lawyer, Bruce Margolin—a longhair interested in Indian gurus—steps forward and offers to defend him pro bono.

The Nixon White House wants Leary punished as quickly as possible, and the trial for his prison escape convenes almost immediately. It is held amid extraordinarily tight security: He's completely manacled, chained neck to foot and flanked by twenty guards as he's transported in a long line of squad cars to the San Luis Obispo courtroom. He has conferred with Margolin and decided that his best defense is to claim that he suffered from an involuntary state of intoxication—LSD flashbacks—at the time of his escape: "*The defendant, by virtue of his experimentation with these drugs, has experienced permanent and irreversible molecular and synaptic brain changes resulting in a state of mind best characterized as altered reality and meta-consciousness.*"

People are wondering if Leary's mind really has been blown by acid. A psychological test is ordered. His IQ registers at 143, still genius level. His creativity leaps off the charts. He's definitely not psychotic, the court-appointed psychologist reports. He feels empathy, love, attachment to others.

He's found guilty on the escape charge and is facing up to fifteen years in prison—and maybe a few decades more if he's prosecuted on the other charges around the country.

The judge issues another thunderclap: Timothy Leary will serve his sentence in Folsom State Prison, the maximum-security fortress opened in 1880 and immortalized in a Johnny Cash song. Folsom is home to the state's hardest criminals, including Charles Manson, the mastermind behind the most grisly murders in recent American history.

Manacled and shackled, Leary arrives at his new home, a place where ninety-three condemned men have been executed over the decades. Thick granite walls surround the perimeter and sharp-shooting guards are stationed atop lookout towers. He is taken to a reinforced lockup zone deep inside Folsom, a heavily patrolled cellblock separated from the rest of the prison by a maze of razor wire. This area is reserved for the most dangerous criminals, men who are kept in solitary confinement.

Tim shuffles inside and is led down a very dark wing. The prisoner in the adjoining cell has been expecting him. He sends over welcoming gifts via a prison trustee: some smokes, paperback books, a small container filled with crackers, coffee, sugar cubes, powdered cream.

Tim and his neighbor can't see each other, but they can converse through an air shaft.

"I've been watching your fall, Timothy," Charles Manson says to him. "I knew you'd end up here."

Tim is astonished. He thanks Manson for the gifts. Beyond that, he is speechless.

Manson continues: "I've been waiting to talk to you for years. Our lives would have never crossed outside. But now we have plenty of time. We were all your students, you know. You had everyone looking up to you. You could have led the people anywhere you wanted...And you didn't tell them what to do. That's what I could never figure out. You showed everyone how to create a new head but you never gave them the new head. Why didn't you? I wanted to ask you that for years."

Tim gingerly replies: "That was the point. I didn't want to impose my realities. The idea is that everybody takes responsibility for his nervous system, creates his own reality. Anything else is brainwashing."

Manson asks Tim about the moment in an acid trip when your ego disintegrates into straight energy in harmony with space and time.

Tim explains: "It's the moment when you are free from biochemical imprints. You can take off from there and go anywhere you want. You should have looked for the energy fusion called love."

Manson thinks about it for a second: "It's all death," he suggests.

Tim corrects him: "It's all love," he says.

In the summer of 1973, the government quietly drops the twenty-nine "Hippie Mafia" indictments against Leary—the ones designed to portray him as the kingpin of the largest, most organized drug-dealing operation in American history. They also drop the record-setting $5 million bond. The charges relating to $75 million in tax fraud are let go as well.

In November, after six months at Folsom alongside Manson, Tim is transferred to another prison midway between Sacramento and San Francisco. Joanna arrives for long visits and she tells him she has taken over the role Rosemary once filled—raising money, trying to sell his writing, talking to supporters. One day he tells her that he is developing a new theory of how life developed on Earth—he is convinced now that the planet was simply a female egg, waiting to be fertilized by a speeding meteor seeded with DNA.

Too, there is that newly discovered comet entering the solar system, Kohoutek, which scientists expect to become so bright that it will be visible to the naked eye during daylight. Tim is now certain that the comet is a sign that humans are ready for the next stage of evolution: space travel.

I'm going to be liberated not just from prison, but from Planet Earth.

Instead, the comet turns out to be a dud.

✻   ✻   ✻

In May 1974, he's told to report to the visitors' room, where FBI agents and federal prosecutors are waiting for him. They want to finish off the Weather Underground, the Black Panthers, and the Brotherhood of Eternal Love. They want to do it by nailing the radical lawyers who represent the underground revolutionaries. They are interested, especially, in the man they think masterminded Timothy Leary's escape: Michael Kennedy, the San Francisco attorney who once summed up Leary's breakout as the perfect marriage of "dope and dynamite."

Tim has been in prison for seventeen months. He knows that other charges can come snarling up. The FBI agents tell him that the only way he'll get out of prison before he is decrepit or dies is to confess everything he knows about the radical groups—and Kennedy's role as the orchestrator of his prison escape.

Tim lets it sink in.

Since he has been in prison, he's been trying to watch the twists and turns of the Watergate scandal—the miasma of lies upon lies from the Nixon White House. Tim has been jotting down some prison notes, meditating on the "seeds of paranoia," trying to address what it means to tell the truth:

> Secrecy is the original sin. The fig leaf in the Garden of Eden...What a blessing that Watergate has been uncovered to teach us the primary lesson...Communication is love...
>
> All FBI files and CIA dossiers and White House conversations should be open to all. Let everything hang open...
>
> There is nothing and no way to hide. This is the acid message. We're all on cosmic TV every moment...
>
> Concealment is the seed-source of every human conflict.

Tim agrees to admit everything to the eager FBI agents and they press the RECORD button on the tape machine. He begins by telling them Kennedy helped arrange the escape and controlled much of it.

The FBI agents are giddy as Tim goes on and on: Kennedy set

him up by sending him to Algeria; he was always ripping Tim off, quashing his manuscript, stealing his house, keeping money that people had donated. The agents press him for information on the Weathermen fugitives, but there's little he can tell them beyond what they know already. His knowledge of many events seems to be hearsay, and the statute of limitations is quickly running out.

From a legal standpoint, Leary's testimony is useless, but the FBI has already secured its higher goal: They've gotten him to cooperate. They are turning the famous Timothy Leary into a government informant. And when word is carefully leaked to the media that he is talking to the FBI, it should cause the counterculture to implode from paranoia.

While Leary meets with the FBI agents, the House Judiciary Committee opens impeachment hearings against President Nixon.

"I'm not a crook," Nixon is insisting, but his administration has been crumbling for months.

His vice president, Spiro Agnew, resigned after being convicted of bribery, tax evasion, and money laundering. His closest aides, including former attorney general John Mitchell, have been indicted for their roles in the Watergate scandal.

Nixon is fighting desperately to stave off impeachment, along with the criminal investigations circling closer to his Oval Office. He fired an independent special prosecutor and now he's battling to withhold White House tapes from prosecutors. Finally, on July 24, the Supreme Court orders him to surrender the recordings. The tapes reveal that the president was intimately involved in a criminal conspiracy from the very beginning.

By now, Nixon is drinking more than ever. One of his press aides sees the president with "a frantic look on his face, wild-eyed, like a madman." The aide immediately calls the defense secretary: "That madman I have just seen has his finger on the red button."

The secretary has already quietly passed word to the joint chiefs of staff: *Ignore military orders from the president.*

Finally, congressional Republicans meet with Nixon at the White House to tell him he can no longer avoid being impeached—and he will likely be sent to prison.

On August 9, the president of the United States addresses the nation. He is announcing his resignation:

> As I recall the high hopes for America with which we began this second term, I feel a great sadness that I will not be here in this office working on your behalf...I would say only that if some of my judgments were wrong, and some were wrong, they were made in what I believed at the time to be the best interests of the nation.

☀   ☀   ☀

The FBI's news about Timothy Leary being a government informant has been carefully leaked to select reporters and the stories are dripping out, one by one, each designed to inflict maximum psychological damage. "Leary is talking, recollecting details and names and faces from the underground," the *Los Angeles Times* reports. In Chicago, the *Tribune* outlines how Leary will be testifying to a federal grand jury about the Weather Underground. The *New York Times* claims that Leary's testimony is expected to be the key evidence leading to criminal indictments of counterculture figures.

By September, the underground press is humming with reports that Timothy Leary has turned into a full-throated narc. The accusations build and build until a group calling itself PILL, People Investigating Leary's Lies, holds a press conference in San Francisco. Yippie leaders, poets, and Tim's twenty-four-year-old son, Jack, are there.

"There's a straight line between Watergate and Timothy Leary," Yippie leader Jerry Rubin announces. "I feel sick for the death of Tim Leary's soul."

His son, who has been taking LSD since he was sixteen and once stripped naked and masturbated in a drugged-out state inside

a jailhouse, was next: "Based on my past experience, I know Timothy Leary lies at will when he thinks it will benefit him."

Suddenly, a man in a massive kangaroo costume bounds forward,
yelling, "This is a kangaroo court." He is holding a thick, creamy
custard pie and he is trying to smash it into Jerry Rubin's face, but his
bulky paws are making it hard to hold. People are yelling, shouting,
and pointing fingers.

Finally, Tim's loyal ally, Allen Ginsberg, appears. He is the poet
laureate of the 1960s counterculture, the link between the psychedelic age and the profound American transcendentalists and thinkers like Emerson, Thoreau, and Whitman. He still thinks that he
and Leary are more American than Richard Nixon—that they are
part of a wild, free, celebratory America...that exultant, adventurous, and exuberant America is in their genetic coding, in their
souls.

Ginsberg looks out at the restless assemblage of activists, radicals, freaks, and seekers who want to crucify Timothy Leary as a
traitor to all that the 1960s embodied. In his barrel-chested voice, he
begins to chant for peace, for calm: "OOOOOOoooooommmm...
AAAAaaaammmm."

Then he speaks: "Does Leary see himself a spiritual president
like Nixon, and is he trying to clean the karma blackboard by creating a hippie Watergate? Will he be pardoned by the next guru?"

❊   ❊   ❊

The FBI has done its work so well that Leary is branded a snitch
inside the prison system. To keep him from being murdered by
other inmates, he is moved constantly from facility to facility
under a code name that winds up on his prison paperwork: *Charlie
Thrush*—like the songbird. Rumors swirl on the outside that the
feds are injecting Leary with powerful drugs, or that he's the target
of assassination plots by lone wolves and prison gangs.

❊   ❊   ❊

In November 1975, Tim receives word that he will be joined by a
new neighbor in prison: Eldridge Cleaver. After fleeing Algeria,

Cleaver ended up in a working-class section of Paris, living in a small house with his wife and children. His royalties from *Soul on Ice* remained frozen by the U.S. government.

Living in Paris, he decided to try his hand at fashion, inventing a set of revealing "codpiece pants" for men. "We've been castrated in clothing and my pants open up new vistas," Cleaver said. "I'm against penis binding." He named the trousers "the Cleavers" and modeled them himself, placing advertisements seeking investors "to revolutionize men's fashion and corner world market. Millions in profits envisioned."

The pants turned out to be a failure, and Cleaver gave up on France—and revolutionary socialism. He began telling journalists that he wanted to return to America, even though he faced up to eighty years in prison. "I'm turning into a patriot," Cleaver said. "I want the U.S. to be vastly improved, not done in."

He arranged to surrender to FBI agents, who accompanied him on his return flight from Paris.

Tim is staggered when he sees Cleaver in the prison. The Black Panther's hair is turning gray and he says he's a born-again Christian and has renounced violence. Cleaver is leading other inmates in prayer, wishing blessings on everyone.

Almost immediately, rumors begin flying that Cleaver had agreed to testify against his former comrades in exchange for leniency. The Black Panther Party issues a statement: *"What is Eldridge Cleaver doing . . . besides sharing holiday feasts with an admitted informer, Timothy Leary?"*

Outstanding charges against Cleaver are soon dropped and he is released from prison in exchange for community service.

❋   ❋   ❋

In early 1976, Tim writes an article for William Buckley Jr.'s conservative *National Review* that tears apart the sixties heroes he'd once bonded with. He mocks Mick Jagger and John Lennon for singing about a "Street Fighting Man" and "Power to the People" while getting insanely rich. He blasts Bob Dylan's *"plastic protest music."* Leary wonders: "Did Dylan stand on picket lines? Get his head busted by company police? March at Selma in the hard rain? Get tear-gassed at Chicago? Sleep in the mud at Woodstock?"

He reserves special venom for "the Outlaw Industry" and the fame-and-money-hungry radical attorneys:

"Surely no one with more than two fingers of forehead ever believed that an armed revolution was possible in America," he writes. "Everyone knows that militancy results not in the overthrow of the government but in the well-publicized court trial."

He's condemning them all, including Bernardine Dohrn, the "witchy goddess" he had once fantasized about fucking while on the run after his escape:

> It is no accident that the Weathermen, the most publicized group of Dylan groupies, a bewildered, fugitive band of terrorists now cut off from their culture and condemned to underground existence, took their name from a depressing Dylan song…surely you *don't* need a Weatherman to know which way the wind blows, and we've all been blown light-years away beyond the rhetoric of violent revolution, haven't we, Bernardine?

Shortly after the article appears, after forty long months in custody, he is finally released on April 21, 1976.

❁   ❁   ❁

Leary faced death threats after leaving prison and entered the Federal Witness Protection Program. He and Joanna lived in a remote cabin in the New Mexico wilderness, but the first time he traveled into Santa Fe his cover was blown and he decided to resurface. After he and Joanna broke up, at a *Star Trek* convention, he moved to Los Angeles, shape-shifting easily from federal prisoner to Hollywood celebrity.

He wrote new books, landed roles in films, and lectured as a "stand-up philosopher." He appeared on television talk shows and spoke to large crowds and received standing ovations. He told interviewers, "People ask me how many times I've taken LSD—and I don't count. But it's the same thing when they ask me how many times I've made love. The answer is, not enough."

By 1977 he was predicting a future world in which personal computers would be connected by a global network, allowing everyone to communicate instantaneously, exchanging text, photos, and videos.

A young man named Steve Jobs, who had attended Reed College in Oregon, where Leary had once lectured on the merits of LSD, eventually dropped acid—and began work on new computers that he thought would revolutionize the world. Jobs told people: "Doing LSD was one of the two or three most important things I have done in my life."

In the early 1980s Leary teamed up with his old archenemy, G. Gordon Liddy, for a series of popular debates at college campuses across the country. He published a memoir, *Flashbacks*, in 1983. He became increasingly fascinated by computers and worked closely with game designers and other programmers of virtual environments. Just as in the old days with John Lennon, famous people—like Johnny Depp—sought him out for revelations about the meaning of life.

❋   ❋   ❋

Leary had a far easier time finding forgiveness than Richard Nixon. For years, Nixon remained mostly hidden, a disgraced symbol of criminality at the highest level in the land. After resigning from office, he tried to destroy the papers and recordings from his presidency. In response, Congress rushed to pass a new law preserving his records as part of the National Archives. While other former presidents established official libraries and museums, Nixon's legacy remained bogged down in court battles over the status of his papers.

Finally, in 1990, the much-delayed Richard M. Nixon Presidential Library and Birthplace opened in Orange County, California. The one-story Spanish-style hacienda was originally built and operated by an independent foundation, not the federal government. This private status allowed the library total control. The executive director informed reporters that visitors "are going to learn *Nixon's* side of the story."

The library held no official papers from Nixon's White House years—those remained under lock and key in Washington. Yet it did display evening gowns worn by his wife, Pat, as first lady. The highlight for many visitors was the interactive "Talking Nixon." After a button was punched for a pre-set question, an electronic Nixon flickered to life on a video screen. When visitors asked about Watergate, the talking Nixon said:

"No one was killed at Watergate. No one profited from Watergate, our scandal . . . was a political shenanigan."

❋   ❋   ❋

Leary remained haunted by his experiences as a fugitive during the Nixon years. He told one interviewer, "Richard Nixon called me the most dangerous man alive, and of course, I tried to be as dangerous to him as I could be."

On a warm Wednesday night in early August 1993, Leary and a thousand of his closest friends decided the time had come to exorcise the demon. They descended on the Nixon Presidential Library and Birthplace. Organizers had arranged to rent out the cash-strapped facility for an ostensibly serious-minded high-technology conference party billed as "Nailed: An Evening on the Cultural Frontier."

Instead, it morphed into a counterculture extravaganza and religious ritual. Nixon Library staffers watched in dismay as a parade of less-than-usual visitors arrived: half-naked Brazilian conga line dancers, sword swallowers, tattooed snake charmers, gypsy fortune-tellers, and Japanese taiko drummers. Many of the strangers were on drugs.

The eighty-year-old former president was nowhere in sight, but some attendees showed up in Nixon masks. The rock band Fishbone was setting up to play, along with a group called Bronx Style Bob. The Red Hot Chili Peppers were scheduled to come on after midnight. Rocker Todd Rundgren was in the crowd—and so was an inventor who was getting very stoned and marveling at what was happening in Nixon's museum: "I felt deeply, spiritually fulfilled by being able to smoke a joint by the reflecting pool at Richard Nixon's library. It's the balancing of opposites over time."

At the center of it all was seventy-two-year-old Timothy Leary, the master of ceremonies, standing in front of Richard Nixon's birthplace:

"In the sixties, we said *power to the people!*" Leary shouted as the crowd urged him on.

"In the eighties, nineties, and twenty-first century, it's *power to the pupil. The dilated pupil!*"

Pot smoke wafted around the grounds. There was a delirious rush to the Nixon gift shop, still open. Drunk and stoned visitors bypassed the eight-volume sets of Nixon's collected works, instead scooping up photographs of Richard Nixon shaking hands with Elvis Presley. Rundgren, the rock star, was drinking in the madness: "You want to do every disgusting thing you ever did at home in here."

Near 2 a.m., the Red Hot Chili Peppers ended their set and began urinating, symbolically, on the U.S. president's floor.

Suddenly, Timothy Leary's voice rose up again. He began leading the final rites of the exorcism. It felt like he was shouting directly at Richard Nixon's face:

The way to program your brain is to use your eyeballs!
Flood your brain with light!
It's called illumination!
It's called perception!
It's called vision!

❈   ❈   ❈

Eight months later, former president Richard Nixon suffered a massive stroke as he sat down to eat dinner. He was conscious but unable to speak.

His brain was flooded with a large blood clot. Doctors reported that he had lost his vision.

Nixon lingered for four days and then finally died.

POST-CREDITS

Timothy Leary was diagnosed with inoperable prostate cancer in 1995 and developed a new philosophy of embracing death: "I'm looking forward to the most fascinating experience in life, which is dying," he told people. "You've got to approach your dying the way you live your life—with curiosity, with hope, with fascination, with courage and with the help of your friends." A few years earlier he had confronted death through his daughter's demise: Susan, declared mentally unfit for trial after allegedly shooting her boyfriend in the head, hanged herself in jail with a shoelace.

Following his cancer diagnosis, he made arrangements to be frozen in cryonic suspension, only to call it off: "They have no sense of humor," he said of the cryonic technicians. "I was worried I would wake up in fifty years surrounded by people with clipboards."

He originally wanted his death aired live on the Internet. Instead, he had it videotaped. With friends and family at his bedside on May 31, 1996, he began to clench his fist and utter: "Why?" Then he clenched his fist again and said: "Why not?" His last word before he died at age seventy-five was: "*Beautiful.*"

A year later, seven grams of his ashes were blasted into space aboard a Pegasus rocket, along with the cremains of *Star Trek* creator Gene Roddenberry. Tim remained in orbit for six years until the rocket burned on reentry to the atmosphere, scattering his ashes around the planet. Several more grams of his remains were carried by the actress Susan Sarandon and laid to rest at the Burning Man festival in 2015.

Stew Albert, the Yippie who almost lost his mind on acid with Tim Leary on an Algerian beach, successfully sued the FBI for placing illegal wiretaps in his house. He moved to Oregon and compiled a documentary history, *The Sixties Papers: Documents of a Rebellious Decade*. In 2005 he published a memoir, *Who the Hell Is Stew Albert?* He died in 2006 at age sixty-six.

Bill Ayers remained a hunted fugitive until 1980, when he and Bernardine Dohrn turned themselves in. They married soon after. The government's charges against the Weather Underground were dismissed because of the FBI's illegal COINTELPRO tactics. Ayers said: "Guilty as hell, free as a bird—America is a great country." He became a professor at the University of Illinois at Chicago, respected for his work in education reform and known for his devotion to double skim lattes at Starbucks. In 1997 he was named Chicago's Citizen of the Year. In 2001 he published a memoir, *Fugitive Days*. His ties to Barack Obama, a neighbor in his affluent Chicago neighborhood, became a major issue in the 2008 presidential campaign.

Terrence Burke, the drug agent who dragged Timothy Leary back to the United States, became deputy administrator of the Drug Enforcement Administration. After retiring, he moved to Colorado and developed his own international private investigative agency. He joined a mountain rescue team and assisted in hundreds of searches and rescues in the Colorado Rockies. He wrote a memoir, *Stalking the Caravan: A Drug Agent in Afghanistan 1971–1973*.

Eldridge Cleaver parlayed his status as a born-again Christian to go on lucrative national speaking tours, billing himself as the "Eldridge Cleaver Crusades." He developed his own religious offshoot called Guardians of the Sperm. Later, he converted to Mormonism and became a conservative Republican. He endorsed Ronald Reagan for president in 1980. He watched as Huey Newton, his old ally and then rival, disbanded the Black Panther Party in 1982. Cleaver ran for U.S. senator from California in the Republican primary in 1986 but was defeated. He and his wife, Kathleen, divorced in 1987. In 1988 he was arrested for burglary—and a year later, he read the news about Newton being shot to death, after leaving a crack house, by a member of a group called the Black Guerrilla Family. In 1992 and 1994 Cleaver was arrested for cocaine possession. He died in 1998 at age sixty-two.

Donald Cox, Field Marshal DC, went into exile in southern France, becoming fluent in French and working as a general contractor and house painter. "It was not government repression that destroyed the Black Panther Party," he said. "I'm convinced that, on the whole, the organization was destroyed by the megalomania of men." He added, "Our chance of survival would be greatly enhanced if men were just completely eliminated from any decision-making process and all decisions were put in the hands of women." DC hoped to be able to eventually return to the United States, but he spent the rest of his life in exile. He died in France in 2011 at age seventy-four.

Bernardine Dohrn was the mother of two children in 1980 when she and Bill Ayers surrendered. Most of the charges against her were dropped, but she served seven months in prison for refusing to cooperate with a grand jury. She worked at a Chicago law firm with connections to Ayers's wealthy father. She later became an adjunct professor at Northwestern University's Pritzker School of Law, founding the Children and Family Justice Center. She has remained active in several causes. In 2010, during Obama's presidency, she said: "The real terrorist is the American government."

Joanna Harcourt-Smith was condemned by some in the counterculture as a government agent who had deliberately led Leary to Afghanistan so he could be captured. She worked passionately to free him from prison, raising money, spending money, consulting anyone she thought could help. When Tim was released in April 1976, their new life together was marred by drinking and fighting. After a few months, they broke up—and Joanna was pregnant. She maintained the child was his but also admitted that she had slept with other men. Her son, Marlon Gobel, was born in 1977. She moved to Santa Fe, New Mexico, and began weaning herself from alcohol and drugs. Her family disinherited her and she worked as a chef. In 2006 she created the *Future Primitive* podcast, spreading her message of positive Buddhism. In 2013 she published a memoir, *Tripping the Bardo with Timothy Leary: My Psychedelic Love Story*.

Michel Hauchard, the ominously suave man Leary dubbed a latter-day Goldfinger, remains as mysterious today as he was in Switzerland in the early 1970s.

Michael Kennedy made headlines suing Donald Trump on behalf of Trump's wife Ivana. Kennedy hosted famous guests in his 1879 oceanfront estate on Long Island, and he had homes in Manhattan and Ireland, and offices on Park Avenue. He also counseled Mafia kingpin John Gotti, but for many political activists, Kennedy remained a revered crusader with a long history of championing counterculture figures and causes. He negotiated Bernardine Dohrn's 1980 surrender (she later said Kennedy's representing Trump's wife was something "no one could have predicted"). A defense lawyer in the film *Presumed Innocent* was inspired by Kennedy. He died in 2016 at age seventy-eight.

Rosemary Woodruff Leary remained underground for more than twenty years. She lived in Canada, Afghanistan, Sicily, Colombia, and then Costa Rica. In the early 1980s, she secretly returned to the United States, telling friends she had water-skied back into the country from a yacht off the Florida coast. She moved to Provincetown, at the tip of Cape Cod, and lived for several years under the name Sarah Woodruff. She worked as an innkeeper and continued to file tax returns using her correct Social Security number. She agreed to meet with Tim in 1992, more than twenty years after their split. He helped her find an attorney who was able to get the old charges against her dismissed. By 1994 she was able to surface and use her real name again. She stayed close to Tim but refused to marry him again. After his death in 1996, she handed out packets of his ashes mixed with glitter to guests at a party in his honor. She died of congestive heart failure in 2002 at the age of sixty-six.

G. Gordon Liddy was convicted of all Watergate charges and sentenced to twenty years in prison. In April 1977, new president Jimmy Carter commuted the rest of his sentence and Liddy was freed after spending more than four years behind bars. In 1980 he published a bestselling autobiography, *Will*. His rollicking campus debates with Timothy Leary were the subject of a 1983 documentary, *Return Engagement*. Liddy later became a syndicated radio talk show host and Fox News commentator. In 2006, at the age of seventy-five, he became the oldest contestant to ever appear on the reality show *Fear Factor*. He was locked inside a maggot-filled isolation pod and bested the competition, winning two custom motorcycles. He retired to Scottsdale, Arizona.

Dennis Martino became an informant for Nixon's newly created Drug Enforcement Administration. He spied on Leary's defense team during the prison escape trial and cooperated in the federal case against the Brotherhood of Eternal Love. He quickly realized the DEA had access to far better drugs than any criminal organization. He became addicted to cocaine. Traveling for the DEA, he always took his beloved Moog synthesizer along. He became lovers with Joanna Harcourt-Smith and hoped to marry her. He followed her to Spain in 1975 and died alone in a hotel room, apparently from a ruptured appendix. He was twenty-nine.

Richard Nixon resigned from office on August 9, 1974, after realizing he would be impeached and possibly indicted. He became gravely ill and word spread that he was on his deathbed. His successor, Gerald Ford, granted him a full pardon. Nixon bounced back from his illness and began plotting his comeback. He lived another twenty years, authoring ten books and crashing innumerable state funerals and other official functions. He died in 1994 at age eighty-one, still regarded by millions of Americans as the most dangerous criminal to ever occupy the Oval Office.

ACKNOWLEDGMENTS

Thank you, of course, to Timothy Leary for leading a very interesting life.

This book would not have been possible without the heroic efforts of Michael Horowitz and Robert Barker to keep Leary's legacy alive. Under great duress, they were able to preserve many of his most important papers. A special thank-you to Michael for also fielding several queries as we worked on the book and then pointing us to valuable information and photographs. Michael has shared many stories of Tim on his website: www.timothylearyarchives.org.

And a note of appreciation to Stacy Valis, our friend from PEN Center USA, who not only knew Timothy Leary but helped introduce us to Michael.

Thomas Lannon, the acting Charles J. Liebman Curator of Manuscripts at the New York Public Library, provided access to the vast Leary archives and then helped us, over and over again, to understand the contents. Thomas offered excellent insights into the history and context of the material, the times, and Leary.

The work done by Joanna Harcourt-Smith to chronicle and interpret her life with Timothy Leary served as a constant touchstone. She was there, she survived it all, and then she had the courage and intellect to try to make sense of it all. We thank her. We're also indebted to Rosemary Woodruff Leary, who spoke openly and honestly about her years with Tim in later interviews and worked on her own memoir, *The Magician's Daughter*, which unfortunately remained uncompleted at the time of her death.

Thanks, too, to James Senner for sharing his experiences and perspectives on life in Afghanistan and Timothy Leary's capture.

Thanks also to John Schewel for patiently responding to inquiries about his relationship with Rosemary Woodruff Leary.

Thank you to research assistants Andy East and Paromita Pain, for working so hard to find documents, comb databases, and dig into the history. We profited enormously from their smarts and great energy. Thank you to Caroline Covington for translating documents. Thanks to Emma Davis, Ashley Mastervich, Michael Marks, Wesley Scarborough, and Heather Leighton for their help.

We would like to acknowledge the many writers and researchers who paved the way examining our subject and the time period. There are too many to mention each one, but we would be remiss if we didn't cite Robert Greenfield, John Higgs, Nicholas Schou, Brian Barritt, Stew Albert, John Bryan, Terrence Burke, and Bryan Burrough.

Thank you to Nancy Glenn Hansen and, by extension, Egil "Bud" Krogh, both familiar with the inner workings of the Nixon White House. Ms. Hansen, a colleague of Krogh's, was kind to entertain our inquiries and point us toward a better understanding of President Nixon and his domestic policies, including the war on drugs—which Krogh helped to lead before he was swept up in the Watergate scandal.

Special thanks to the archives staff at various institutions: Lee Anne Titangos at the University of California, Berkeley's Bancroft Library; Jon Fletcher and Carla Braswell at the Richard Nixon Presidential Library and Museum; Tim Noakes at the Stanford University Libraries; Rebecca Hankins and Pilar Baskett at Texas A&M University's Cushing Memorial Library and Archives; Kelly D. Barton at the Ronald Reagan Presidential Library and Museum; Christina Violeta Jones at the National Archives and Records Administration; and Kate Hutchens at the University of Michigan Library.

Bill Minutaglio thanks five late friends who serve as daily inspirations: Louie Canelakes; Anne Lang; Chuck Nevitt; Augie, who loved the Llano River and knew the right time to make his move; and Perseus, who saw things no one else could. Also, Ed Timms, John Branch, Dave Garlock, Brad Buchholz, Alicia Dennis, and Hans Martin-Leibing. Thanks to Dennis Darling and Nancy Schiesari from the University of Texas at Austin. Warm thanks to the legendary Bob Compton.

Steve Davis thanks his friends and inspirations: Sam Pfiester, Ron Querry, Marc Simmons, Theresa Chambers Stolte, Mary Lou Comparetto, Bill and Sally Wittliff, Kip Stratton, Eddie Wilson, Mark Busby, and Camille and Emily Rosengren. Also the late Bud Shrake and Larry L. King. Thanks to the wonderful Liz Rogers for providing a writing retreat in Alpine. Special thanks to colleagues at the Wittliff Collections at Texas State University: David Coleman, Katie Salzmann, Carla Ellard, Lyda Guz, Teri Werlein, Lauren Goodley, Tabitha Dunn, Todd Richardson, Michele Miller, and Ramona Kelly. Thanks to Texas State for providing a sabbatical to work on portions of this book, and to Joan Heath, Carl Van Wyatt, Ken Pierce, and President Denise Trauth.

We are exceedingly fortunate to work with a world-class editor, Sean Desmond, who also happens to be a world-class friend—always extending his intelligence, good cheer, and guidance. His insights and wisdom did so much to improve this book. All authors should be lucky enough to collaborate with him and his brilliant colleagues at Twelve, including Paul Samuelson, Libby Burton, Rachel Kambury, and Carolyn Kurek. Special thanks to Elisa Rivlin for her cogent analysis and to our amazingly talented copy editor and fact-checker, Laura Cherkas. Thank you to Howie Sanders, Kassie Evashevski, and David Hale Smith.

Minutaglio thanks the inner Italian circle: Tessie, Francis Xavier, Frank, Bob, Tom, and John. He thanks Linda Smeltzer, Martha Williams, and Tom Sheehy. He offers love to his wife, Holly Williams, and their talented children: Rose Angelina Minutaglio and Nicholas Xavier Minutaglio.

Steve Davis thanks his loving family: wife Georgia Ruiz Davis, daughters Natalie and Lucia, and the canine tricksters, Truman, Louie, and Ralfred.

A NOTE ON SOURCES / BIBLIOGRAPHY / ENDNOTES

Our research for this book is based primarily from examining thousands of pages of contemporaneous primary-source materials found in the following archives: the Timothy Leary Papers at the New York Public Library; the Richard Nixon Presidential Library and Museum; the National Archives and Records Administration; the Presidential Recordings Program of the Miller Center at the University of Virginia; Federal Bureau of Investigation papers on Timothy Leary; the U.S. Department of State Archives; the Eldridge Cleaver Papers at the University of California, Berkeley; Federal Bureau of Investigation papers on "Black Extremists"; Nixon Administration national security files relating to Algeria (via NARA); the Ronald Reagan Presidential Library and Museum; the Eldridge Cleaver Collection at Texas A&M University; the Dr. Huey P. Newton Foundation Inc. Collection at Stanford University; the Clayton Van Lydegraf papers at the University of Washington; and the Stew Albert and Judy Gumbo Albert papers at the University of Michigan.

This archival research was supplemented by hundreds of newspaper articles, dozens of books, and interviews. A complete list of endnotes is provided on the authors' websites:

www.billminutaglio.com
www.stevenldavis.org

The major books, articles, interviews, websites, films, and research databases used in the research are identified on the following pages.

Many contemporaneous newspaper and magazines were searched through ProQuest, EBSCO, LexisNexis, and Google, which allows historical access to papers ranging from the *New York Times* and *Washington Post* to alternative media such as the *Village Voice* and *Berkeley Barb* (1965–1980).

Books

The Sixties Papers: Documents of a Rebellious Decade by Judith Clavir Albert and Stewart Edward Albert. Praeger, 1984.

Who the Hell Is Stew Albert?: A Memoir by Stew Albert. Red Hen Press, 2004.

Nixon: The Triumph of a Politician 1962–1972, volume 2, by Stephen E. Ambrose. Simon & Schuster, 1989.

Peace, War, and Politics: An Eyewitness Account by Jack Anderson. Forge, 1999.

Fugitive Days: A Memoir by Bill Ayers. Beacon, 2001.

The Road of Excess: A Psychedelic Autobiography by Brian Barritt. PSI Publishing, 1998.

Smoke and Mirrors: The War on Drugs and the Politics of Failure by Dan Baum. Little, Brown and Company, 1996.

Outlaws of America: The Weather Underground and the Politics of Solidarity by Dan Berger. AK Press, 2005.

The Nixon Tapes: 1973 edited by Douglas Brinkley and Luke Nichter. Houghton-Mifflin, 2015.

A Taste of Power: A Black Woman's Story by Elaine Brown. Pantheon, 1993.

Whatever Happened to Timothy Leary? by John Bryan. Renaisence Press, 1980.

Stalking the Caravan: A Drug Agent in Afghanistan 1971–1973 by Terrence Burke. La Plata Books, 2015.

Days of Rage: America's Radical Underground, the FBI, and the Forgotten Age of Revolutionary Violence by Bryan Burrough. Penguin, 2015.

Governor Reagan: His Rise to Power by Lou Cannon. PublicAffairs, 2003.

Sixties Radicals, Then and Now: Candid Conversations with Those Who Shaped the Era by Ron Chepesiuk. McFarland, 1995.

Eldridge Cleaver: Post-Prison Writings and Speeches by Eldridge Cleaver. Random House, 1969.

Soul on Fire by Eldridge Cleaver. Word Books, 1978.

Soul on Ice by Eldridge Cleaver. McGraw-Hill, 1968.

Target Zero: A Life in Writing by Eldridge Cleaver, edited by Kathleen Cleaver. St. Martin's Griffin, 2006.

Liberation, Imagination, and the Black Panther Party: A New Look at the Panthers and Their Legacy by Kathleen Cleaver and George Katsiaficas. Routledge, 2001.

Destructive Generation: Second Thoughts About the '60s by Peter Collier and David Horowitz. Free Press Paperbacks, 1996.

White Hand Society: The Psychedelic Partnership of Timothy Leary & Allen Ginsberg by Peter Conners. City Lights Books, 2010.

The Nixon Defense: What He Knew and When He Knew It by John W. Dean. Viking, 2014.

Sing a Battle Song: The Revolutionary Poetry, Statements, and Communiqués of the Weather Underground 1970–1974 edited by Bernardine Dohrn and Bill Ayers. Seven Stories Press, 2006.

Poisoning the Press: Richard Nixon, Jack Anderson, and the Rise of Washington's Scandal Culture by Mark Feldstein. Farrar, Straus and Giroux, 2010.

Timothy Leary: Outside Looking In edited by Robert Forte. Park Street, 1999.

How We Got Here: The 70's: The Decade That Brought You Modern Life (For Better or Worse) by David Frum. Basic Books, 2000.

The Last Days of the Late, Great State of California by Curt Gentry. Ballantine, 1975.

Bringing Down America: An FBI Informer with the Weathermen by Larry Grathwohl. Arlington House, 1976.

A Day in the Life: One Family, the Beautiful People, and the End of the Sixties by Robert Greenfield. Da Capo Press, 2009.

Timothy Leary: A Biography by Robert Greenfield. Harcourt, 2006.

Mystic Chemist: The Life of Albert Hofmann and His Discovery of LSD by Dieter Hagenbach and Lucius Werthmüller. Synergetic, 2013.

The Haldeman Diaries: Inside the Nixon White House by H. R. Haldeman. G. P. Putnam's Sons, 1994.

Tripping the Bardo with Timothy Leary: My Psychedelic Love Story by Joanna Harcourt-Smith. CreateSpace Independent Publishing, 2013.

Strictly Ghetto Property: The Story of Los Siete de la Raza by Marjorie Heins. Ramparts, 1972.

Political Violence and Terrorism in Modern America: A Chronology by Christopher Hewitt. Praeger Security International, 2005.

I Have America Surrounded: The Life of Timothy Leary by John Higgs. Thistle, 2013.

Huey: Spirit of the Panther by David Hilliard with Keith Zimmerman and Kent Zimmerman. Thunder's Mouth Press, 2005.

The Autobiography of Abbie Hoffman by Abbie Hoffman. Da Capo Press, 2000.

Rational Mysticism: Spirituality Meets Science in the Search for Enlightenment by John Horgan. Houghton-Mifflin, 2003.

An Annotated Bibliography of Timothy Leary by Michael Horowitz, Karen Walls, and Billy Smith. Archon Books/Shoe String Press, 1988.

Chasing Shadows: The Nixon Tapes, the Chennault Affair, and the Origins of Watergate by Ken Hughes. University of Virginia Press, 2015.

The Way the Wind Blew: A History of the Weather Underground by Ron Jacobs. Verso, 1997.

Abbie Hoffman: American Rebel by Marty Jezer. Rutgers University Press, 1993.

The Black Panther Party (Reconsidered) edited by Charles E. Jones. Black Classic Press, 2005.

A Radical Line: From the Labor Movement to the Weather Underground, One Family's Century of Conscience by Thai Jones. Free Press, 2004.

Waiting 'Til the Midnight Hour: A Narrative History of Black Power in America by Peniel E. Joseph. Henry Holt, 2006.

The Briar Patch by Murray Kempton. E. P. Dutton, 1973.

The First Family Detail: Secret Service Agents Reveal the Hidden Lives of the Presidents by Ronald Kessler. Crown Forum, 2014.

1973 Nervous Breakdown: Watergate, Warhol, and the Birth of Post-Sixties America by Andreas Killen. Bloomsbury, 2007.

The Long March: How the Cultural Revolution of the 1960s Changed America by Roger Kimball. Encounter Books, 2001.

The Skies Belong to Us: Love and Terror in the Golden Age of Hijacking by Brendan I. Koerner. Crown, 2013.

Paul Krassner's Psychedelic Trips for the Mind edited by Paul Krassner. High Times Books, 2001.

Integrity: Good People, Bad Choices, and Life Lessons from the White House by Egil "Bud" Krogh. PublicAffairs, 2007.

Acid Dreams: The CIA, LSD and the Sixties Rebellion by Martin A. Lee and Bruce Shlain. Grove Press, 1985.

Will: The Autobiography of G. Gordon Liddy by G. Gordon Liddy. St. Martin's Press, 1980.

Conversation with Eldridge Cleaver: Algiers by Lee Lockwood. McGraw-Hill, 1970.

A Piece of Tape: The Watergate Story: Fact and Fiction by James W. McCord. Washington Media Services, 1974.

Eldridge Cleaver Reborn by John A. Oliver. Logos International, 1977.

MH/CHAOS: The CIA's Campaign Against the Radical New Left and the Black Panthers by Frank J. Rafalko. Naval Institute Press, 2011.

Out of the Whale: Growing Up in the American Left: An Autobiography by Jonah Raskin. Links, 1974.

President Nixon: Alone in the White House by Richard Reeves. Simon & Schuster, 2001.

January 1973: Watergate, Roe v. Wade, Vietnam, and the Month That Changed America Forever by James Robenalt. Chicago Review Press, 2015.

The Age of Paranoia: How the Sixties Ended by the Editors of *Rolling Stone*. Pocket Books, 1972.

The Strong Man: John Mitchell and the Secrets of Watergate by James Rosen. Doubleday, 2008.

Subversives: The FBI's War on Student Radicals and Reagan's Rise to Power by Seth Rosenfeld. Farrar, Straus and Giroux, 2012.

Eldridge Cleaver by Kathleen Rout. Twayne Publishers, 1991.

Underground: My Life with SDS and the Weathermen by Mark Rudd. William Morrow, 2009.

Sixties Going On Seventies by Nora Sayre. Arbor House, 1973.

Orange Sunshine: The Brotherhood of Eternal Love and Its Quest to Spread Peace, Love, and Acid to the World by Nicholas Schou. St. Martin's Griffin, 2011.

Seize the Time: The Story of the Black Panther Party and Huey P. Newton by Bobby Seale. Random House, 1970.

Timothy Leary's Trip Thru Time by R. U. Sirius. www.timothyleary.org, 2013.

Timothy Leary, the Madness of the Sixties and Me by Charles W. Slack. P. H. Wyden, 1974.

Steal This Dream: Abbie Hoffman and the Countercultural Revolution in America by Larry Sloman. Doubleday, 1998.

An International History of the Black Panther Party by Jennifer B. Smith. Routledge, 2015.

With the Weathermen: The Personal Journal of a Revolutionary Woman by Susan Stern. Doubleday, 1975.

Storming Heaven: LSD and the American Dream by Jay Stevens. Grove Press, 1998.

The Arrogance of Power: The Secret World of Richard Nixon by Anthony Summers. Penguin, 2001.

The Brotherhood of Eternal Love: From Flower Power to Hippie Mafia: The Story of the LSD Counterculture by Stewart Tendler and David May. Cyan Communications, 2007.

Fighting Injustice by Michael E. Tigar. American Bar Association, 2003.

Can't Find My Way Home: America in the Great Stoned Age, 1945–2000 by Martin Torgoff. Simon & Schuster, 2004.

Radicals on the Road: Internationalism, Orientalism, and Feminism During the Vietnam Era by Judy Tzu-Chun Wu. Cornell University Press, 2013.

Full Committee Consideration of Report of Intelligence Subcommittee Regarding G. Gordon Liddy. U.S. Congress. July 1973.

Hashish Smuggling and Passport Fraud: "The Brotherhood of Eternal Love": Hearing Before the Subcommittee to Investigate the Administration of the Internal Security Act and Other Internal Security Laws of the Committee on the Judiciary, United States Senate, Ninety-Third Congress, First Session, October 3, 1973. U.S. Congress.

Bringing the War Home: The Weather Underground, the Red Army Faction, and Revolutionary Violence in the Sixties and Seventies by Jeremy Varon. University of California Press, 2004.

One Man Against the World: The Tragedy of Richard Nixon by Tim Weiner. Henry Holt, 2015.

Flying Close to the Sun: My Life and Times as a Weatherman by Cathy Wilkerson. Seven Stories Press, 2007.

Nixon Agonistes: The Crisis of the Self-Made Man by Garry Wills. Mariner Books, 2002.

The Final Days by Bob Woodward and Carl Bernstein. Simon & Schuster, 1976.

Eldridge Cleaver: My Friend the Devil: A Memoir by Marvin X. Black Bird Press, 2009.

The Parisian Jazz Chronicles: An Improvisational Memoir by Mike Zwerin. Yale University Press, 2005.

Books by Timothy Leary (in chronological order)

Interpersonal Diagnosis of Personality: A Functional Theory and Methodology for Personality Evaluation by Timothy Leary. Ronald Press, 1957.

The Psychedelic Experience: A Manual Based on the Tibetan Book of the Dead by Timothy Leary, Ralph Metzner, and Richard Alpert. University Books, 1964.

The Politics of Ecstasy by Timothy Leary. Putnam, 1968.

High Priest by Timothy Leary. NAL, 1968.

Jail Notes by Timothy Leary. Douglas Books, 1970.

Confessions of a Hope Fiend by Timothy Leary. Bantam Books, 1973.

Neurologic by Timothy Leary, Joanna Leary. 1973.

StarSeed by Timothy Leary. Level Press, 1973.

What Does WoMan Want? by Timothy Leary. 88 Books, 1976.

Neuropolitics: The Sociobiology of Human Metamorphosis by Timothy Leary. Star-Seed/Peace Press, 1977.

The Game of Life by Timothy Leary. Peace Press, 1979.

The Intelligence Agents by Timothy Leary. Peace Press, 1979.

Changing My Mind Among Others by Timothy Leary. Prentice Hall, 1982.

Flashbacks by Timothy Leary. J. P. Tarcher, 1983.

Turn On, Tune In, Drop Out by Timothy Leary. Ronin Publishing, 1999.

The Politics of Psychopharmacology by Timothy Leary. Ronin Publishing, 2001.

Leary on Drugs: New Material from the Archives! Advice, Humor and Wisdom from the Godfather of Psychedelia by Timothy Leary. Re/search Publications, 2009.

Articles

Newspapers and magazines consulted:

Berkeley Barb

The Black Panther

East Village Other

LA Weekly

Life

Los Angeles Free Press

Los Angeles Times

New York Times

Newsweek

Ramparts

Rolling Stone

San Francisco Chronicle

San Francisco Examiner

Time

Village Voice

Washington Post

Specific articles of note:

"Nixon Gives Elvis a Narcotics Badge" by Jack Anderson. Clipping in Timothy Leary Papers.

"Race, Rage & Eldridge Cleaver" by Jervis Anderson. *Commentary*, 1968.

"Panther Rift Rocks Whole Radical Left" by Ross K. Baker. *Washington Post*, March 21, 1971.

"Revolution on Ice: How the Black Panthers Lost the FBI's War of Dirty Tricks" by Lowell Bergman and David Weir. *Rolling Stone*, September 9, 1976.

"Comrades Recall Stew Albert" by Richard Brenneman. *Berkeley Daily Planet*, June 16, 2006.

"Tim Leary and the Long Arm of the Law" by Bill Cardoso. *Rolling Stone*, March 15, 1973.

"A Revolutionary Bust in Algiers" by Rudolph Chelminski. *Life*, March 26, 1971.

"Souled Out" by Kate Coleman. *New West*, May 1980.

"Getting High with Jennifer" by Jennifer Dohrn. *Good Times*, January 8, 1971.

"Laguna on Acid: The Great Hippie Christmas Invasion of 1970" by Bob Emmers. *OC Weekly*, December 24, 1998.

"Huey Newton: Twenty-Five Floors from the Street" by Tim Findley. *Rolling Stone*, August 3, 1972.

"Our Other Man in Algiers" by Sanche de Gramont. *New York Times*, November 1, 1970.

"Why Eldridge Cleaver Is a Wife-Beater" by Warren Hinckle. Clipping in Huey Newton Papers.

Interview with Albert Hofmann by Michael Horowitz. *High Times*, November 1976.

"4 Kent State Students Killed by Troops" by John Kifner, *New York Times*, May 5, 1970.

"Panthers Open International HQ" by Elaine Klein. *Guardian* (UK), October 3, 1970.

"Anita and the Blow-Up Doll: Death of a Yippie" by Paul Krassner. *Tikkun*, May/June 1999.

"How Our Paranoias Are Hyped for Fame and Profit" by Timothy Leary. *National Review*, April 16, 1976.

"Tim Leary, Won't You Please Come Home?" by Alan Levy. *Penthouse*, March 1973.

"The Decline and Fall of Eldridge Cleaver" by Claude Lewis. Philly.com, June 10, 1992.

"A Soul on Ice, a Life on Hold: Eldridge Cleaver's Failure" by Claude Lewis. Philly.com, May 13, 1998.

"Uptight in Babylon: Eldridge Cleaver's 'Cold War'" by Sean L. Malloy. *Diplomatic History* (2013) volume 37, no. 3: 538–571.

"With the Panthers in Algiers" by Robert Manning. In Alternative Features Service, volume 2, packet 72, November 10, 1972. Berkeley, CA: privately published, 1972.

"The Exiles: An Interview of Kathleen Cleaver" by Madeline Murphy. *Chicken-Bones*, August 2, 2011. Originally published in *Madeline Murphy Speaks*, C. H. Fairfax, 1988.

"Eldridge Cleaver in Algiers: A Visit with Papa Rage" by Gordon Parks. *Life*, February 6, 1970.

"Leary in Limbo" by Donn Pearce. *Playboy*, July 1971.

"The President, Politics, and the Police: Consequences of the 1970 'Stoning' of Richard M. Nixon at the San Jose Civic Auditorium" by Kathryn Collins Philp. Privately printed, April 15, 2005.

"William Eagleton Remembered as Adventurous Spirit, Skilled Diplomat" by Elaine S. Povich. *Journal Star* (Peoria), July 16, 2011.

"Stew Albert's Radical Life, 1939–2006" by Michael Simmons. *Counterpunch*, February 2, 2006.

"Old Con, Black Panther, Brilliant Writer and Quintessential American" by Harvey Swados. *New York Times Magazine*, September 7, 1969.

"Bring Me the Head of Timothy Leary" by Craig Vetter. *Playboy*, September 1975.

"North Korea and the American Radical Left" by Benjamin R. Young. Wilson Center North Korea International Documentation Project, February 6, 2013.

"Soul on Acid, Leary in Algiers" by Michael Zwerin. *OZ* volume 33, 1971.

"Free Tim, Again." *Berkeley Barb*, February 5–11, 1971.

"Algerian Acid Cap-Tives: Free Tim, Again. Free All Political Prisoners." *Berkeley Barb*, February 5–11, 1971.

"Suppressed Issue: Guerrilla War in the USA." *Scanlan's*, January 1971.

"Eye on Kathleen Cleaver." *Women's Wear Daily*, November 21, 1968.

"Remembering Stew Albert." www.emptymirrorbooks.com/thirdpage/stew rememberance.html.

Other Sources

Timothy Leary Archives, website maintained by Lisa Rein and Michael Horowitz: http://www.timothylearyarchives.org.

Numerous recordings of Leary interviews, speeches, and talks can be heard at the *Psychedelic Salon* podcast: https://psychedelicsalon.com.

Association for Diplomatic Studies and Training Foreign Affairs Oral History Collection. Ambassador Allen C. Davis, interviewed by Peter Moffat, 1998. Laurent E. Morin, interviewed by Charles Stuart Kennedy, 1992. Philip C. Brown, interviewed by Charles Stuart Kennedy, 2012.

Global Terrorism Database: https://www.start.umd.edu/gtd.

Joanna Harcourt-Smith's *Future Primitive* podcast: www.futureprimitive.org.

Interview with Rosemary Woodruff Leary: "The Magician's Daughter." http://www.mavericksofthemind.com/rosemary.htm.

"An Interview with Donald Cox, former Field Marshall, Black Panther Party" by Safiya Bukhari. http://www.itsabouttimebpp.com/DC/htm/In_Memory_Of_Exiled_Fallen_Black_Panther_Party_Field_Marshall_Donald_DC_Cox.htm.

Interviews with Eldridge Cleaver in *Playboy* and *Rolling Stone*.

Interviews with Timothy Leary in *Playboy*.

Interview with James Senner by authors via email.

Interview with John Schewel by authors via email.

Interview with Joanna Harcourt-Smith: *Psychedelic Salon* podcast #303, March 12, 2012.

What I Remember About My Life by David F. Phillips, 2010. www.radbash.com/autobiography.

Field Marshall Donald Cox. Produced by Roz B. Payne. Newsreel Films, 2006.

Eldridge Cleaver, Black Panther directed by William Klein, 1970.

The Weather Underground directed by Sam Green and Bill Siegel. Independent Lens, 2002.

Return Engagement directed by Alan Rudolph, 1983.

INDEX

ABOUT THE AUTHORS

Bill Minutaglio's work has appeared in the *New York Times, Guardian, Newsweek, Bulletin of the Atomic Scientists*, and many other publications. A University of Texas at Austin professor, he and Steven Davis collaborated on *Dallas 1963*, recipient of a PEN Center USA award. He has written the memoir/anthology *In Search of the Blues* as well as acclaimed books about George W. Bush, the writer Molly Ivins, and America's greatest industrial disaster. www.billminutaglio.com.

Steven L. Davis is the PEN USA award–winning coauthor of *Dallas 1963* (written with Bill Minutaglio). He has authored two other acclaimed books on Texas and has edited several more. He is the president of the Texas Institute of Letters and is a longtime curator at the Wittliff Collections at Texas State University in San Marcos, which holds the literary papers of many leading Southwestern authors. He lives with his family in New Braunfels, Texas.